Are We Still Rolling?

Studios, Drugs and Rock 'n' Roll - One Man's Journey Recording Classic Albums

Phill Brown

BENNION KEARNY

Published in 2024 by Bennion Kearny

ISBN: 9781915855244

Phill Brown has asserted his right under the Copyright, Designs and Patents Act, 1988 to be identified as the author of this book.

Copyright Phill Brown 2024. All Rights Reserved. No part of this publication may be reproduced, stored in a retrieval system, or transmitted in any form or by any means, electronic, mechanical, photocopying, recording or otherwise, without the prior permission of the publisher.

This book is sold subject to the condition that it shall not, by way of trade or otherwise, be lent, re-sold, hired out or otherwise circulated without the publisher's prior consent in any form of binding or cover other than that in which it is published and without a similar condition including this condition being imposed on the subsequent purchaser.

Bennion Kearny, 6 Woodside, Churnet View Road, Oakamoor, ST10 3AE, UK

The first edition of the book was published by Tape Op.

Credits

Art Direction by John Baccigaluppi

Editing by Larry Crane, Caitlin Gutenberger & John Baccigaluppi

Graphic Design by Scott McChane

Proofreading by Caitlin Gutenberger

Legal Counsel by Alan Korn

Front Cover photo by Roger Hillier

Phill would like to thank James Lumsden-Cook of Bennion Kearny, Larry Crane and John Baccigaluppi of Tape Op Books, Roger Hillier, Julian Gill, Robert Palmer, Barbara Marsh, Dana Gillespie, John Fenton, Terry Brown, Ray Doyle, and Steve Smith.

To Sally:

Thank you for everything.

I could not have achieved as much without you.

"There's my truth,
there's your truth,
and then there's The Truth."
Steve Smith

"This is my truth,
some may disagree."
Phill Brown

In memory of musicians, producers, family and friends: Robert Ash, Jeff Beck, Mark Bolan, John Bonham, John Bindon, Lenny Breau, Linda Brown, Vicki Brown, Elsie and Leslie Brown, Jenny Bruce, David Byron, Alan Callan, Tim Cross, Sandy Denny, Dave Domlio, Jim Capaldi, Mongezi Feza, Lowell George, Mick Greenwood, Keith Harwood, Alex Harvey, Ritchie Haywood, Bill Hicks, Mark Hollis, Nicky Hopkins, Andy Johns, Brian Jones, Paul Kossoff, Keith Grant, Vincent Crane, Graham Leaver, Ronnie Lane, John Martyn, David Malin, Bob Marley, Steve Marriott, George Melly, Jimmy Miller, Denise Mills, Willie Mitchell, Roy Morgan, Mickie Most, Harry Nilsson, Kenji Omura, Robert Palmer, Mike Patto, Cozy Powell, Keith Relf, Lou Reizner, Nigel Rouse, Del Shannon, Norman Smith, Steve Smith, Alan Spenner, Guy Stevens, Peter Veitch, Kevin Wilkinson, Paul and Suzanne Wightman, Chris Wood, and Maxi Jazz.

Foreword

This is not a technical manual (although it will certainly function as one) – it's a contemporary thriller. Phill Brown is a sound engineer. It's a mystery, even to people in the music business, as to exactly what a sound engineer does – are they part of the creative process or merely technicians? In the past 30 years, recording studios have moved from the engine room of a submarine to the bridge of a starship – baffling the outsider – although recording music will always be the same un-guessable adventure. That's what Phil Brown has written here – an adventure story.

Look at the chapter headings. Laid out in the form of a diary, he takes us through the crazy journey that is making music. Not as an academic journal, but as a spiritual experience. With his laconic navigation, we're steered through the centre of the ego hurricanes of creative madness. He is the Jiminy Cricket of recording sessions, and his excellent recollections of the excesses of morons and geniuses involved in creating melodies and rhythms for us to enjoy are sheer entertainment. It's a "how-to" book and a love story! A self-driven need to understand why creative people do what they do, and how to survive it and them.

Robert Palmer, 9 September 1997

Table of Contents

Introduction 1
Chapter 1. Olympic Studios (part one) 9
Chapter 2. Olympic Studios (part two) 17
Chapter 3. The Rolling Stones 27
Chapter 4. Canada 35
Chapter 5. Island Studios 49
Chapter 6. Jeff Beck 61
Chapter 7. Harry Nilsson 69
Chapter 8. Murray Head 73
Chapter 9. Bob Marley & The Wailers 87
Chapter 10. Joe Brown 95
Chapter 11. Robert Palmer 99
Chapter 12. Dana Gillespie 109
Chapter 13. Robert Palmer 121
Chapter 14. Pink Floyd 137
Chapter 15. Stomu Yamashta and Rock Follies 141
Chapter 16. Robert Palmer 153
Chapter 17. Joe South 161
Chapter 18. Steve Winwood 169
Chapter 19. John Martyn 183
Chapter 20. Shakin' Stevens 195
Chapter 21. Roxy Music 203
Chapter 22. Paul Carrack 213
Chapter 23. Murray Head – On the Road 223
Chapter 24. Red Box 235
Chapter 25. Go West 241
Chapter 26. Talk Talk 245

Chapter 27. Talk Talk 255
Chapter 28. Alan Spenner 267
Chapter 29. .O.rang..271
Chapter 30. Throwing Muses 277
Chapter 31. Fusanosuke Kondo 285
Chapter 32. Mark Hollis 297
Chapter 33. Dido...311

Epilogue..321
Glossary 326

Introduction

In the spring of 1995, I was in hospital having 12 inches of colon removed – an experience I can't recommend despite the considerable skill of Mr. Chilvers, the surgeon at St Anthony's Hospital, Cheam, in Surrey. It seemed that my lifestyle had finally caught up with me. The two consultants and the other doctors I came into contact with were all in agreement about the cause of my predicament. As one of them said, "Mr. Brown, this situation has been created by your long working days, poor diet, sedentary lifestyle and the combination of continuous adrenaline rushes and intense stress. The old saying 'bust a gut' comes to mind."

During my seven-day stay at St. Anthony's and previous two weeks of purgatory in a hospital in Tunbridge Wells, I had plenty of time to contemplate what I realised with surprise was nearly 30 years in the music industry. The doctors were right – my present poor state of health was in many ways the legacy of this career. However, considering the abuse that my system had suffered and the high casualty rate among my many friends and acquaintances, I reflected that my situation could have been a lot worse. At least I was still alive, which was a good position from which to start my recovery. While lying in my hospital bed with a drip in my arm and a cocktail of, for once, completely legal drugs pouring through my body, I consoled myself by recalling the more enjoyable projects I had been involved with. I had worked with some of the greatest acts in the business, including Jimi Hendrix, Joe Cocker, Traffic, Spooky Tooth, Jeff Beck, Led Zeppelin, Robert Palmer, Bob Marley, Steve Winwood, Harry Nilsson, Atomic Rooster, Stomu Yamashta, John Martyn, Little Feat, Roxy Music and Talk Talk.

Now, in my hospital bed in 1995, I was unable to work at all for the first time in years, and my thoughts inevitably turned once again to past events. It seemed a good moment to look at my entire "story" so far.

When I began work at the bottom of the studio hierarchy as a tape operator, I discovered that there was an informal system of apprenticeship in the recording industry. I was expected to learn by watching and listening while I made tea and performed other mundane jobs about the studio. However, I never resented being the "dogsbody". To work in a studio and to train under such engineers as Keith Grant, Glyn Johns and Eddie Kramer was a privilege, and I gained a unique approach and attitude towards recording that I carried with me through the next 30 years. Although in those early days everything seemed strange and new, I could have no notion of the crazy sessions that lay ahead, the extraordinary people I would work with or the wildly varied types of music I would help to create.

The sequence of events that led me to become a sound recording engineer began when I was still at school in the early 1960s. In 1964, my elder brother Terry started working at Olympic Studios in London as a trainee sound engineer. Since leaving school, he had been working at the post room of J. Walter Thompson, the advertising agency where our father had worked for 15 years. My brother was expected to rise through the ranks and become successful in the advertising industry. To me this seemed a dismal fate. However, one day Terry delivered a package to Olympic Studios. He caught a glimpse of an exotic world of unconventional characters, mysterious equipment and most attractive of all, exciting music. He decided to ask for a job at Olympic. My parents were not keen on this idea. They were conventional and careful in outlook and were concerned that Terry would lose his pension and security.

At that time, I was 13 years old and in my third year as a day pupil at Stanborough Park, a private day and boarding school in Garston, Watford. The school was run by the Seventh Day Adventists – a non-conformist Christian sect with a firm moral code and strict principles. Children from all over the world were sent to Stanborough Park by parents who upheld these religious beliefs, but the school was also attended by local children. Most of these had failed their 11-plus examinations, an ordeal to which all children in state schools were subjected at the time. The successful minority was creamed off to a grammar school. The rest, which included me, would have to make do with "secondary modern" education. The only alternative was to opt out. This is what my parents decided I should do, due to the poor reputation of the three secondary modern schools within the area.

I found the combination of religion, strict morals and discipline that was enforced by Stanborough Park very difficult to deal with, particularly during my final two years at the school. I resented all the trivial rules and regulations: "Don't be out of bounds. Wear a cap at all times when off the school grounds. Keep hair short, clean and tidy." Plus, I didn't like being force-fed religious dogma and moral values. Each day there was a half-hour morning assembly, with a strong emphasis on religion. Once a month, we would "march" into assembly to the music *Triumphal March* from Aida (by Giuseppe Verdi), and then a guest speaker would preach to us all. It may have been a Seventh Day Adventist parson from the other side of the world, or perhaps a local policeman.

Once a year there was "Health Week", where assembly became two hours long. Jars containing hearts, lungs and brains from both the healthy and the sick would be held up in front of the entire school to illustrate the perilous effects of smoking and drinking. One teacher, Mr. French, fainted onto the piano on his first viewing. Whether or not this experience affected him permanently, I have no idea, but as for the pupils, the effects usually faded by the third viewing. This bizarre and gross annual performance did nothing to put me off smoking or drinking, and as with many a child, the effect of such an exacting and inflexible regime at school was more or less the opposite of what was intended. I developed a lifelong attitude towards rules and authority that has always been sceptical, to put it mildly.

When Terry left the advertising agency and started working at Olympic Studios, I began to see that there might be alternatives to the rigid attitude of mind promoted by my schoolteachers. Beyond that, I saw a possible way of avoiding the kind of working life that was led by my father and by other adults in my family – a life that appeared to me to be boring in the extreme.

After he had been at Olympic for about four months, Terry asked me if I would like to travel to work with him to see the studio. I was delighted. At the time, my brother drove a 1947 Triumph Roadster, a large, low-slung two-seater that looked unusual among the family saloons of the day. One Saturday morning, we both got into the car and set off for London, leaving behind the semi-detached house in North Watford where our parents had lived for

20 years. In retrospect, it seems like the first step of a very long journey.

I can't remember exactly what I was expecting Olympic Studios to be like, but it wasn't a narrow, three-storey, bizarre-looking building. It was in a mews off Carlton Street. Evidently, it had been used previously as a Jewish synagogue and later as a mortuary. Terry parked the car outside the studio in the mews – at that time there were fewer restrictions on car parking in central London. He unlocked the street door, and we found ourselves in a small reception area.

It was a Saturday, so there was no one at the reception desk, and the building was strangely quiet. Part of Terry's job was to prepare the studio for the day's session an hour or so before the musicians and the rest of the staff arrived.

Terry showed me the main studio – Studio One – which ran the whole width of the building. The walls, ceiling and isolation screens were all covered in cream-coloured acoustic pegboard tiles. The hushed atmosphere was now even more noticeable because of the "dead" acoustics of the recording room. In one corner, there was a grand piano, a Hammond organ and a large collection of mic stands, cables and headphones.

Down in the basement I was taken through a series of small rooms, including ones used for maintenance, tape copying and tape storage. All these rooms had un-plastered brick walls, painted white. Fixed to them (but not concealed) were all the audio, telephone, electricity cables and air conditioning ducts for the offices and studio. It was an untidy and dirty area.

On the first floor was the control room. This was set parallel to the studio and looked down into it. Like the studio itself, the walls were covered in off-white pegboard acoustic tiles. There were four large loudspeaker cabinets standing on the floor against the wall. These, I learned, were Tannoy/Lockwood monitors. Years later, in the mid-1970s, these became my favourite monitor speakers for recording and mixing. Immediately in front of the Tannoys was the sound desk. By today's standards this was extremely small and basic, with just 12 input channels. Each input had six large, Bakelite knobs to control top, mid and bass EQ, feeds for the headphones and a track/record selector switch. In the centre of the desk were four round VU meters and below these, four toggle switches to select monitors. Cables and wires oozed from the back of the desk and disappeared into either the wall or boxes lying on the floor. To the left of the desk was a small window giving a restricted view down into the studio room. To the right was a small seating area for about three or four people. On the remaining wall and floor space was the large 4-track tape machine and a couple of 1-track, mono machines, all housed in metal cabinets. Wires ran from these, connecting to a patchbay, amps and meters in metal cabinets on the wall. It all looked very dirty, with lighter patches on the wall where equipment had once been but was now removed, and there were badly worn areas of carpet, especially directly behind the desk.

In a separate building across the mews was Studio Two, where there was basic equipment for jingles and voiceovers, plus tape copying and editing facilities.

During this and many subsequent weekend visits to Olympic Studios, I gradually formed a picture in my mind of how the studio was laid out and began to make sense of what, at first, looked like a confused jumble of equipment. Olympic, then, was perhaps a bit seedy, especially when compared to some of the studios I eventually worked in, but for me at the age of 13 it was an Aladdin's cave. For some months, I spent every available weekend with Terry, soaking up the atmosphere at the studio and sitting in on sessions with such artists as The Yardbirds, Marianne Faithfull and P. J. Proby. I met several musicians, notably members of The Yardbirds, (including bassist Paul Samwell-Smith and Keith Relf, the harmonica player and singer), Big Jim Sullivan, who was a session guitarist for P. J. Proby, and Clem Cattini, a session drummer and previous member of The Tornados and Johnny Kidd & the Pirates. I would come to work with all these people in the years ahead.

One Sunday in 1965, I was at the studio when The Yardbirds were there to record a single. They were young and brimming with enthusiasm. By the end of that one-day session, they had recorded, overdubbed and mixed *For Your Love*, which soon became their first Top 10 hit. Such a feat would be almost impossible today. Suddenly, all I wanted to do was to be in that environment and record music all day – I was convinced that it would be brilliant fun and far better than "working" for a living.

Terry introduced me to many people from the world of music, including two staff members at Olympic, who in later years were to have a significant influence on my career: Keith Grant and Frank Owen. I would often sit in Studio Two with Frank while he mixed voiceovers on commercials or edited 1/4-inch tapes together for shows on Radio Luxembourg. He showed me how the tape machines and desk operated. All the projects were usually mixed to mono, as the wonders of stereo were still in their infancy. For voiceovers, a backing track would be played and this, along with the live vocal, would be recorded onto a second mono machine. I was intrigued by these aspects of the job just as much as the "glamour" of the band sessions.

In time, Frank taught me how to edit 1/4-inch tape. I returned home and tried editing tape recordings of the Top 20 on my Brenell mono tape machine. It was a great experience watching Frank and Terry making records on what would now be considered to be antiquated 4-track equipment. Even then, I realised that with this way of working, it was very important that the performance, the sounds and any necessary mixing were correct at the source. With more than one instrument recorded on each track, there was little that could be changed later. By watching them work and talking to Terry on the drives home to Watford in his Triumph, I learnt a great deal. By today's standards Olympic would be little more than the equivalent of a basic demo studio, but at the time the banks of equipment and machines looked impressive. In addition to Marianne Faithfull and The Yardbirds, The Rolling Stones, Dusty Springfield and Jonathan King had all worked at the studio during the mid-'60s.

After recording many classic records, including *Substitute* by The Who and *Everyone's Gone to the Moon* by Jonathan King, Terry left Olympic in 1965. Moving up the career ladder, he went to work as an engineer at Lansdowne Studios in Notting Hill Gate, under its studio manager and owner Adrian Kerridge. I still went and sat in on sessions with Terry whenever I could. During one of the visits to Lansdowne, I watched a session for The Smoke as they recorded *My Friend Jack*. This was the first time I witnessed a stereo mix. The single was immediately banned by the BBC, as the lyrics were said to promote drug abuse ("My friend Jack eats sugar lumps").

Meanwhile, the path of my career at Stanborough Park is described by my school reports, which began with "a promising term" in 1962 and ended with "seems to have thrown in the towel" in 1967. By June 1967, when I had finished my exams and left, I had decided to be a sound recording engineer.

Having left Stanborough Park School and needing to support myself, I began working in the gents' outfitters department of the Co-operative store on St Albans Road in North Watford. The shop has long since disappeared. I sold the full range of collarless shirts, Y-fronts, thermals, suits, cufflinks, tie pins and such. It was interesting for the first two weeks, but then it became the most boring, dead-end job imaginable. I would arrive at 8:30 a.m. and make tea for Mrs. Metcalf. She was a large woman, about 50 years old, who smoked Craven A cigarettes. We had access to a backroom that contained a single gas ring, two chairs, a table and a shelf with a kettle and two mugs on it. There was a curtain that screened this room off from the shop. The weekdays were slow, with little to do except talk to Mrs. Metcalf. On Fridays and Saturday mornings, we would be very busy, and the time would go quickly. The only real action and excitement that ever occurred was one Friday morning after the store had been burgled during the night.

Mrs. Metcalf had a habit of finishing sentences by saying, "...I've worked in retail all my life." I soon became determined that whatever else might happen, this would not happen to me. I didn't like the way I was told what to do – it was too much like school.

However much I hated the work, I was cheerful about the future because I had already asked Keith Grant about the possibility of a job at Olympic when I'd seen him at Terry's wedding (to Linda Knowles) in September 1966. Keith had said that as soon as a vacancy came up he would let me know. At the time, unemployment figures were low. There was a general feeling of "get out there and do it", and as with many a 16-year-old, the idea of failure never entered my head. I was pleased but not surprised therefore when, four months, later Keith offered me a job as tape op. "I've got a trainee job going. I'll pay you £10 a week. Are you interested?" he asked.

I started on the 2nd of November 1967 at Olympic Studios, which by then had moved to Barnes, just over the river from Hammersmith, West London. By this time, my brother Terry had left Lansdowne and was building Morgan Studios on Willesden High Road for a partnership consisting of Barry Morgan, Monty Babson and Leon Calvert. He still worked occasionally as a freelance engineer at Olympic Studios, and we worked together on various projects, including *Gorilla* by The Bonzo Dog Doo-Dah Band and the second, self-titled Traffic album. We got on very well – we always had – and there were no ego or big brother problems. When we were working together on sessions, we were often referred to as "The Brown Brothers".

The new Olympic Studios were built in 1966 in a converted cinema on Church Road, Barnes, London, just 100 yards from the Red Lion Public House. In this studio, at the beginning of November 1967, I began my training as a sound recording engineer.

Chapter 1. Olympic Studios (part one)
2 November 1967

At Olympic Studios, I joined the staff of Keith Grant, Vic Smith, Alan O'Duffy and Eddie Kramer – engineers; Anna Menzies – studio booker; Sandra Read (whom I was later to date) – assistant; Dick Swettenham, Jo Yu, Hugh Tennant and Clive Green – maintenance men. Swettenham and Green went on to build Helios and Cadac desks; Jo Yu helped build Island Studios, Basing Street during 1969; and Hugh Tennant built RAK Studios for producer Mickie Most in the early 1970s. There were also Andy Johns and George Chkiantz – at that time referred to as tape ops (in later years this designation was replaced by the term "assistant engineer"). I started on the 2nd of November 1967 for a wage of £10 per week.

I spent the first week sitting in on Keith Grant's sessions. Keith was about 26 years old, 5 feet 9 inches tall, with short, dark hair, piercing eyes, goatee beard and a large beer gut, and he reminded me of the actor James Robertson Justice. He had an easy humour out of the studio, but at work had strong views on everything and was opinionated and strict. I spent my first couple of days sitting with the clients on the couch in front of the console, facing the control room window, just watching and listening. There was a great deal to take in, but fortunately because of my visits to studios with Terry over the past three years, it was not all foreign to me. Sometimes, I would help Kevin Hewitt make tea for the musicians or move isolation screens between sessions. Kevin – an Irishman then in his late 40s – helped set up the studio for big orchestral sessions and served as tea boy during the Musicians' Union's prescribed breaks. I was a little nervous on sessions at first and spent most of my time quietly adjusting to this new environment. It was the complete opposite to my sheltered years at Stanborough Park School. I was now around people who smoked and drank heavily, spoke with sharp, aggressive wit and appeared to spend most of their time bent on enjoying themselves. It was a different world, and I found it refreshing and intensely exciting.

During my second week, I learned to load and operate the Ampex 4-track tape machine and began to gain a basic understanding of the desk. There was a great deal of information to remember during sessions, but almost immediately I learned Keith's number one rule: "Don't speak unless spoken to. Otherwise keep quiet." Within two weeks, I had learned about the range of different types of microphones and their positioning, the assortment of leads and power packs, how to edit 1/4-inch tape and make tape copies. I began working on Keith's sessions, the first of which was for Anita Harris and the album *Just Loving You*, recorded with an 80-piece orchestra. Alan Tew and David Whitaker were the musical arrangers, and Mike Margolis (Anita's lover, whom she later married) produced the album. The first time Keith called out, "Okay Phill, record," and then down the studio talkback, "Okay guys, we're rolling. Take one." What a buzz!

Anita Harris was small and attractive, with medium length, light chestnut brown hair, big brown eyes and a wonderful smile. She was a happy, friendly woman – as soon as she arrived each morning, she would come straight into the control room in a cloud of exotic perfume and give everyone a big kiss. She had no discernible ego, worked hard and treated all those involved as being equally important to the project. This included me, and I soon felt I was one of the crew.

The sessions were certainly "in at the deep end" for me. I would arrive two hours before the session was due to start and help Kevin to set up the screens, microphones, music stands, chairs and ashtrays. During the session itself, my job was to operate the buttons for record, rewind and playback on the 4-track tape machine, and to keep a list of takes, marking them either "F/S" (False Start), "B/D" (Break Down), "C" (Complete) or "Master". I also replaced any broken headphones and made tea. It was common practice for Keith to record an 80-piece orchestra in stereo on two tracks of the 4-track machine, leaving the other two tracks for vocal overdubs. It was impossible to change the balance of any instrument later (there was no control over the level of the recorded bass drum or hi-hat, for example), and any solo rides, echoes or individual effects that were required were added live to this stereo mix as the musicians played. Despite these limitations, the results were often impressive and remain so even when compared with recordings made with the advanced 48- and 56-track computerized technology of the 1990s.

Anita's project was followed almost immediately by another large orchestral session, this time with Dusty Springfield for the album *Dusty... Definitely*. She appeared just as she did on her television shows, with blonde, backcombed hair and eyes made large with heavy mascara and eyeliner. Only her clothes were different, as instead of her usual dresses, she wore shirts and cord trousers. Dusty had originally been very successful with the group The Springfields in the early '60s and had her first solo hit in 1963 with *I Only Want to Be With You*. Since then, she had had at least 13 Top 20 hits and had appeared in her own television show. In contrast to the work with Anita, these sessions were more difficult. This was mainly due to Dusty keeping herself somewhat withdrawn from the proceedings and from the people involved. She sang very well, but appeared unhappy and troubled and was often in tears. She did not seem to enjoy male company, and mainly dealt with her manager, Vicky Wickham. Keith made up for the lack of humour on the sessions by doing cartwheels across the floor of Studio One and showing blue movies to selected members of the orchestra in his office during lunch.

I also worked on a great many recordings of advertising jingles, often with musicians such as Jimmy Page, John Paul Jones, Ronnie Verrell, Tony Meehan, (one half of the early '60s duo Jet Harris and Tony Meehan), Nicky Hopkins, Big Jim Sullivan and Clem Cattini. Within two years Page and Jones would be in the biggest rock band in the world – Led Zeppelin – but there was no hint of this in 1967. Some of the jingle sessions started as early as 8 a.m., and this would entail a 5 a.m. departure from Watford for myself. Once set up, I would operate the Ampex 4-track machine on commercials that were usually 30, 25 or seven seconds in length. A seven-second track was particularly difficult to balance and mix, for obvious reasons. There were no desk remote controls in that era, so I would be cued by Keith to record, play back or drop in. I worked with Keith on most of his sessions from November 1967 to January 1968. As well as Anita and Dusty's projects, there were albums with Leonard Cohen and Harry Secombe, jingles for Kellogg's and my old employers the Co-op, and film scores with John Barry. It was the best possible education for microphone technique and speed of working. When not on a session, I would be given the job of looking after the copying room, where I would spend hundreds of hours copying, editing and splicing leader tape onto copies of jingles, singles and finished albums.

Once I knew the ropes and was considered "safe", I was allowed to work with other engineers – initially mainly Vic Smith and Alan O'Duffy. At the time, the Musicians' Union stipulated a maximum continuous work period of 3 hours for musicians during recording sessions, after which there had to be a break – also, the ACTT (Association of Cinematograph, Television and Allied Technicians – the film and engineers' union) had strict rules for overtime pay. However, Olympic was not an ACTT union studio and did a large amount of work for the rock world, usually at night when everything was looser. Not being union controlled, the sessions almost invariably exceeded the prescribed limit many times over. It became common practice to work for 15 to 18 hours in a solid stretch, with food breaks in the control room. At weekends, there were often 24-hour sessions. The most extreme example occurred one weekend when I was working with my brother Terry and the band Freedom. We started work on a Saturday afternoon and the session became quite complicated. Before long, we were working with three 4-track machines and creating tape phasing while mixing. We eventually emerged at 7 a.m. on Monday morning, 40 hours later.

Of all the staff I saw socially, I spent the most time with George Chkiantz. He was 20 years old, about 5 feet 10 inches tall, often unshaven with an unruly mass of dark brown curly hair. He chain smoked cigarettes and could stay up for days without sleep, fired by an intelligent and bizarre sense of humour from some other planet. He was a wonderful combination of technical boffin and seat-of-your-pants engineer and had accomplished a great deal of work with Jimi Hendrix, The Rolling Stones, Family and the Small Faces as an assistant engineer. He pioneered the tape phasing effect used on *Itchycoo Park* by the Small Faces in the summer of 1967. George had given this new effect to Glyn Johns, who had recorded *Itchycoo Park* as a freelance engineer. It was rumoured that this had annoyed Eddie Kramer, the house engineer at Olympic, as Eddie thought that the effect should have been given to him first, for use with Jimi Hendrix.

George helped me to understand the studio equipment and could always answer any technical questions I might have. He lived with his girlfriend in a house in Bennerley Road, Wandsworth. It was full of loudspeakers, amplifiers and odd bits of electrical equipment laid out on tables. On the third floor there was a music room with a homemade valve amplifier and large 12" speakers. The "furniture" consisted of mattresses and cushions strewn on the floor, and there were beads and bells hanging from the windows, doorframes and mantelpiece. We would sometimes end up in this room late at night after sessions, drinking tea, listening to Simon & Garfunkel's *Bookends* and Family's *Music in a Doll's House* and smoking a sticky black hash that I later found out to be opium. We talked about sessions, the reasons for placing a microphone in a certain position, musicians, sounds and the spiritual world. He was a great source of inspiration to a 17-year-old, despite being only 20 himself.

As I came to the end of my first three months at Olympic, the traveling back and forth to Watford and the shortage of time for any social life were my only areas of complaint. To make it easier to get around, I started driving lessons in London, having arranged with the studio booker Anna Menzies to have the odd hour off work when necessary. The problem with my lack of social life was more difficult to resolve, as I was working between 80 and 100 hours a week. There were no nights out with the boys to the pub, no movies or dancing. The few times I saw old friends they seemed very childish, and I slowly drifted away from them.

About 10.30pm on the 21st of January 1968, Eddie Kramer telephoned the studio. He was at a party in the West End with Hendrix, and wanted to know who was in Studio One. I was stripping down a string session with Alan O'Duffy. I explained the situation and he said 'Great, we are on our way down'. Eddie turned up with Mitch Mitchell, Dave Mason and Brian Jones. I helped Eddie Kramer to set up the studio. Mitch's drums were set up on a drum riser in the middle of the studio and were mic'ed with Neumann U67s for overheads and an AKG D 12 on the bass drum. Dave Mason, the bass player from Traffic, was playing acoustic guitar. I did not realise it at the time, but Hendrix was already moving away from his original Experience trio. There was no sign of Noel Redding, and Hendrix was playing the bass guitar himself. Noel Redding later wrote 'Yeah, we were at this party and a bit drunk, I did not see the point of going'.

In the control room there were about half a dozen people, including Eddie, Brian Jones, a girlfriend of Brian's named Linda Lawrence and Roger Mayer. Roger was a technical boffin who made electronic gadgets, including distortion boxes and wah-wah pedals. George Chkiantz was a Tape-op, but in reality, he was a key influence in the discussions with Roger about fuzz boxes and various effects, and made a significant contribution towards the sounds that were achieved by Hendrix. There was an easy and relaxed atmosphere. Although Hendrix appeared to be a little shy, he was also warm and friendly. He was wearing dark satin trousers, a psychedelic paisley shirt, blue jacket, beads, a black hat, a collection of large rings on his fingers, a scarf tied to his wrist and another one 'round his forehead. Brian's style was rather different. On this occasion, he looked very dapper in a black jacket, white trousers and ruffled white shirt. George turned up, and as I had an early start the next day, I left at about 2 a.m.

A few days later, Eddie Kramer asked if I would be able to assist him with further work on the track they had recorded that night. Evidently, George would not be available on the 26th of January when Jimi planned to return to Studio One. Although wary of Eddie (I had only worked with him once before, during Traffic's *Mr. Fantasy* album), I immediately said yes. On the 26th, I set up Studio One with Eddie, and we loaded up the master take of *All Along the Watchtower*. The song had Mitch on drums, Jimi on bass, Dave on acoustic guitars and Jimi's guide electric guitar track. Over the years since his death, there have been many stories about Jimi that describe "party" recording sessions, with the studio full of people, wild drug abuse and recordings made under the influence of acid. There was no hint of such chaos during the two days I worked with Hendrix. On the contrary, the sessions were completely free of liggers, and there were no visible signs of serious drug use by Jimi. Most of the time, there was just Eddie, Jimi and myself in the studio, with the occasional visit from Roger Mayer. There was little conversation apart from the occasional polite request from Hendrix or a terse command barked at me by Kramer. These were the complete opposite to the Traffic party-style sessions I was soon to work on. With Hendrix the emphasis was strongly on getting results – both musically and sonically.

The recording equipment at Olympic in January 1968 was still only 4-track and very limited. This meant that many decisions about final sounds and levels had to be made while recording the basic instruments. It was common practice to record between two 4-track machines, bouncing the four tracks from one machine to two tracks (stereo mix) of another, allowing more tracks for overdubbing. The setup for Hendrix's electric guitar overdubs was achieved simply by placing a Vox AC30 amplifier in the studio, close to the control room window. We then placed Neumann U67s both close and distant, with an AKG C 12A close to the amp. From the control room it was difficult to see what Jimi actually did with his hands while he played guitar. He was hunched over the amp with his back to the control room window, his head bent low. We tried out numerous guitar ideas and sounds – desk distortion, fuzz box, wah-wah, Leslie cabinet, harmonising, ADT, phasing, Pultec filtering, repeat echoes and backwards effects. Most of this technique was outside my experience and way above my head, so I just followed Eddie's commands.

The two days flew by. Jimi was gone, taking with him a rough mix. A few months later at the Record Plant in New York, the recording was transferred to a recently installed 12-track tape machine – state-of-the-art at the time. After the overdubbing of percussion, vocal and more guitars, the track was finished, mixed and finally issued as a single in October 1968, reaching #5 in the UK charts. Initially, many people did not realise it was a cover version of a Bob Dylan song, and subsequently Dylan's own performances of the song were heavily influenced by the Hendrix version. The track also appeared on Hendrix's *Electric Ladyland* album. During the recording, *All Along the Watchtower* had sounded amazing on the Tannoy Red monitors in Studio One. For me, it was a magical and intense sound – even when unfinished, the track created a great rush when played loud in Studio One. Within months, the finished track was being played constantly on the radio. It remains one of my favourite recordings for the way it never fails to trigger an emotional surge.

Phill, Olympic Studio One, with Homemade 'Helios' Desk

Terry and me at his Wedding. Terry was 19 and I was 15

Chapter 2. Olympic Studios (part two)
26 May 1968

It was George Chkiantz who recommended and introduced me to Glyn Johns – one of the first freelance recording engineers in the UK, then at the peak of his career. During the early 1960s, he had had a limited singing career before training at IBC Studios and going on to work with an amazing collection of high-profile artists like The Rolling Stones, The Who, the Small Faces, The Beatles and later with the Eagles. He was confident and relaxed in his recording abilities, although I think some people might have misinterpreted this as arrogance.

Glyn and I got on well immediately, and it was a relationship that lasted until I left Olympic in December 1968. Although he was a bit of a taskmaster, he was straightforward and very good to work for. Just by watching and working with him I learned a great deal about microphone placement and technique, plus how to deal with the assortment of egos and personalities in the studio environment. During the following nine months we worked together on the Small Faces' *Ogden's Nut Gone Flake* album, The Move's single *Yellow Rainbow*, Steve Miller's *Sailor* album, The Rolling Stones *Beggars Banquet* and Traffic's second album, *Traffic Two*.

The first time I assisted on a session with Traffic had been on the 17th of November 1967 with Eddie Kramer engineering and Jimmy Miller producing. We were finishing off overdubs and working on the final mix of the song *Heaven is in Your Mind* for the album Mr. Fantasy. I was only on the session by default, as Glyn's younger brother Andy was to assist on the session but had not turned up. Initially, Eddie asked me to simply help him set up a couple of mics and find some headphones, but I ended up working with him for the whole session – albeit somewhat timidly. Eddie had come to London from South Africa in 1960. He had worked for an assortment of top artists and record companies and had done many sessions for Island Records. During my first two weeks at Olympic I had seen very little of him, and on the few occasions when I did see him, he had appeared to be blunt and offhand. I found him conceited and aggressive. On this occasion, however, he was friendlier and guided me through the session. Traffic's *Mr. Fantasy* album was released just one month later in December 1967.

I had been a fan of Steve Winwood for the previous two years. Steve had been the singer and keyboard player for the Spencer Davis Group since the age of 15. He was a brilliant musician and could play almost any instrument – bass, piano, organ and electric guitar – but it was his voice I particularly loved. This was the voice that had brought such a distinctive vocal sound to the singles *Keep on Running* and *I'm a Man*, both of which I thought were excellent. He was only two years older than me, and this made his success and achievements at the age of 19 seem even more impressive. On leaving the Spencer Davis Group in early 1967, he had formed his own band, Traffic, with Jim Capaldi on drums, Chris Wood on sax, and Dave Mason on bass.

At 23 years old, Jim Capaldi already looked old and weathered; his untidy black hair, beard and moustache accentuating his vagabond image. He had a great deal of nervous energy and consumed Valium like sweets. Nevertheless, he was a tight and excellent drummer. Jim was funny, friendly and open. Years later, while working on his solo albums *Short Cut Draw Blood* and *Sweet Smell of Success*, he would tell me stories about touring in America with Traffic and the endless rounds of traveling, groupies and drugs. He would try to describe to me the nights when he played drums while watching himself from high above the stage, after being given some form of acid or a mystery pill.

Dave Mason was a much harder guy to get to know. Thin, wiry and quiet, he had been a roadie for the Spencer Davis Group and became good friends with Steve Winwood, which led to the formation of Traffic. He had written *Hole in My Shoe* (a #2 single in the UK charts) but had briefly left the band after their first LP, *Mr. Fantasy*, to pursue other interests, including work with Jimi Hendrix and production for the band Family. However, despite Dave's continuing success with various solo projects, he was now back for Traffic's second album. He was only 21 years old.

Chris Wood was friendly, charming, mellow and the most accessible of the band members. He would come and sit by the tape machines and with eyes closed, nod his head to playbacks or quietly chatter away during breaks. After Winwood, he was my favourite musician, and during the next 10 years, could often be found hanging out at Basing Street Studios, always ready for a sax, flute or keyboard overdub. Once, when I had brought him into Studio Two for a sax solo, he was so wasted on drugs or alcohol that he just laid on his back on the floor and played. It was still beautiful.

Twenty years later, as Talk Talk struggled with their Variophon sax sound, with its intermittent split notes and flashes of magic, producer Tim Friese-Greene suddenly said, "It sounds just like Chris Wood." The name stuck and was written on the track sheet for the song *I Believe in You* as "Chris Wood". Unfortunately, Chris passed away in the early 80s.

The second Traffic album was to be recorded in short bursts over a period of a few months, starting in February 1968. The sound engineering was shared between Glyn Johns and Eddie Kramer, depending upon who was available. When neither was, my brother Terry or Brian Humphries would take over the job. I worked with all of these engineers on an assortment of songs for the album, including *(Roamin' Thru the Gloamin' with) 40,000 Headmen, Feelin' Alright* and *No Time to Live*. Each session seemed to differ in every way from the previous one, partly due to the diversity of the songs, but also because of the different working methods of each engineer. Some nights, I would set up screens and booths across the middle of the studio and we would record full electric band tracks with drums, bass, Hammond and sax. Other times everyone would sit in a circle on carpets on the floor, and we would record acoustic guitar, percussion, flute and piano. Despite these differences, there seemed to be no problem with continuity on the finished album.

It was important to create the right sounds on the instruments from the start, as little could be changed later. Although the studio seemed well equipped at the time, there were relatively few effects. By the mid-1980s, technical innovation made it possible to control and modify recorded sound in ways that were previously undreamed of. By that time, it was possible to process a signal using digital effects machines (Yamaha SPX, AMS, Lexicon) to simulate a wide variety of acoustic environments, from a small, wood-panelled room to a giant concert hall or church. In 1968, however, the only artificial reverberation we had was created with EMT echo plates, spring reverbs, primitive tape echo devices or naturally reverberant spaces such as corridors and stairwells.

The sessions with Traffic had a very "down home" air, with friends, girlfriends, roadies and hangers-on all sitting around the studio. Having this many people on the session sometimes caused distraction, noise and disruption, but most of the time the visitors helped to produce a relaxed and creative environment. Traffic liked to recreate the atmosphere of their rented Berkshire cottage, and while working in the studio they would burn incense and work in almost total darkness. The band, roadies and friends were an excellent bunch of characters, and for me, the sessions were thrilling. With this number of people around in the building, it meant that there was always something happening somewhere. From time to time, I would come across a small group of people sitting on the back stairs or in the maintenance room, playing acoustic guitars, eating hamburgers or rolling joints.

The band, Glyn Johns, and producer Jimmy Miller, knew exactly what they were aiming for and worked hard to achieve it amid the party atmosphere. Some songs had tight, worked-out arrangements, while others were captured after a lengthy jam. Jimmy was skilled at keeping the momentum of sessions up and was always ready to play percussion on a track or come up with a rhythm idea when the need arose. He was a large man, about 6 feet 2 inches tall with a solid build, long, dark hair and a moustache. He had a loud voice, was quick witted, sharp, and possessed an excellent sense of the bizarre. He always appeared to get the best out of people and would take control of the situation, patiently and calmly, pointing people in the right direction. During my year at Olympic, I worked with him on albums for Spooky Tooth and The Rolling Stones, in addition to the album for Traffic. I loved his approach. Jimmy was a wonderful inspiration to all involved on these albums and probably one of the best two all-around producers I have ever worked with – the other being Steve Smith. Jimmy treated me well, and we often played table tennis together at the back of Studio One after the Traffic sessions had ended – a ritual that continued right through the Stones' sessions for *Beggars Banquet*. He usually won.

Around this time, Dr. Squires, my local general practitioner in North Watford, placed me on prescription Valium. I had consulted him about a nervous feeling in my stomach, and after a few questions about my work hours, sleep patterns and diet, he diagnosed "tension" and prescribed 10 milligrams a day. I now feel, with information gleaned during 1994 and '95 and my subsequent operation, that this could have been the start of severe colon problems, but ignorance is bliss, and I swallowed the Valium daily. Unfortunately, I was on this drug for 10 years before getting myself cleaned up.

By March 1968, I was feeling comfortable in my knowledge of the studio equipment and had adjusted to the atmosphere of rock sessions. The studio employed two new assistants – Keith Harwood and Roger Quested. Andy Johns left Olympic to join my brother Terry at Morgan Studios in northwest London. I was now considered to be an experienced tape op, but there was no pay rise from Keith Grant. Over the next few months this began to annoy me.

I worked with George Chkiantz (who by now had been promoted to the job of junior engineer) on the promotional films for The Rolling Stones' songs *Jumpin' Jack Flash* and *Child of the Moon*. These films were directed by Michael Lindsay-Hogg, a prominent television director of the day. The idea of making such a film was a radical one – at that time only The Beatles had issued promotional films, and it would be at least 10 years before the music video became an important adjunct to the release of a single.

Jumpin' Jack Flash was filmed in Olympic's Studio One. The film crew built a large stage in the middle of the room and covered the walls with black fabric. The Stones then had their faces painted and were filmed by two camera crews as the band mimed to the backing track, played loud on the Tannoy/Lockwood studio monitors. *Child of the Moon* was filmed outside on location in the country (I forget where) and entailed my spending the day in a ditch with a Nagra portable tape machine and a shotgun microphone pointing up at Mick Jagger's mouth. This may sound easy, but I remember being extremely bored and very uncomfortable. At one point, George and I were asked for our ACTT membership numbers, and when neither of us could "remember" them (neither of us was a member), there were threats that George, myself and Olympic Studios might be blacklisted by the union. Keith Grant managed to smooth things over, and we heard no more about it. I decided at that point never to join a union that could be so officious, and subsequently have been involved with many films and videos "illegally".

In the spring of 1968, the new Ampex 8-track machine was delivered and installed into Studio One. In contrast to the old, weathered, portable 4-track machines, it was large, heavy and gleaming. The Small Faces' *Ogden's Nut Gone Flake* was one of the first albums to be recorded on this new 8-track equipment, with Glyn Johns engineering. The band had been formed in 1964 and signed up with manager Don Arden, an old-school hustler. They were not a group of intellectuals, but a bunch of East End soul boys – pint-sized herberts. They were all small-framed and dressed in a similar way, in crushed velvet trousers or white jeans, tailored flowered shirts, chiffon scarves, felt hats, soft, Italian shoes and fur coats. They had thin, drawn faces, mod haircuts and childlike smiles. The band was made up of Steve Marriott on guitar and vocals, Ronnie Lane on bass and vocals, Kenney Jones on drums and Ian McLagan on keyboards.

By the time I worked with the Small Faces in the spring of 1968, they had already had nine Top 20 hits and had been touring continuously. However, 25 years later in a Channel 4 television programme, they said that they had received no royalty statements and no fees for gigs. Instead, they were paid just £20 a week and given accounts in all the trendy Carnaby Street shops – Lord John, John Michael, Tomcat and Topper shoes. Their manager, Don Arden, justified this by saying, "I've never exploited anyone who didn't want to be exploited. I only exploited people for their own benefit."

Ogden's Nut Gone Flake was a tongue-in-cheek, hippie concept album, and side two featured Stanley Unwin reciting the story of *Happiness Stan*, who was looking for the missing half of the moon. The side began with the phrase, "Are you all sitting cumftibold two-square on your botty? Then I'll begin..." I was already a big fan of Stanley Unwin from watching him over the years on the television programme *Hogmanay* on New Year's Eve and was thrilled to be working with him. From a basic storyline written by Marriott and Lane, Unwin would transpose the words to his own style and language. His vocal was recorded wild on a mono 1/4-inch machine and was flown in during the mixing. He was a naturally humorous, charming and polite man who generated respect. My memory of Stanley Unwin is of him sitting at a Neumann U67 microphone in the vocal booth of Studio One, wearing a tweed jacket and trousers, looking completely relaxed, talking gibberish and smiling a lot.

Partly due to the zany nature of the material, the sessions for *Ogden's Nut Gone Flake* had a great atmosphere and were full of humour. Steve Marriott and Ronnie Lane had written the majority of the songs and were producing the album with Glyn. They were much influenced by old music hall traditions, and this showed in the way they used rhythms, melodies and character vocals. Marriott had been brought up on musicals and played the Artful Dodger in the musical *Oliver!* when he was 12 years old. He was sharp and clever, cheeky, hilariously funny and had an irresistible personality. He was a fireball, always talking and up to some practical joke; a natural at amusing people and enjoying life. Marriott and Lane were particularly funny and engaging and stormed through the sessions with little regard for conventional studio procedure or technicalities. Working in Studio One, we laid down songs as a band with drums, bass, guitar and piano or organ set up according to Glyn's tried and tested layout. As we were no longer limited to four tracks, each instrument now had a track of its own, and this left four tracks to overdub vocals, solos, effects and orchestral arrangements. Lead and backing vocals were usually recorded at the same time in this loose party atmosphere, with Marriott and Lane intermittently playing some form of percussion or random finger snaps. I loved this approach, and I liked the way they would find things in the studio to hit or play at random. I was reminded of this many years later when working with Talk Talk.

The members of the band were endlessly messing about, forgetting the lyrics and musical parts. The key word at times like that was "nice". They would look at each other, smile, say "Nice" and then have another go, trying not to laugh. When Marriott sang, the veins would stick out on the side of his neck like twigs, and in between verse, chorus and solos he would dive off the microphone and fool around in an exaggerated, theatrical manner. Some songs were recorded in sections and were then edited together on the 1-inch 8-track. The band used all the tricks of the day, including heavy compression, tape phasing, wild panning and feeding guitars and vocals through a Leslie speaker. There were harp, flute and cello arrangements as well, which were all overdubbed. We used every possible space within the building to record in, including the corridors and toilets. I thoroughly enjoyed this approach. There was a strong feeling of freedom on these night sessions, with no office staff and no 80-piece orchestra to look after. Working with just four or five band members (who did not sight-read music) was easier, much more fun and had less predictable results – I particularly enjoyed that aspect of it. The album ends with Stanley Unwin's voice – "So I hope you'll turn out three quarters half as lovely won't you wouldn't half and enjoy it. Stay cool won't you?"

Drugs in the form of speed and dope were in abundance on Small Faces sessions. In some corridor, empty office or sitting behind a studio screen, it was not unusual to find a roadie or one of the band with a joint in his hand or a pill in his mouth. When we worked late into the night, the roadies occasionally offered me a toke or a blue. I did have the odd blast from a joint, but being wary of pills, I had never tried the blues. Glyn Johns did not approve of drugs, even spliffs. Ironically, he often worked on heavily drugged sessions with artists such as the Steve Miller Band, The Rolling Stones, Traffic, the Eagles, and The Beatles, but he did not indulge himself. He never made a big thing about the use of drugs, and where clients were concerned, he turned a blind eye to the matter.

On the 26th of May, I was back working with Glyn and the Traffic sessions. We were recording the song *No Time to Live*. This was a beautiful, haunting song, but complicated in its arrangement and difficult to perform as a live band. The intro had a thin, ghostly Hammond part and a wonderful, warm, drifting flute that was prominent throughout the song. The other instruments were drums, timpani, bass and piano. We had recorded at least eight takes in the dark and druggy environment of Studio One and were playing back our chosen master. It had been a long day and it was now around 2 a.m. I was particularly tired and had been fighting off sleep since midnight. One of the roadies saw me nodding off at the 8-track machine, came over and handed me a black pill. I felt a bit doubtful, but the roadie said, "Don't worry, it's fine. It will just help you to stay awake." This allayed my fears and I swallowed the pill. The effects came on surprisingly slowly, but after a while I began to appreciate being back in control of my eyelids. The pill helped me through to the end of the session. I then packed up and drove home to Watford, getting there at about 6 a.m. I lay in bed, now wide awake, until midday before getting up, bathing and driving back to Olympic at 5 p.m., to set up again for another evening session with Traffic. By now I was beginning to feel a little wired, but I was certainly not tired, and eating little I sped (literally) through the evening. By 2 or 3 a.m. most of the bad side effects of the speed had hit me. I felt grubby and itchy, and my scrambled brain was darting from one subject to another. It was difficult to work, and I was pleased when we finally finished around 4 a.m. The roadies thought it was very amusing and as I left for home they informed me that they had given me a black bomber – a particularly strong form of speed. After being up for about 38 hours, I finally managed to sleep. Although I later took speed in the form of the milder blue pills, this experience made me avoid anything stronger, like sulphate and especially black bombers.

Glyn was pleased with my work and attitude during the Traffic sessions and asked me to work with him, Jimmy Miller and The Rolling Stones on their next LP – *Beggars Banquet*.

Chapter 3. The Rolling Stones 10 June 1968

The Rolling Stones' album *Beggars Banquet* was recorded over a three-month period between April and June 1968 in Olympic Studios' Studio One.

The Stones appeared to be split into two camps. In one camp were Bill Wyman (quiet and laidback) and Charlie Watts (the perfect gentleman, always polite and friendly, with a warm, dry slant on life). In the other camp were Mick Jagger (who although sharp and amusing, I found distant and arrogant) and Keith Richards (who came over as being very intense and aggressive). Brian Jones struggled between these two partnerships, having what appeared to be a difficult time. He often looked wasted on drugs or alcohol but was usually friendly and easy-going. Over the previous few months, he had been trying to give up various drugs, including marijuana, alcohol and LSD. It was rumoured that Brian was swallowing speed and drinking two bottles of Scotch per day. He appeared by far the most talented of all the members of the band, and could play multiple instruments – sitar, marimba, sax, harmonica and wonderful slide guitar. Although he had originally led the Stones, it was clear that he had now been demoted, and Jagger and Richards rarely appeared to listen to what he had to say. It has been suggested by writers over the years that he was suffering from paranoia and believed the rest of the Stones were trying to get him out of the band. I was not aware of this at the time, but I did feel sorry for Brian. He was clearly in a very depressed state of mind.

He spent a lot of time crouched on a low chair in his booth, hunched over his guitar, which he held high on his chest. He looked as though he was having difficulty keeping up with what was going on, or even breathing properly. By contrast, Jagger pranced about in a white ruffled shirt, oozing confidence. I had most contact with Bill, Charlie and Brian. They were friendly, with no ego problems and behaved just like ordinary guys. In stark contrast, I had very little communication with Jagger and

Richards. Mick treated me as a lackey, and I was very wary of Keith.

Charlie was set up in the permanent drum booth on the right-hand side of the studio (seen from the control room), with three other booths built out of screens in the centre of the room, to accommodate Mick, Keith and Bill. In the large area in front of the control room window, we put the piano, the Hammond organ and a booth for Brian. This still left enough space for acoustic set ups and overdubs. Our start time was any time after 2 p.m., as we had a 24-hour lock out. The setup was Charlie on drums, Bill on bass, Brian on acoustic guitar, Keith on electric guitar, bass and percussion, and session musician Nicky Hopkins on piano and organ. Mick played various percussion instruments, the occasional acoustic guitar and sang guide vocals. Nicky was an absolute sweetheart, mellow and relaxed – a real gentleman. Jagger and Richards, along with producer Jimmy Miller, took control of the sessions for feel, approach and arrangements.

Each song was first run through and rehearsed with Brian, Mick and Keith. Bill and Charlie were not usually involved until the structure of the verses and choruses had been agreed upon. We tried out every possibility when recording songs. *Street Fighting Man* was transferred to 8-track from a basic cassette demo of Keith's. Some songs, like *Sympathy for the Devil*, went through many different styles and feels before the band settled on a final version. Because of the limited selection of studio effects then available, sounds had to be created at the source, so we tried different guitars, amps, microphones and various unusual locations in the studio building – such as recording overdubs for in the stairwell. When recording songs played on acoustic instruments, Glyn would use a mic setup similar to the one he used with Traffic. The band would be in a circle on the floor in front of the studio window, on a 12-foot square rug, with African drums, tablas, congas, tambourines, acoustic guitars, bottleneck, bass and piano.

Jagger still sang guide vocals as the song was being recorded or played along on percussion. Brian's depression would often cause low points during a day's recording. To my surprise, however, he appeared to deal extremely well with his ex-girlfriend, Anita Pallenberg, being at the studio, even though she was now living with Keith. Brian was emotionally very up one night and played a beautiful slide acoustic guitar on *No Expectations*. Magic. A few days later, on May 21st, Brian was busted for the second time for possession of cannabis.

Some vocals were kept – especially on acoustic numbers – while they were re-recorded on other songs such as *Sympathy for the Devil* and *Street Fighting Man*. The sessions were crowded with maybe 20 or 30 people at a time, and there would be mountains of coffee cups, Coke bottles, roaches and dog ends to be removed from the studio each morning after the session. The visitors were usually smartly dressed, with the men in white or flowered shirts, ruffled cuffs, black trousers or suits. Most of the women also wore trousers, apart from Anita Pallenberg, who favoured Indian-style flowing dresses, either with or without underwear.

A similar crowd appeared almost every night and included among them various close friends of the band, Anita, Andrew Loog Oldham, Tony Sanchez and Marianne Faithfull. Of all the women there, I thought Marianne was by far the most beautiful. She was the classic English Rose, with long, blond hair, pale skin, a wide mouth, cute nose and large, sad eyes. She had a slight frame and wonderfully long legs, usually concealed by a pair of trousers. Although she was then only 21 years old, Marianne appeared worldly and experienced in life. She was very friendly, amusing and intelligent and seemed always to be carrying a book around with her.

It was during these sessions for *Beggars Banquet* that I first experienced a particularly deep and intense enjoyment of music in the studio. On rare occasions, usually during an exceptional performance by a musician, a feeling would occur of being transported and becoming unaware of my surroundings. This wonderful, detached feeling took over, for example, while I was listening to *Parachute Woman* loud at 3 a.m. with 20 people in the control room. Then it was everything – romantic, happy, sad, all-powerful – a great rush. This feeling would sometimes be recalled over subsequent years during a particular artist's performances – in the '70s with Murray Head's, Robert Palmer's or Steve Winwood's vocals, and with Lowell George's guitar playing. There were other similar moments while recording with Talk Talk, David F. Malin and Paul Roberts during the '80s.

On the 4th of June, about two months into the recording of *Beggars Banquet*, the film director Jean-Luc Godard turned up with a full crew to film the recording of *Sympathy for the Devil* for the movie *One Plus One*. The film, later re-titled *Sympathy for the Devil*, was about glamour and violence in the 1960s, and in retrospect provided an interesting archive of the recording of a Rolling Stones' classic. The crew laid a rail track for the camera in a semicircle around our main setup and ran the camera back and forth continuously. Extra lights were set up on poles around the studio and in the roof, with light-diffusing paper over them. The control room was in complete darkness, with no filming taking place in there. The cameras and crew filmed every other night, and different versions of the song were recorded both on tape and on film during a six-day period.

The first version of the song started off lightweight – almost as a country ballad – with Jagger, Richards and Jones all playing acoustic guitars, Nicky on Hammond, Bill on bass and Charlie playing side stick. Apart from an AKG C 12A microphone on the bass amp and a D 224 on Jagger's vocal, all instruments were mic'ed with valve Neumann U67s. They tried a 6/8 tempo with Keith moving to electric guitar, and then progressed to Bill playing a cabasa, while Keith played bass. All through these rehearsals and early takes, crewmembers and friends were sitting around in the studio. The sessions progressed slowly, as the band worked out different arrangements and approaches. After a few days, the drum booth was enlarged to accommodate two extra percussion booths and its roof was extended.

We recorded all rehearsals and run-throughs either as a reference or (in case we were lucky) recorded a master. Jagger grew impatient at the slow progress, while Bill said almost nothing night after night. The rhythm patterns were constantly changing, and Charlie appeared to be struggling from time to time, while Brian sat for hours in his booth, strumming his acoustic guitar and chain-smoking cigarettes. Jagger and Richards worked closely together, with Keith acting as musical director.

After two or three days they tried taking a completely different route and moved to the acoustic setup in front of the studio window. Charlie was now playing an African drum, with Bill and Brian on acoustic guitars, Keith on electric guitar and Nicky on electric piano. They used this setup to play through several different rhythms and tempos, as Jagger and Richards were still not completely happy with anything they had yet recorded. Once this approach had been exhausted, they went back to the previous setup.

With these constant changes of instruments, I was kept very busy and rarely sat down for longer than a few minutes. Unusually, due to all the running about, I operated the 8-track machine while standing. By contrast with the portable Ampex 4-track machines, the 8-track was a monster. It resembled a 6-foot high, floor-standing cooking stove on castors, with deep, 1-inch tape spools and large, illuminated transport switches in different colours. There were polished metal arms to prevent the tape from snagging, glistening rollers, a brass capstan and a hum guard that closed over the tape heads. There were rows of switches marked "Record", "Playback" and "Sync", and pots marked "Record Level", "Playback Level" and such. Most obvious of all were the eight backlit VU level meters with their needles jumping erratically as the tape was played.

A major breakthrough in recording *Sympathy for the Devil* occurred once the band began to play the song at a faster tempo. They brought in a friend, Rocky Dijon, to play percussion, and changed the drum pattern. With Wyman now on maracas, Richards on bass, Jagger on African drum and guide vocal, Rocky on congas and Hopkins moving over to play the piano, the track suddenly developed a hard, sinister feel, and the next night it was mastered. Jagger's lead vocal and the backing vocals of "Woo-woo, Woo-woo" were all recorded simultaneously, with Mick singing on one side of a sound screen and Nicky, Charlie, Marianne, Brian, Bill, Keith and Anita chanting on the other. Keith gave them their cue and pointed into the air every time he wanted them to change key. It was 4:30 a.m., and there were about nine other people in the control room besides Glyn and myself. These included Jimmy Miller who, as ever, kept up the momentum of the session and was always ready to play any of a multitude of percussion instruments. In the main studio area, there were a further 20 people – cameramen, sound guys, assistants and roadies who worked quietly around the Stones.

On the evening of the 10th of June, as Jagger was repairing the vocal track, I saw Marianne Faithfull write *Burn Baby Burn* in red lipstick on the control room window. This was written in mirror writing so that Jagger could read it on the other side of the window. This turned out to be strangely prophetic. Sometime later, in the middle of a take, there was a loud "pop" and I noticed Jagger look up to the ceiling and step to one side. Down floated a piece of burning paper, followed by some small pieces of debris. Now everyone in the studio was looking up towards the ceiling. Whatever was going on was happening directly above our main setup of amplifiers, piano and Hammond. I stopped the tape machine and looked over to Glyn. "I think we have a fire," he said, "We'd better get out there."

Glyn and I entered the studio and for the first time saw flames. We began to realise the seriousness of the situation. A bulb had set fire to the diffusing paper, which had in turn set alight a hessian panel and then the insulation in the roof. I began moving mics away from the area directly below the fire. The film crew removed their equipment and turned off some of the lights, while the Stones and their roadies and friends grabbed guitars and tried to move amplifiers. It soon became a very dangerous area, and only the guitars and smaller amps were rescued. We had no time to try and move the Hammond, piano or any of the larger amps. Glyn went down to reception and called the fire brigade.

Jimmy Miller, as usual remaining cool and in control, had just one thing on his mind. By the time I returned to the control room, he had spooled off the 8-track tapes and was collecting boxes of masters together. He asked me to help him carry them down to reception, to retrieve other Stones masters from the tape store and to call a cab. Within 15 minutes from the moment the lamp burst, Jimmy was gone with all the tapes. The liggers had packed up and left. The area had also been cleared of some of the film and studio equipment, and the Stones had dispersed, leaving Stu (Ian Stewart – friend, roadie, manager, gofer, organiser and former pianist with the Stones) to sort things out as usual. Meanwhile at the back of the studio, Glyn was in a deep conversation with Jean-Luc Godard. At the front of the studio, the roof was very much alight and by the time the fire brigade arrived there was a considerable amount of debris falling to the floor, most of it on fire.

Three fire engines arrived with sirens blaring. The fire fighters ran their hoses across the wide pavement, in through the front door and up the stairs to Studio One. Fire escape doors were opened to the street, and all those still left in the building were now evacuated. Glyn and I stood in Church Road and watched the proceedings. There was a great deal of noise and yelling as people ran about and the fire fighters got to work.

Although the flames could not be seen from the street, there was a huge amount of smoke billowing into the air and a roaring sound that made conversation difficult. Flashing blue lights were reflected in the water that streamed across the road while the police directed traffic. After a short while, lights began to come on in neighbouring windows. I noticed that one of the fire engines was being used to spray water directly onto the roof. This was a large building, a former cinema, and part of a larger cluster of shops and flats all now under threat from water damage if not from the fire.

The fire was put out in less than 30 minutes, and Glyn and I were allowed back into the building. There was a strong smell of burning, and the studio floor had a covering of wet soot. More importantly, there was now a large hole in the roof through which the sky could clearly be seen. There were fragments of charred debris all over the place. Some items of equipment, including amplifiers, the Hammond organ and some of the photographic gear, were damaged and sat more or less where they had been left, soaked with dirty water. I was a little shaken by these events and just stood there looking out through the hole to the night sky. "What are we going to do now?" I asked Glyn aimlessly. He did not answer.

Glyn and Jimmy took the tapes to America and *Beggars Banquet* was finally mixed in Los Angeles. Godard did not return to Olympic to resume shooting, and the film was completed using the footage he had shot before the fire occurred.

The hole in the roof remained for a week or two. We had to stop recording whenever a plane flew over.

Chapter 4. Canada
28 June 1969

After a year of being paid £10 per week, I eventually confronted Keith Grant about a pay rise. He called my bluff and I left. Despite my years' experience working at Olympic, to my surprise I found it impossible to find another job as assistant engineer, apart from an occasional day's recording at Jack Jackson's Studio in Rickmansworth, Hertfordshire. Finally, under pressure from my parents, I reluctantly took a job as a security guard. For six months, I spent 12 hours a night trudging around factories, warehouses and a former mill that had been converted into a film store. For protection, I had a gun that fired a bright blue dye and a large German Shepherd dog – fortunately for me she was not as fierce as she looked.

But in 1968 an event changed both my brother Terry's and my futures. While working on a session at Morgan Studios, Terry met Mort Ross and Doug Riley, two musicians and songwriters who were over from Toronto, Canada, to record a collection of beer commercials. Mort and Doug loved Terry's work and were impressed by his track record (The Who, Manfred Mann and Traffic). They offered him the chance to become involved in the setting up of a record company – Revolution Records – and to build the first 16-track studio in Canada. Terry went for a week's visit to Toronto. On returning to London, he decided that this was where his future lay and telephoned Mort and Doug, taking them up on their offer.

Terry and his wife Linda emigrated on the 1st of January 1969, and soon after their arrival Terry began working on designs for Revolution Sound Studios (soon to be renamed Toronto Sound). Meanwhile Terry, Mort and Doug formed the record company and signed their first two artists – Diane Brooks and the band Motherlode. Both acts brought success almost immediately. Ray Charles heard Diane's first album and was impressed – evidently he remarked, "This is the greatest voice I've heard since Dinah Washington." He arranged for the album to be released on his Tangerine label in the USA. Motherlode followed this with a triumph of their own when their single, *When I Die*, became a hit in America. The success of these first two projects, especially in America, was reflected in good sales figures for both records, and the record company's share of the royalties was used to help pay for building the new studio.

Further capital having been secured, the plans for the studio were finalised and a suitable building was rented at Thorncliffe Park, a modern estate of shops, offices and light industry in the central east suburbs of Toronto. Terry then offered me a job as a junior engineer, and I flew to Canada to join him on the 28th of June 1969. Terry and Linda met me at the airport. They were keen to show me the site of the new studio, so we immediately drove to Thorncliffe Park.

The building, which was on Overlea Boulevard, was a large hangar of a structure and as yet little more than a shell. Although there was nothing to see inside, its sheer size was impressive. Clearly there was plenty of space for the two studios that they hoped to build. The first one would be capable of recording 25 musicians and the second one, when financed and built, would be sufficiently large enough to hold 60 musicians.

I moved in with Terry and Linda at Woodlawn Avenue on the ground floor of a duplex. It was a large, detached house near to the convergence of Yonge Street and St. Clair Avenue, containing three bedrooms, two living rooms with large bay windows, a bathroom with a sunken bath and a fully fitted kitchen. There were wooden beams across the ceilings and a beautiful wooden staircase. Mort Ross and his family lived in the apartment above.

On my first weekend, two days after I arrived, a barbecue had been arranged so that I could meet some of the local musicians and those closely involved with the studio – Barry Tallman, Steve Kennedy, Brian and Brenda Russell, Diane Brooks, Gee Chung and, of course, Doug Riley and Mort Ross. For the barbecue, they had chosen a wonderful location about a two-hour drive north of Toronto. I travelled with Doug and his girlfriend in their brand-new black Chevrolet Camaro. It was a beautiful, hot summer's day, and we soon covered the 120 miles, arriving at a large lake surrounded by trees. With friends, husbands and wives, there were about 25 of us altogether. We set up the barbecue, laid out blankets, unloaded the picnic coolers and put up umbrellas to create some shade. We ate fish, hamburgers and fresh corn on the cob that we had bought on our way from a stall at the side of the road. We drank beer and Coke and smoked a little grass. It was a marvellous way to meet everyone.

During the afternoon, Barry produced some Microdot acid and offered it around to all the men. The women were not included in this ritual, and at first knew nothing about it. I had no idea what I was taking, but I found the effects were pleasant, with mild visual hallucinations and a heightened awareness of the surrounding sounds. The weather was wonderful, the landscape beautiful and my new acquaintances sharp and amusing. We played tapes, talked easily about the many artists that had been recorded at Olympic Studios and discussed plans for the future.

After a few hours, we packed up our belongings and went go-kart racing at a local circuit. It was total madness, hurtling around a track at 40 mph out of our heads. There were shunts, spins and crashes, but everyone survived, and as it became dark, we headed back to Toronto with just the odd bruise to remind us later of what we had done. That night, as I lay in bed listening to CHUM FM and enjoying the last few effects of the acid (floating off the bed, near to the ceiling), I relived my first 48 hours of being in Canada – the acid, the weather and the attitude of my weekend companions had set up a very positive feeling for me that would last almost a whole year in Toronto.

During my first three months in Canada, I had plenty of time on my hands to soak up the atmosphere of Toronto, especially during the evenings. I found myself with more freedom than I had ever experienced before, and at almost 19 years old I was ready for it. For the previous two years, I had given up any form of social life in favour of my ambition to become a sound engineer, working consistently for 80 to 100 hours a week. Now, however, until the studio was complete, the whole of July, August and September of this year was time out for me. Toronto in 1969 was a remarkable place to be. During that summer, thousands of American draft dodgers were swarming into Vancouver, Toronto and Montreal. Acid, hash and drugs in general were in abundance and there was a strong youth culture.

One of my new friends, trombone player Barry Tallman, decided to visit his parents in Winnipeg, some 1,200 miles or so to the west. He planned to drive across Canada in his black 1962 Fleetwood Cadillac and invited me to go with him. As I had nothing specific to do, I said yes. It seemed an excellent opportunity to see some of the Canadian interior – the wide, endless prairies, forests, rivers and lakes. I thought the car was brilliant – massive with huge tail fins, lots of chrome and by British standards, many unusual gadgets, including a device that dipped the headlights automatically when triggered by the lights of an approaching vehicle. I was highly impressed.

We set off during the third week of July, with Barry's supply of speed, mescaline and hash hidden under the dashboard. We travelled north to Barrie and Sault St. Marie. Here we crossed over the US border into Michigan and drove west through Marquette, Duluth, Grand Rapids and Thief River Falls, Minnesota. It was one visual treat after another, as large American trucks travelled in convoy, six-lane highways crisscrossed each other and weaved through the vast open spaces, and the beautiful, clear, peacock-blue sky stretched on forever.

We occasionally pulled into truck stops to get coffee and food and to be insulted by the local rednecks for having long hair. We did the 1,200-mile drive in about 26 hours, taking turns to drive and to sleep. For me, it was very exciting driving through the night on single track highways in such a beautiful car. We arrived in Winnipeg and had a few days of staying with Barry's parents and visiting friends before driving northwest to Dauphin. Here we spent time at the 75th National Ukrainian Festival, which took place during the first three days of August.

The Festival site was spread over a wide area, with many different activities and events taking place simultaneously with local orchestras, choirs and dancers. The *Echoes of Ukraine* theme was exhibited by shows of spinning, weaving, beadwork, ancient Easter egg decorating and cultural displays. Being high summer, the weather was extremely hot, and there was a lazy, mellow atmosphere amongst the groups of people who wandered amidst all the marquees and tents. While strolling around the Festival, we came upon a band who were playing and performing sketches on the grass near to a lake where people were fishing, swimming, water skiing and boating. During a break, we got into conversation with the band, and were invited back to their house, where we enjoyed a marvellous evening of music with singing, jokes and mime sketches. They were an enormously creative bunch, with a talent to entertain without apparent effort – particularly two of them, Cathy and Dave.

At some point, it was agreed that we should all take some LSD and go over to the attic den of one of the band members to continue the party. Windowpane acid was duly distributed, and we headed across town in two cars. We climbed the five flights of stairs to the attic hippie den and settled in. I found that the acid took effect quickly, probably because I hadn't eaten very much during the day.

We listened to music played at very high volume and smoked a particularly strong type of hash. Within an hour of arriving in the room, I was very stoned, very high and beginning to have the occasional panic attack. At some point, in my head, the music and the people faded away, and I was left sitting alone. When I came back to my senses things were not as they should have been. I was sitting on the floor in the middle of the attic as before, but when I looked around the room, to my horror, I saw that all my new friends had vanished and, in their place, sitting against the walls around the room, were skeletons. The image was so hideous and so real that my only thought was to get out as quickly as possible.

The next thing I became aware of was sitting on the pavement in the street. Barry and Cathy were talking to me and trying to get me to stand up. There was a police car parked over the other side of the street and Barry was worried that I might attract their attention, although I'm sure I already had. Fortunately, I was beginning to feel better and finally stood up and began the long six-hour comedown to normality. It was a really unpleasant experience, and I have no idea why it happened. Perhaps it was triggered by claustrophobia in the tiny attic room, too much hash or the acid – I never really knew.

Barry had previously taken me through his list of "dos and don'ts" for having a successful trip – don't take it unless you feel really positive, don't stare in any mirrors once you are tripping, and don't go to a party where there are lots of unfamiliar people. The "dos" included drinking plenty of orange juice and water and avoiding alcohol. I suppose a score of four out of five from Barry's checklist wasn't too bad – my mistake was probably to take the acid with people I didn't know.

The next day, in a somewhat delicate state, we loaded up with food supplies and beer and drove southwest to the Riding Mountain National Park. Barry had a friend who was living in a motor home near Clear Lake for a few weeks, so we decided to pay him a visit. Chas and his wife Jenny made us very welcome. We stayed for about three days, eating pasta, drinking beer, taking long walks, lying in the sun, listening to music, smoking homegrown grass and talking. It gave me a chance to calm down after my experience in Dauphin and to come to terms with having had a bad trip.

The location was breathtakingly beautiful – a large, freshwater lake surrounded by conifers and a collection of scattered bays and inlets. Here we lunched on wonderfully delicious fish, drank beer and margaritas and rented a powerful speedboat to explore the lake. In the late afternoon, we threw caution to the wind, took our last tabs of mescaline and dived into the crystal-clear lake. In contrast to the air temperature of 90-plus degrees, it was cold but exhilarating. I enjoyed being underwater and watching the effects of the sunlight as it scattered in all directions. It was only afterwards, when we were sitting on the grassy bank soaking up the sun and the glorious scenery, that I remembered I could not swim. We spent the evening lying on our backs at the side of the lake and watching the stars.

We drove back to Winnipeg and that evening Barry took me to see Lenny Breau, an old friend of his from the past who lived in the northern suburbs of Winnipeg. He was a guitarist with whom Barry had played in various bands before moving to Toronto. Both Barry and my brother Terry had previously referred to Lenny as "that brilliant technician of a guitarist." There were a couple of other people there, including Lenny's sister Geraldine, a sultry woman in her mid-20s with long ebony hair. They were all smoking opium and invited us to partake. I had not had any opium since the days with George Chkiantz at Olympic some 18 months before, and after my recent experience with the acid I decided to be careful and not have too much. Unfortunately, Barry was not so cautious and spent most of the evening throwing up in the toilet while I listened to blues records and talked with Geraldine and Lenny. Around 11 p.m. Geraldine led me out into the large, tree-lined garden and in the humid summer heat seduced me on the long, soft grass lawn. Could this trip get any better?

From the age of 10, Lenny had taught himself to play guitar by listening to records and local radio stations. As a child, he had not realised that there was often more than one guitarist playing on a record, and he developed a style that was unique, playing the rhythm and lead parts as one. (I would later work with Lenny Breau in Toronto, and he truly was a formidable guitarist. Unfortunately, his career was short-lived, as he died of a heroin overdose in the mid-1980s.)

Barry and I said goodbye to Lenny and headed back to Toronto, again driving nonstop for 1,200 miles with both of us feeling mellow, fragile and very tired. The little amount of speed we had left helped to get us home. Barry and I continued to spend time together. He was always an excellent companion for an evening's entertainment in Toronto and initiated me into the drug subculture of the city – going to showings of *2001: A Space Odyssey* on mescaline and visiting the dark, cellar jazz bars. The people I was spending time with were very positive in their attitude towards drugs, both at work and play, and everyone I met during my first three or four months in Canada seemed to be using them.

During August and September, the building work went to plan and the studio began to take shape. The insulated walls and ceiling went up, offices were built, and equipment was ordered. Then problems appeared almost overnight. The finances of the new company seemed to be in disarray, and when this was investigated, the rumour was that Mort Ross had spent a good deal of the money that had been set aside for the studio to finance his heroin habit. By the time Terry and Doug found out there was not enough money left to pay the builders, Terry offered the builders a deal – either the studio could declare bankruptcy and they would not be paid, or they could finish the studio and be paid out of the income from sessions once the studio was in operation. The main builder, Gerry, accepted the latter choice and continued working with two assistants. Terry and I started to do more of the physical work, laying glass fibre on the walls and in the plate reverb room and running mic lines and cables for the desk and outboard equipment. Terry and Doug pulled out of their involvement with Mort and looked for new financial backing to salvage the part of the business concerned with the recording studio. The record company, Revolution Records, died a natural death. At the same time, Terry and Linda looked for a new apartment. They had fallen out badly with Mort over the finances and drug situation and wanted to move away from him as soon as possible.

Despite these upsets, I was still enjoying being in Toronto. With the international success of such Canadian musicians as Joni Mitchell, The Band, Neil Young, Gordon Lightfoot and Motherlode, it was hoped that the city would become another music capital – perhaps fourth in line after London, Los Angeles and New York. It was a wonderful time to be there, and because I was helping to build the studio, it felt as though I was at the forefront of the action. I hooked up with a crowd of expatriates and local musicians: Spyros Lagoudontis, Frank Lee, Pat Coffey, Gary Mertz and two French Canadian women – Ginette Roy and Francine Gagnon. We spent most of our evenings and nights together at clubs and discos in downtown Yorkville or in the acid clubs of East York.

These clubs were decorated wildly with oil-lights projected onto the walls and ceiling, and sponge mattresses on the floors. We were all very white and middle class and partied a great deal, meeting at a club at 10 p.m. and then moving on to the next one at about 1 a.m. We usually ended up at someone's apartment by 3 or 4 a.m. The favourites were Ginette and Francine's apartments on Jarvis Street, where we would smoke dope and take downers before weaving our way back to our homes at around 6 a.m. As I did not drink much alcohol, I would often drive Spyros home in his white Dodge. We all used the same drug dealer, Alan, who was English and older than we were – closer to 30 years old. He was a typical dealer – quiet, mysterious and giving little indication as to his background or beliefs. For me, it was an easy life. I would help out at the studio between 2 p.m. and 8 p.m. and then party from 10 p.m. to 6 a.m.

The Cadac desk (one of the first desks built by Clive Green, previously a maintenance man at Olympic Studios) arrived from England and was stored in its polythene cover at the building site. Everything was coming together well, but it was a slow process. Terry and I were still working alongside the three professional builders, but we were about two months behind the original schedule. This meant more time out for me.

I was still living with Terry and Linda, now in a house on Foxbar Road. Although sometimes I would stay in and talk to Terry about the studio and any new plans that were being made, my evenings were nearly always free. Most of the time, I was out with Barry Tallman, Steve and Sharon Kennedy, or Francine and the usual crowd. There were parties everywhere – in Yorkville, onboard ships at the Toronto docks and out in Queens – and it was wild. Terry continued to do a great deal of public relations work and was often on the radio and doing press interviews.

Meanwhile, at home, friction was beginning to develop between Linda and me over my friends, my use of drugs and the hours I kept. Terry got caught up in it all and backed Linda, much to my annoyance. Terry knew I smoked a fair amount of dope and that sometimes I took acid, and he did not really approve of it either. He had not taken acid since the barbecue back in June. I tried to explain to him that after the stifling years at Stanborough Park School, the job at the Co-op and the hard work at Olympic, I was just making up for some of my lost youth. It was just a bit of fun letting my hair down, and I would stop taking acid once the studio was opened. Terry seemed unconvinced, and as I was under 21, he was responsible for me. I didn't think it was such a big deal.

Around this time, I started to have severe stomach pains. After seeing the doctor, I was given a barium meal, an X-ray and treatment for an ulcer. I was advised not to drink alcohol or eat spicy, fatty foods, and I had to swallow a collection of chalk pills and medicines. At the time, I felt it was an inconvenience, but nothing too desperate, as I drank very little alcohol anyway. Life carried on much as before.

Finally, the studio was finished and opened in November of 1969. We were busy from day one and recorded an assortment of projects with Lulu, Ray Stevens, Motherlode, Perth County

Conspiracy, Edward Bear, Count Basie and various jingles. It was wonderful to be back working in the studio environment again and to say down the talkback to Count Basie, "Okay, we're rolling," as he counted in his 17-piece band. Life was great.

One night in late October, I was in a club in Yorkville with Francine, Frank Lee, Ginette, Spyros, Spyros' girlfriend Susan, Alan (our dealer) and his girlfriend Carol. I had been rehearsing all day with Frank and Spyros and the band they had now formed, called The Robert E. Lee Brigade. John Williams, an A&R man and musical director for Columbia Records, had signed the band and was now acting as their executive producer. The rehearsals were for a future album they wanted me to produce, and we had spent the evening discussing songs, schedules and drummers. As I had no track record at all at this point, it was amazing that I had been offered the job – I think it was purely because it was known that I had assisted on Jimi Hendrix, The Rolling Stones and Traffic sessions, and that I was one of the team that was building the "new studio in town". Because of all this, I was getting a great deal of attention, and I certainly had no intention of dampening their enthusiasm. The album was not due to be recorded until the spring, so there was little sense of urgency. The rehearsals, which took place either in Toronto or an hour north at Tom's house, were as much social as musical gatherings after which the fun usually continued, either at a club or a nearby bar.

On this particular occasion, I was ready to call it a night by 1 a.m., but some of the others wanted to continue socializing, so as we left the club, we split into two groups. I got a lift with Alan and Carol, along with Susan, who needed to be up early. We were all heading in the same direction, but the group that went with Frank and Spyros were intending to stop at a bar for one last drink. Before long, I was wishing I had joined them.

We headed out of Yorkville and onto Yonge Street in Alan's brown Pontiac LeMans. Something was about to happen that caused me to remember exactly what everyone was doing at that moment. I was in the back with Susan and was leaning against the door with my eyes half closed. Susan was searching in her bag for a cigarette, while Alan was talking to Carol about – of all things – buying some cat litter. As we reached Yonge Street and St. Clair

Avenue, just around the corner from my drop off point, all hell broke loose. I saw the first Royal Canadian Mounted Police car pull across in front of us and come to a stop with its lights flashing. I failed to see the second one until it had parked behind our car. Before I could take it all in, the four policemen were already out of their cars and running, guns in hand. We were ordered out of the car at gunpoint and made to stand with hands held up in front of us. The streets were deserted. There were no sirens blaring, and everything seemed strangely quiet apart from the shouting of the policemen. I had no idea why we had been stopped and did not, at first, connect it with drugs. We were then taken downtown, two in each police car. The police drove Alan's car to the same location, where it was taken apart and searched.

Once at police headquarters, we were immediately separated, taken to individual interview rooms and frisked. I was put into a small, rectangular room that had brown painted woodwork and cream walls. It was completely empty except for two chairs, a table and an ashtray, with the proverbial single light hanging from the centre of the ceiling. There were no windows, and apart from a city map of Toronto the walls were bare. Dozens of police officers buzzed around the building, but only three of them dealt directly with me.

Over the next five hours, they played the usual games, including the nice guy alternating with the bastard during the interviews, as in all great police dramas. I was clean – I had no dope on me – but they had found 2 ounces in the car. I told them I knew nothing about the drugs and that I was just getting a lift home with Alan. I stuck to that story all night, even when they burst into the room and made remarks like, "Okay, we've found 2 ounces in the car, and you'll all go down for this one." Later they came back and said, "Your friends have owned up, so come on, tell us the truth. You might as well make it easier on yourself."

The night dragged on. From time to time there would be visits to tell me what the others were supposed to have said. More than once I was left alone for 30 minutes to an hour to sweat it out. There was one overweight officer, aged about 40, who appeared to take great delight in reminding me, "You're going down." I stuck to my story, which was basically true, although I guessed

Alan had probably been carrying something. By 6 a.m., although I was beginning to think I would probably be arrested and fined, the possibility of a prison sentence seemed remote. At around 7 a.m., the man that appeared to be in charge came in and said, "Okay boy, you can leave."

When I arrived at the main desk, Susan was standing there waiting, looking more pissed off than scared. "Well, at least you're up early," I said, "Everything okay?"

"Yeah," answered Susan, "but this is typical of my luck at the moment. Spyro told me only last week to be careful with Alan."

Evidently, the police had been after Alan for a while. He was eventually charged with possession with intent to supply and went to prison for five years. I went home to Foxbar Road to explain to Terry and Linda what had happened. They had not been worried by my being out all night, as this was quite normal. However, when I told them what had happened and that I had given Terry's name and address as a reference, they were extremely angry. Linda, although fond of a drink herself, was becoming very anti-drugs. When Geraldine from Winnipeg turned up, it was the final straw. I was given an ultimatum.

"This is your final warning," Linda said, "Clean up your act, or you're out."

Postscript:

Terry went on to have great success with Toronto Sound Studios, and engineered and produced at least five Rush albums during the 1970's and 1980's.

Terry and me at Revolution Sound Studios, Toronto, recording Edward Bear, 1970

Revolution Sound Studios, with Edward Bear, 1970

Phill, Sly Stone, and Bob. Studio Two, Island, 1970

Wedding guests, April Fool's Day, 1972

Chapter 5. Island Studios
21 July 1970

I arrived at Island Studios Basing Street, Notting Hill Gate, on the 21st of July 1970 for a meeting with Frank Owen. I carried with me a 15 ips 1/4-inch tape of the work I had completed in Toronto, hurriedly put together with the help of Ervin Copestake the night before I left Canada. It was a last-minute gut feeling that I should take with me a tape of some of the tracks I had engineered from January to June 1970 at the finally-completed Toronto Sound Studios (briefly known as Revolution Sound).

The tape included jingles for the Ford Meteor and Ban deodorant and tracks by Mother Tucker's Yellow Duck, Motherlode and Edward Bear. I found Frank Owen was still the perfect gentleman – courteous and considerate. As he chain-smoked Rothmans cigarettes and ate Veganin we talked about Terry, Toronto, the work I had done in Canada and the plans for Island Studios. I was shown around the building – the two studios, control rooms, tape store and library, plate reverb room and some offices. My overall impression was of a very large, three-storey church with corridors, spiral staircases and nooks and crannies all over the place. In a small, 5-by-8 brown-carpeted office with a skylight to the pavement outside sat Frank's assistant and studio booker, Sally Wightman. She was a classic looking, 1960s hip London chick in an impossibly short, dark brown Biba dress with long, dark blonde hair. She looked like Marianne Faithfull – or more accurately Joni Mitchell. She was beautiful, but she was also very distant and removed.

In the kitchen, I was surprised to find Kevin Hewitt, who previously had been tea maker and caretaker at Olympic Studios, and Jo Yu, ex-Olympic maintenance man. It was like coming home to a brand new Olympic. The whole building was painted inside in cream with mosaic-styled tiles on the walls and soft, subtle lighting sunk into the walls and ceiling. In Studio Two, the walls had a painted beach scene with a few palm trees, an ocean and a big yellow sun to give the impression of being on a tropical island. This studio was already finished and in use while Studio

One was in the final stages of wiring. Both control rooms had brown-carpeted walls, floors and ceilings, and were equipped with custom-built 24 in/16 out Helios desks, Tannoy monitoring in Lockwood cabinets and 3M 16 and 8-track machines. There was an excellent collection of microphones, and for outboard equipment there were harmonisers and ADTs, UREI compressors, Kepex gates and Pultec EQ units – most of the effects and processors available at the time. There were also four full-sized EMT plate reverbs, two of which I would later discover sounded particularly beautiful. Each studio had a Hammond C3 organ and a Steinway grand piano, with the bonus in Studio One of a small pipe organ. Frank said they were looking for a junior engineer, took my reel of tape and said he would listen to it, speak to Chris Blackwell (the owner of Island Records) and "be in touch in a day or so."

After two days Frank telephoned me as promised, and I was offered the job of junior engineer. I joined the newly opened Island Studios on the 25th of July 1970 on a wage of £25 for a 40-hour week. For the first few days, I assisted Frank Owen on his sessions. This was to give me time to adjust to where everything was, to understand how the Helios desk worked and to meet the rest of the studio staff. Besides Frank, who was studio manager and chief engineer, there was Brian Humphries the senior engineer, Roger Beale, Clive Franks and Max Whittaker as assistant engineers, and Jo Yu, Bill Masterson, Paul Bennett and Paul Livesey on maintenance. Sally Wightman, besides being Frank's secretary, was the studio booker – and Dee Simpson was the receptionist. In addition, there was "Digga" (Richard Digby Smith), who had arrived from Birmingham and sat outside reception for days on end until he was finally given the job of runner and van boy. As Island Records also operated from this building, there was the Island Records staff of John Glover and Alec Leslie, who ran the Island Artists' management office and arranged gigs. There was also Muff Winwood, Guy Stevens and Denise Mills working in A&R, David Sanderson and Sue Humphries in the press office and Chris Blackwell's personal secretary, Elsa Peters. The majority of the staff was between 18 and 26 years old and was a great collection of characters. The atmosphere and working conditions appeared extremely relaxed.

Once I started to engineer on sessions, events happened very quickly. My first session at Basing Street was with Third World War, produced by John Fenton, who also heavily influenced many of the band's lyrics. John was about 5 feet 10 inches tall, 28 years old and was bright, speedy and anti-establishment. He had a skinhead haircut – a style that was extremely unfashionable in the music scene of 1970. He had made money both from his involvement with Seltaeb (the Beatles merchandising company) and from Aaron Schroeder Publishing. Third World War had been formed in 1968 at the height of flower power, with Fenton eager to work on something he himself described as "new, positive and aggressive."

On day one of the recording sessions, with a joint in his hand, he looked me straight in the eye and announced, "I'm fed up with all that love and peace shit and then having them massacre four at Kent State University. Look at the deaths of Janis Joplin, Brian Jones and Otis Redding. It's all the rock 'n' roll/CIA/Johnson/Vietnam conspiracy. I want a no-bullshit, working-class band. I've had enough of all this pseudo peace crap." I thought, "Ah, here's a calm, reasonable fellow who has a definite opinion, smokes dope, is left field and obviously likes to control situations. This could be fun." I liked John immediately. We got on very well and have stayed friends ever since.

The band set up in Studio Two with instruments all over the place. I used a selection of mics that I was familiar with from Canada. These included AKG D 12, AKG D 224, Neumann U87 and Shure SM57 microphones. John did not believe in screening people off, so they just set up wherever they felt comfortable. The band consisted of Fred Smith on drums, Jim Avery on bass, Terry Stamp on vocals and "chopper" guitar and Mick Liber on lead guitar. In addition, there were some heavyweight session musicians, including Jim Price and Bobby Keys on brass, Tony Ashton on piano and John "Speedy" Keen on percussion. Terry, the singer and bandleader, was a 15-stone lorry driver. He played the guitar by smashing the strings with his fist. The music was raw, noisy and uncomfortable to listen to, but at the same time I found it strangely addictive. The band was a real bunch of characters, dedicated to having a good time. They also liked to shock whenever possible. The songs they recorded had such titles as

Preaching Violence, Shepherds Bush Cowboy, Toe-Rag, Ascension Day and *Teddy Teeth Goes Sailing*. I thought John's general approach – particularly the lyrics – were excellent. With hindsight, Third World War was probably the first punk band – unfortunately six years too soon – but with more melody, coherent lyrics and musicianship than would have been required in the punk era.

I got into the sessions easily. There was a large amount of drink and drugs around, and the sessions went on all night. We would start at 2 p.m. and often work through until 6 or 7 a.m. I would take a cab home to Hammersmith and play mono copies on my Brenell tape recorder to my girlfriend, Sandra Read, while she got ready for work at Olympic. I then slept and returned to the studio at 2 p.m. Our tape assistant, Clive Franks, fell asleep at the wheel of his car while driving home one morning and crashed. Fortunately, he was unhurt and was back at work by 2 p.m. – what a trouper. In a matter of days we had cut all the backing tracks for the whole album. It had a great atmosphere. The whole approach was extremely live – talking and mistakes were left in, and with the raw sound and the content of the lyrics, the overall effect was complete anarchy. With references to queens, poofters, the Monarchy's arse, unions and violence, the songs were in complete contradiction to the ethos of the times. Twenty years later they would have been described as "politically incorrect" in the extreme.

Some mornings I would go back to John's home in Knightsbridge. He rented a large flat on the second floor of an old apartment block near Harrods. There were three bedrooms and two large reception rooms, all of them full of belongings – books, boxes, amplifiers, papers, tapes and mattresses. A long, winding hallway provided access to all the rooms. This hallway was papered from floor to ceiling with news cuttings, headlines and photographs – including a set of Keith Moon and Vivian Stanshall dressed as Adolf Hitler and Hermann Göring. Reminding me of a film set from some 1960's movie, it was a wonderful flat, and we would sit and discuss ideas for overdubs and mixing late into the day. John wanted to put a low frequency (7 cycles) on the record that would destroy the stylus at the end of the album or make people feel nauseous or shit themselves. Unfortunately, although the theory was good, all these ideas were impossible on vinyl and probably illegal anyway.

We had recorded most of the lead vocals live at the same time as the backing tracks. For this reason there was very little overdubbing, which mostly consisted of brass and string arrangements. By the middle of August, the album (*Third World War*) was overdubbed, mixed and finished – all within two weeks. At the time, we all thought it would be massively successful, but unfortunately it received little or no airplay and the press didn't like it.

Third World War toured the UK and Europe. This turned out to be an expensive enterprise and costs began to escalate. By the time the second album (*Third World War II*) was released in 1972, John had accumulated personal debts of £28,000. At this point, events took a decidedly negative turn. The BBC banned airtime for the group, and they found it impossible to get any form of sponsorship. In addition, there was always a great deal of violence at the gigs. This peaked in 1973 at the 10th anniversary party for Time Out magazine in a club in Leicester Square, and soon afterwards the group disbanded. The press described the road crew – Liverpool Bobbie, Karate Burt and Roger the Roadie (aka Roger the Hat) – as "...the most vicious road crew in the history of music" after a punter had part of his ear bitten off. The record company did not want to renew the contract, and the project ran out of energy.

At the beginning of September 1970, I found work was going very well. I recorded albums with Tim Rose and the group Axiom, both produced by Shel Talmy (the producer of several 1960s hits for The Kinks and The Who), followed by a couple of tracks with Mott the Hoople for the album *Wildlife*, with Guy Stevens producing. From the little I had seen of him around the Island offices, I thought Guy was brash, hyper and probably mad. He was always flamboyantly dressed, often wearing skin-tight red trousers and wild t-shirts. Guy appeared to be from the John Fenton school of production – a talented person, but often completely out of it on alcohol or drugs. After working with him for a couple of days, I came to the conclusion that he was an amazing guy with hundreds of ideas and an open-minded approach to projects. However, I still thought he was probably mad.

With Mott the Hoople's line up of Ian Hunter on piano and vocals, Mick Ralphs on guitar and vocals, Pete "Overend" Watts on bass, Verden Allen on organ, Dale "Buffin" Griffin on drums and guest singer Jess Roden, we set up in Studio Two. Because of a large drum kit, 4-by-12 speaker cabinets for the guitar amplifiers and additional screens, space was at a premium. I had now progressed to using two Neumann U87s on drum overheads to give a better stereo picture, but I still did not mic the hi-hat separately. Being new to the studio rooms, I was still finding out about the possibilities for different sounds. Most sessions were fast and efficient, with engineers, assistants and maintenance staff all geared up to making things run smoothly. In those days at Island Studios, we tended to talk in terms of making something sound brighter, fatter, fuller, more ballsy or less honky, and we did not talk about frequencies. It was more common to change the position or sound in the studio room and adjust microphones accordingly, rather than attempt to boost frequencies in the control room.

During the recording of the song *Lay Down*, Guy was so stoned he rolled off the desk riser in his chair and crashed to the floor. He was right in the middle of explaining to the band what sounds would be best to use for the backing vocals. "It'll be great," he was saying. "We'll make the voices warm and lush; y-y-you know – fat, but with strength. We can get Jess on the top line." He hardly faltered – just carried on talking on his side, on the floor. The band and I were all in fits of laughter. It really was a great atmosphere to record in.

The studios were now working 24 hours a day with two 12-hour sessions in both rooms. The name was now changed from Island Studios to Basing Street Studios. During October, we took on more staff, including junior engineer Tony Platt, who came from Trident Studios in St. Anne's Court, Soho, and assistant engineer Jerry Russell from America. Tony and I had a very similar approach to sessions and eventually worked on many of each other's projects, including Bob Marley & The Wailers. Ron Fawcus, now our van driver, was promoted to assistant engineer.

We had the occasional full staff meetings with Frank, Sally, all the engineers and assistants and everyone from maintenance. We would discuss any problems that had arisen in the studio or how we could make sessions run more smoothly. It was a relaxed bunch of people, and there were no big egos to deal with. For the first two years, it felt like a continuous party.

Most of my time was taken up with back-to-back sessions. I worked on tracks with the American singer/songwriter/producer Scott English and an album with Read and Tom, produced by Tony Cox. Read and Tom were an acoustic, Simon & Garfunkel-styled duo. They were a couple of nice guys, though their music was a little bland. I learned a great deal about recording acoustic instruments during those sessions.

Sometime in November, I tracked and mixed a single for David Bowie, recorded with some of the members of the band Blue Mink. Their bass player, Herbie Flowers, was producing. The single was called *Holy Holy*, and on release was immediately banned by the BBC due to its sexual content. Unfortunately, as in the case of Third World War, this did not make it a hit. David Bowie, a pretty boy with long blonde hair, turned up at the studio wearing a silk shirt, velvet trousers and highwayman's boots. He said little on the sessions and gave off an air of haughty reserve. This project was after his *Space Oddity* hit single, but before his worldwide success with the album *The Rise and Fall of Ziggy Stardust and The Spiders From Mars*. I was not particularly impressed with his performance on the *Holy Holy* single and was surprised when he shot to fame just one year later.

After *Holy Holy*, I immediately started work on an album with the folk/rock band Renaissance. Formed in 1969, the group consisted of Keith Relf on vocals, Jim McCarty on drums (both ex-Yardbirds), John Hawken on keyboards (ex-Nashville Teens), Louis Cennamo on bass, and Keith's sister Jane on vocals. They were a lovely bunch of people – easy-going, friendly, hardworking and excellent musicians.

The sessions were a little different from the norm for me, as besides drums, bass, guitars and keyboards, the album featured unusual overdubs, including harpsichord and vibes. I now used more microphones on the drums and had finally started to mic the hi-hat separately. The band played at a lower volume than I was used to, and this created less leakage, allowing us to replace individual instruments without creating a "ghost" doubling effect. They still all played together for the feel but would often replace various instruments to tighten things up. I used up tracks on the 16-track machine very quickly, and often had more than one instrument sharing the same track. This made mixing harder, but members of the band would help out by controlling specific faders, EQ or echoes. When we all got it right, this hands-on approach was very satisfying.

As December arrived, I was back in Studio Two and began working on tracks with Sly Stone. I was already a big fan of Sly & the Family Stone and had spent many a night in Toronto with Francine listening to the album *Stand!*. Sly and his sister Rose had just arrived in London from Germany, where he had been laying down various rhythm box backing tracks for a new album. This was one of the first times a drum machine was used on a pop recording. In time, these tracks would become the album *There's a Riot Goin' On*, featuring the hit single *Family Affair*. The LP received mixed reviews, varying from "violent and controversially militant" to "having a softer, more personal feel." With Bob Potter assisting, we set up for bass guitar and keyboard overdubs in the control room. The procedure was for Sly to choose one of the many drum machine rhythm tracks and try out ideas on Hammond, Farfisa organ or his Fender Mustang bass guitar. These ideas would be recorded to tape.

Sly was dressed all in white, and most of the time wore a brown woollen hat and dark glasses. Rose took loads of Polaroid photographs of the proceedings, while Sly took loads of cocaine from a large plastic bag that sat on the end of the desk. Throughout the sessions, he snorted a line every half-hour. He was a very friendly man and always offered a line to Bob and me. I was not used to doing cocaine, and even though I refused every other line, within a few hours I had become completely wired. Bob, however, adjusted well to his new benefactor. The days rolled into one another with Sly, Rose, Bob and me all in Studio Two working through various rhythm tracks and putting down ideas on bass, electric guitar, Hammond, Farfisa and vocals, all the while consuming vast amounts of cocaine from the plastic bag.

After a week, I had had enough of being that strung out and handed the project over to Bob to engineer with Max Whittaker to assist him. I left the sessions with a bleeding nose, a blurred memory of half a dozen songs and two Polaroid photos of Sly and me.

A couple of months previously, I had split up with Sandra and moved in with my co-workers Jerry Russell and Sally Wightman, who shared a flat in Chelsea off the Kings Road. Jerry moved out, and Sally and I soon became lovers and the sole occupiers of 21 Walpole Street, paying an extravagant £18 a week. The flat was on the second floor of a row of three-storey, terraced houses and consisted of one large room, divided off at one end. An archway through the partition led into a kitchen area. The walls were painted a typically 1960s shade of orange, disguised only slightly by a few Motherlode and Island posters and an Indian bedspread. There were two large, un-curtained windows overlooking Walpole Street, and the room contained a Victorian fireplace. Despite not having seen a real fire for many years, this fireplace remained the focal point of the room. The bathroom was one flight down and always freezing, although there was the consolation of a massive iron bath. The flat was very stark and cold, with almost no furniture except for the enormous double bed where we spent most of our time, either on it or in it, as this was the warmest place to be. Neither of us thought of the flat as home, but we spent a memorable six months there, and despite the spartan living conditions, we were quite content.

By now, Basing Street had acquired a collection of liggers who spent most of the evenings and nights at the studio hanging out, playing pool and watching television. These included musicians, wannabes and dealers, among them Lucky Gordon (who enjoyed brief notoriety in the Christine Keeler/Profumo Affair), Mike Harrison (the former singer with Spooky Tooth), Chris Wood (the flute and sax player from Traffic), Steve Brickle (a short, stocky Welsh dealer), "Wild" Bill Cody (a security guard) and various local Rastafarians. The Island staff were all liked and accepted in the area around Portobello Road and Basing Street. This was some time before riots disrupted the Notting Hill Carnival in the mid-1970s – it was still a relaxed, cool place to be. We often ate at the soul food restaurant, the Mangrove, or drank in the Apollo pub, both in All Saints Road. It was now very easy to score drugs from one of the many dealers that hung out at Basing Street, where the menu consisted of hash (Nepalese temple ball, red Lebanese, Moroccan or Afghani black), grass (African or Jamaican), speed (French blues or black bombers), downers (Mandrax or Seconol), acid (windowpane, Microdot), MDA and mescaline. Occasional additions to the list were cocaine and elephant tranquilizer.

I was getting used to working for five to 10 days on 18-hour sessions. These would often finish on a Monday morning at 9 a.m., and by 2 p.m. or 7 p.m. the same day we would be set up ready to start a whole new project. It was an incredibly heavy schedule. Over the coming months, I continued to work hard and spend 100 hours a week at the studios.

In May, Sally received a phone call from Peter Grant, the manager of Led Zeppelin. He wanted to book five days for the band to work on overdubs for a new album. Sally told him about me and my experience at Olympic Studios and in Toronto. I think Grant and the band confused me with my brother Terry, because on arriving in Studio Two Jimmy Page said, "Oh, you're not who I thought you were at all. Oh well. Whatever." This threw me immediately, and I was unnerved from then on.

The full band were there – John Bonham, Robert Plant, John Paul Jones, Jimmy Page, and East End heavy, Peter Grant, with a couple of minders. Peter was vast, probably over 20 stone, and had difficulty squeezing into the luxurious, high-backed leather chairs that were positioned on the riser behind the Helios desk. To me he appeared very seedy, with thinning long hair, sweaty skin and ill-fitting clothes. He dealt with me and the other minions around him in an offhand manner and gave off a somewhat threatening vibe. Control Room Two was not a large room, measuring only 15 by 20 feet. With the brown-carpeted walls on the floor and ceiling, dull lighting, desk and machines, nine people (band, manager, minders, myself and an assistant) and this strange, aggressive attitude, the sessions were immediately claustrophobic and scary.

The members of the band, apart from Bonham, had long, flowing curly hair – looking like Jesus or some Greek gods. Jones was friendly, polite and on another planet altogether. Bonham and

Plant were relaxed and relatively easy to deal with, but Page was dark, moody and difficult. I found him particularly hard to communicate with. He was self-centred and into some form of weird, spiritual crap. A great fan of the writings of Aleister Crowley, he owned Crowley's old residence, Boleskine House.

We worked mainly on two songs: *Four Sticks* and *Stairway to Heaven*. The backing tracks had drums, bass and some guide guitars already recorded, and there were good vocals on both tracks. We spent most of our time working on *Stairway to Heaven* – trying out flute parts on the introduction with John Paul Jones, and overdubbing guitar ideas and solos with Jimmy Page. We worked on lead guitar parts to *Stairway to Heaven* endlessly, trying out different styles, sounds and effects. Page sat on my right at the Desk, with Grant on my left. His guitar was sent through tie-lines to an amp in the studio live room. We tried the guitar through Leslie, desk distortion and various pedals and recorded takes continuously. The guitar overdubs took days to perform and get right, and I was constantly dropping in on certain sections. Page would just say 'again', 'again', at the end of a take. Listening to the final version of *Stairway to Heaven*, it's hard to imagine how bad some of the playing and tuning was. There were many loose timing mistakes and wrong notes from Page, and the control room atmosphere remained intense.

There was very little direct communication from any of the band, and having Peter Grant sitting beside me did not help. I found him belligerent and rude, and aware of the many stories about Grant's well-known bullyboy techniques, I was disturbed by his presence. On his death in 1996, there were glowing obituaries in newspapers and music magazines, describing him as "always being on the side of the artist" and "fair". I would have first-hand knowledge of this so-called fair attitude to artists later, while working with Jeff Beck.

The sessions with Zeppelin were long with no convenient breaks, and I would be at the desk for some 15 to 18 hours a day. I had to maintain a constant level of high concentration and vigilance during this time – it was not easy. You couldn't fuck up on projects like these. It was very tiring, and the severe atmosphere generated by Peter, his minders and the band did not leave me with warm memories. I thought Page was a good guitarist, but not on a par with Jeff Beck, Jimi Hendrix or Eric Clapton. I was relieved when the Zeppelin sessions were over, and I could return to projects that were more laid back and easy-going. However, I couldn't really complain – in my first year at Basing Street I had worked on 12 albums and at least eight singles, plus odd bits of television and film – an approximate average of one complete track, recorded, overdubbed and mixed every two and a half days. I was slowly making a name for myself.

Penny Hanson, who had worked for Island Records in London before moving out to Jamaica, took over from Sally, who now left Island and went to work at B & C Records. Allegedly, Penny had previously had some form of a nervous breakdown and was found unconscious on the runway at Kingston Airport. She joined Basing Street amidst much rumour and gossip about these events – I never found out what really happened. Her flirtatious manner and dress sense made it obvious that she was a very different person to Sally. It also became clear that, in the studio environment, she would be much more difficult to deal with.

Postscript:

I found out in 2001, while working with Robert Plant, that Jimmy Page constructed guitar solos by trying out many ideas. He would then learn his preferred parts and play it as a complete solo. Unfortunately, this was never explained to me at the time of working on the guitars on *Stairway to Heaven*. Had it been, I would probably have enjoyed the process more.

Chapter 6. Jeff Beck
9 August 1971

In July 1971, the newly arrived studio booker, Penny Hanson, told me that I would be working with Jeff Beck on an album for Epic Records, part of the CBS group. Jeff had originally made his name with The Yardbirds, replacing Eric Clapton in 1965 and for a while playing alongside Jimmy Page. Jeff had commercial success as a solo artist after leaving the band in late 1966 and had gradually built up a reputation as an excellent guitarist, although he was thought by some to be unreliable and difficult. The new LP was to be Jeff's third solo album, although the first with this particular band of musicians. Previous albums included *Truth* (1968), with Rod Stewart on vocals, Nicky Hopkins on piano, Mickey Waller on drums and Ron Wood on bass, and *Beck-Ola* (1969) with Tony Newman replacing Mickey on drums. The compilation album *The Most of Jeff Beck* was also released in 1969, which included the hit, *Hi Ho Silver Lining*. Production on all these albums was credited to Mickie Most.

The drums were set up in the middle of Studio One and were divided off with full-height, sound absorbing screens at the back and sides. There were half-height screens at the front of the kit to form a complete circle. Seen from the control room, the bass was boothed off to the right and the guitar to the left, with the piano directly in front of the control room window. These booths were all made with half-height screens. This was my "classic rock" setup, lifted from Glyn Johns during the Olympic Studios years of 1967 and '68. The microphones used were AKG D 12 on the bass drum and an AKG D 224 on the snare, with Neumann U87s for the rest of the kit (toms and overheads). For the bass guitar, we used an AKG D 12 and DI (direct injection), with U87s on Jeff's guitar amps. The piano, also mic'ed with two U87s, had the lid down and was covered with blankets and the thick piano cover to eliminate as much drum leakage as possible. For guide vocals, there was a choice of the booth in the control room (with visual contact to the studio), the void between the two sets of doors leading to the studio from the control room, or a handheld Shure

SM57 in the studio, which gave the vocalist freedom to wander at will while recording.

The band consisted of Cozy Powell on drums, Clive Chaman on bass, Max Middleton on piano, Alex Ligertwood on vocals and Jeff on guitar. They were all exceptional musicians and real characters: Cozy was speedy and gregarious, Max was the eccentric professor, Clive was shy and gentle, and Jeff, who was then 28 years old, was tall and thin with straight, black hair and gaunt features. He was laidback and friendly, cheeky and an easy-going personality. This was both a surprise and a relief to me. Jeff had a reputation for unpredictable behaviour and for being difficult and fiery, so I had prepared myself for a much darker character. He wore jeans and old T-shirts that often showed signs of faded oil stains, and his appearance was always slightly dishevelled. Although quite subdued for most of the time, he came to life once he was strapped to a guitar, and his personality and playing style then became loud, aggressive and on-the-edge – a brilliant English guitarist.

This was to be Jeff's first recording since his recovery from a bad car crash in 1970. He had taken many months to recuperate, and now seemed pleased to be back in the studio working again, particularly with this band. Our days started at 7 p.m. and we would finish about 4 a.m. Jeff lived in Sussex – a 50-mile journey from the studio – and he was often late arriving. When he eventually turned up, he would be covered in apologies, grease and oil. His passion was building and modifying American hot rod cars, and this took up most of his daylight hours.

The sessions started easy, with mutual respect shown by all involved. Jeff had a varied collection of songs, riffs and ideas to work on. Working together, the band tried out numerous versions and arrangements, and then recorded the most successful ideas to tape. The days were productive and enjoyable, with songs, jams and riffs permeating Studio One. Sometimes Jeff's girlfriend, the model Celia Hammond, would turn up and add some glamour to the proceedings.

Having recorded for about two weeks, we had 10 tracks down with most of the overdubs completed. There were some solos to do and then the final vocals and mixes, but we had made very good progress. It was a great band.

Late one afternoon, I turned up an hour before the session as usual. Dave Hutchins, the assistant, went to the store to collect the master tapes, while I checked that all the microphones were still in position and plugged in before going to the control room to make sure that they were all still working. Dave came back some minutes later in confusion saying the 2-inch tapes were not in their usual place. I went to speak to Dee, the receptionist, to see if I could track down the missing masters. She was busy giving information about the evening's sessions to Bill, the night security man. Early each evening, all the night staff were given details of who was working in each studio and who might be in the building. This was part of a procedure that had only been in place for a few months, following one evening in February when the studio had been busted by the police. There had been an anonymous tip-off by a drug dealer who felt he had been unfairly treated. In case there should be another raid, each control room was now fitted with a flashing red warning light that could be triggered from reception.

"Oh, they were picked up earlier today by the management," said Dee when asked about the master tapes.

I waited for Jeff to arrive as there was little else I could do. When he did arrive, he made a couple of frantic telephone calls, and without explaining, told us that we should all go home for the night – but we would resume the next day. I went home to my new basement flat at 28 Monmouth Road, Notting Hill Gate, and spent the evening with Sally. This event gave us an unexpected evening together.

The next day, we gathered in the control room, where the conversation went something like this:

"Okay, sorry about last night," said Jeff. "My management contract is up for renewal, but I'm not sure I want to sign it."

"What's that got to do with us?" asked Cozy.

"Well, taking our tapes is probably some form of insurance," replied Jeff.

"This is all very cryptic. What do you mean? What's the story with the tapes?" continued Cozy.

"Well, if I sign, I'll probably get the tapes back," said Jeff. He sounded surprisingly relaxed.

"That's crazy," continued Cozy. "They can't do that."

"Ah, don't worry. It's cool. It ain't gonna happen. Fuck them. We'll just record the tracks again."

"Fuck off, you've got to be joking. That's two weeks work down the pan."

"Oh, least of my problems," said Jeff calmly, sounding almost detached. "I either sign or re-record. I'm not going to sign, so I guess we re-record."

"What the fuck is all this?" muttered Cozy. "Phill, are you really sure you've checked the tape store?"

This whole event was hard for me to take in. I had never before been in a situation where the master tapes for a session were removed without the artist knowing. After much discussion, we agreed to re-record the album and started immediately, feeling the need to keep up some kind of momentum. A couple of days later, while we were recording a new backing track, the telephone rang. It was the night security man.

"There are three guys down here to see Jeff," he said.

"Okay, send them up," I replied, thinking nothing of it. The door swung open and in walked three "heavies".

"Good evening, gentlemen," said one of the guys. "I wonder if we might have a little chat?"

Two of them went off with Jeff and had a talk in the studio while the tape op and I were left with the third one in the control room. He came and sat beside me at the desk.

"Difficult to engineer with broken fingers, I guess," he said in a normal "how's-it-going?" kind of voice. I just stared ahead at the desk meters, not wanting to know what he looked like, and said nothing. Through the oblong window in the control room door, I could see Cozy with Max, the pianist, standing on the stairs looking worried. I couldn't see him, but it later became clear that one of the guys who had left the room with Jeff was doing all the talking. The visit lasted for 15 minutes and then they were gone. We were all in chaos. What a nightmare.

"Hey, those guys were carrying baseball bats," said Cozy. "These are not half measures."

We were all scared by these events, but due to the shock of it all, behaved in a rather detached manner and never let on to each other how we felt. Jeff never said a word about his "meeting" in the studio. Later that evening, Jeff had a phone call from his management office and the shit really hit the fan – evidently he no longer owned the songs we had recorded. Jeff was adamant. "I still ain't gonna sign," he said. "If need be, we'll just have to record a completely new album."

We took a couple of weeks off, hoping the situation could be resolved. I went to Scotland, camping with Sally at Dunlichity in the hills south of Loch Ness. It was a beautiful spot, deserted for miles around – just heather, hills and lochs. It was very hot. During the days, we fished in the lochs, collected firewood, swam and lay in the sun naked. In the evenings, we cooked our dinner over an open fire, got stoned and made love. On the 9th of August, a few hours after we had called at a house for fresh water, we had unexpected visitors. We had just had our first joint of the day, had brewed a cup of tea and were deciding what to do and where to go, when a light blue Ford Anglia pulled off the narrow, single-track road and parked next to my blue Citroën 2CV. It was the police. I quickly stashed our grass and MDA under the sleeping bags, convinced they were looking for drugs. Red-eyed and nervous, I came out of the tent to meet them.

"Good morning Sir, Madam. How are you both? I wonder if we could ask you a few questions?"

The police informed us that an old man had been injured (maybe killed) during a robbery just a few miles down the road and that the suspects wore long hair and blue jeans – a description that fitted us well at the time. They talked to us for about 30 minutes.

"Who are you?"

"Er... Phill Brown and Sally Wightman."

"Where are you from?"

"Er... London."

"What are you doing?"

"Mmm... holiday, camping."

"How long have you been here?"

"Oh, about four days," I answered, feeling the intense panic that had gripped me on their arrival slowly lifting. I now felt they were not here about drugs.

"What do you do for a living?"

"I'm a sound engineer." (Oops. Don't they know everybody in the music business takes drugs?)

"Oh. Worked with anyone famous then?"

"Anita Harris and Harry Secombe," I answered like a flash – thinking this was safer than saying Jimi Hendrix, The Rolling Stones or Led Zeppelin.

"Where were you this morning?"

"Apart from collecting some water at a house on the way to Inverness, we've been here, just fishing."

"You won't catch much in that loch, it's far too cold. Do your parents know you are here?"

"Er, no. But I'm almost 21 – we live together."

They were nice guys and seemed amused by it all. "Make an honest woman of her," they said as they left.

We rolled a joint, lay back in the sun and talked about our situation in London, work and our rather gloomy flat in Monmouth Road. Although what the policemen had said had only been a joke, it started us talking about our feelings for each other and our future hopes. We had not yet been together for a full year, but there was a calm and safe feeling between us. We were each other's best friends. As for the idea of getting married – well, maybe. Why not? As to getting out of London – definitely.

When I met Jeff and the band again at Basing Street's Studio One, there had been a few changes. We now had a lawyer in a three-piece suit sitting in on all the sessions and someone from Securicor would come and pick up the master tapes at the end of each session, delivering them back the next night. That meant that, at any given time, the master tapes were either in the control room or with Securicor. We set up the instruments and studio to our original layout and started recording. Jeff had written four new songs, and with some riffs and a few jams, we rattled through eight tracks in a week. The material was not of the highest quality, but the playing was excellent. Tight, hard, loud drums from Cozy; smooth, huge bass from Clive; the added delight of Max singing and moaning along with his wonderful piano playing and Jeff – working fast while laying down the backing tracks and then doing one-take overdubs. The atmosphere was excellent, with everyone positive and highly charged.

Once we had all our tracks recorded, we moved downstairs into Studio Two to finish the guitar solos, lead vocals and to do the final mixes. There was still little outboard gear, limited to harmonisers and ADT, UREI compressors, and Pultec and graphic EQ units. There were, however, the four beautiful EMT echo plates to choose from and various tape delay effects. I plugged up three echo plates and a vari-speed tape repeat echo. We worked fast, mixing three songs a day. By mid-September, we delivered to Epic Records the aptly named album, *Rough and Ready*.

Rough and Ready could hardly be called a classic, but it did help to put Jeff back on the map. It was followed a year later by the more successful *Jeff Beck Group* album, produced by Steve Cropper and recorded at Steve's TMI Recording Studio in Memphis, Tennessee, with the same band members, but with Bobby Tench replacing Alex on vocals.

Postscript:

In November 2007, I ran into Jeff by chance at Wadhurst railway station – we were both going up to London for meetings. We chatted for the one hour journey, catching up on the past 35 years and recalling the events of 1971. We laughed at both being at Mickie Most's funeral ("What were we doing there?"), although he had stayed with Peter Grant as manager. He confirmed my memory of events, but he was unsure, however, about the "heavies". "Surely if that was the case," he said, "Cozy and I would have had 'em."

Sally in LA, 1972

Sally and Phill, North Lodge, 1973

Chapter 7. Harry Nilsson 29 February 1972

During my first 18 months at Island Studios, I recorded albums with Tim Rose (produced by Shel Talmy), Renaissance (with the ex-Yardbirds singer Keith Relf), Amazing Blondel (produced by Paul Samwell-Smith, ex-Yardbirds bass player), Kenny Young (writer of *Under the Boardwalk*) and Jeff Beck. I also recorded tracks for Mott the Hoople (with Guy Stevens producing), Led Zeppelin, Cat Stevens and Sly Stone, and singles with David Bowie, Jimmy Cliff, Atomic Rooster, Harry Nilsson, Suzi Quatro, Mud and The Sweet.

I found that I could happily listen to and work with many different musical styles and approaches, from the serious rock sessions of Led Zeppelin and Jeff Beck to commercial, one-day singles with bands like Mud and The Sweet. Nevertheless, some sessions were more enjoyable than others, as some seemed to me to be more artistically worthwhile, and I often worked on recording backing tracks and songs that I would not normally listen to outside the studio environment. Two examples were the groups The Sweet and Mud, both produced by Phil Wainman, with Pip Williams as musical director. I found the music crass and commercial, but the sessions were fast, furious and (initially) fun. However, most enjoyable for me had been working with Tim Rose, Amazing Blondel, Kenny Young, Jeff Beck, Jimmy Cliff and Harry Nilsson.

On the 29th of February 1972, I received a phone call. I was informed that I had won an award presented by The New Musical Express, under the category of Best Engineered Record of the Year. I assumed it would be for Harry Nilsson's *Without You* (written by Tom Evans and Pete Ham of the group Badfinger), which I had over-dubbed and mixed. It had charted No. 1 in February and was in the charts for 20 weeks.

Without You came from the album *Nilsson Schmilsson* and was mixed in December 1971 at Studio Two at Basing Street, with Richard Perry producing. Richard was a reserved, self-contained American from Los Angeles with a silver cigarette case containing pre-rolled, single-skinned grass joints and a separate phial of cocaine. He periodically attacked these, but never shared or offered them around. Richard had been successful with an assortment of artists during the 1960s and early '70s, including Captain Beefheart, Tiny Tim, Ella Fitzgerald, Carly Simon and Barbra Streisand. Despite his success, I found Richard Perry to be arrogant, and he rarely listened to other people's opinions. In contrast, Harry Nilsson seemed happy and friendly. He had a wacky sense of humour and never appeared to take himself too seriously. He had made his name as a songwriter in the late 1960s, and enjoyed a limited success with his work being covered by The Monkees, Three Dog Night and The Yardbirds. In Los Angeles, Nilsson was good friends with John Lennon, and the two often spent nights out on the town drinking during Lennon's "Lost Weekend".

Nilsson's album had been started at Trident Studios, Soho, in June with engineer Robin Geoffrey Cable, but after a severe car crash put Robin out of the picture, the overdubs and mixing were finished with Bill Price at AIR Studios and me at Basing Street. The musicians used included top players such as Jim Gordon, Klaus Voorman, Chris Spedding, Herbie Flowers, Jim Keltner, Gary Wright and Paul Buckmaster. I had worked on overdubs for *Gotta Get Up*, *Coconut*, *Jump into the Fire* and *Without You*. Richard Perry was a tough taskmaster, and during the vocal session for *Without You* had managed to reduce Nilsson to tears. When I came to mix in December 1971, nothing had changed, but this time I was on the receiving end of Richard's working style. We were in Studio Two working on 2-inch, 16-track tape and mixing manually on a Helios 24-channel desk. After three hours of mixing, Richard said, "Yeah, it's feeling good," and then zeroed the faders, instantly undoing the mix and 60% of my work. I'd never had such an experience before and felt somewhat bemused. We set up again – piano, vocal, strings, bass and drums – and after another two or three hours it felt really good. Richard agreed, but said it was "missing something" and zeroed the desk again. I flipped.

I found it extremely hard work mixing manually for three or four hours, and I had felt we were very close to a good result. This time I said, "What the fuck are you doing Richard? It would help if you kept me informed of what you want." He and I then had a full-blown argument, both yelling at each other – pure emotion. He finished by saying, "I just love you frustrated engineers." Richard

Perry was almost 30 years old at the time and very experienced, with a large collection of hit albums to his credit. I was just 21 years old and a relative novice, but I still felt I could deliver what he wanted if only he would tell me what that was.

We took a break, and I went upstairs to the dubbing room at the back of Studio One, where Tony Platt was busy making tape copies. After 45 minutes, I returned to find Richard sitting calmly at the desk. Nothing was said, and we began setting the mix up for the third time. Although the track was surprisingly sparse, with just piano, bass, drums and strings, the vocal recordings were complicated – recorded on two tracks, with a crossfade required during the mixing.

After a further three hours, we finally captured the mix and it felt brilliant. There were no effects or echoes, just a tape-delayed EMT plate reverb on the vocals. I thought it sounded beautiful and timeless. It had taken almost 10 hours – the longest manual mix I had ever done. Richard bore no grudge, and we worked together again with the all-female band Fanny the following year.

My award came through. It was for *Co-Co* by The Sweet, which had charted #2 in June 1971.

Editing 2" Tape, about 1974

Barry, Phill, Robert, Mobile, *Sneakin', Sally*...

Chapter 8. Murray Head
1 September 1972

On the 1st of April 1972, Sally and I were married at St. John's Parish Church, Shirley, and a reception was held at the Selsdon Park Hotel. It was a wonderful day, with a wild collection of characters – family, friends and many of the Island staff. The group photograph looked like some form of bizarre fancy dress party, with half of us in top hat and tails and the remainder wearing either hippie clothes or Marks & Spencer's two-piece suits. Ron Fawcus (now an assistant engineer at Basing Street) had emptied the contents of 20 Rothmans cigarettes and substituted neat grass to make "having a smoke" a little easier. The champagne flowed constantly, and within a couple of hours Ron could be seen offering his doctored Rothmans to anyone who asked for a cigarette.

After our week's honeymoon at the Mermaid Inn, Rye, and hiking round Romney Marsh, I returned to work and recorded singles for Samantha Jones and The Sweet. At the beginning of May, I was contacted by actor/singer Murray Head, who explained that I had been recommended to him by producer Shel Talmy. I had worked with Shel a few times during my first two years at Island, and we'd always had a good relationship. Murray invited me to visit his flat, Toad Hall off Fulham Road, to discuss recording his first solo album – to be called *Nigel Lived*.

When I met Murray, he was 25 years old. A handsome charmer, he was already successful, having starred with Peter Finch and Glenda Jackson in the recently released movie *Sunday Bloody Sunday*. Before that, he had been in the hugely popular musical stage shows *Hair* and *Jesus Christ Superstar*, and appeared with Hayley Mills in the film *The Family Way*. To my relief, I found him to be self-assured, but not self-centred.

At the time, Murray had shoulder-length black hair, which made a strong contrast with his pale complexion. I was immediately aware of his powerful nervous energy, no doubt fuelled by his recent triumphs and expressed by sweeping hand gestures while he was talking. He was the epitome of the glamorous pop star, and was married to Susan Ellis Jones, a model who appeared in advertisements for Oil of Ulay.

During subsequent years, I came to know Murray well. He had spent some of his childhood in France and as a result was bilingual – he later became very successful in France and French-speaking Quebec, Canada. His spoken English had a home-counties accent, while his singing voice had a similar range and tonal colour to that of Steve Winwood. He exuded an aroma that was a mixture of tobacco and grass – Murray was always puffing at a hand-rolled cigarette, joint or small cigar. His clothes usually consisted of jeans, t-shirts, shirts and often a fleece-lined, brown leather flying coat from World War II, cracked and worn with age. He was rarely to be seen without a black and brown leather bag (I began to refer to this as the TARDIS) from which spilled cassette tapes, headphones, broken lighters, lyric books and sheet music. In the months to come, this would be unpacked within minutes of his arrival, and he would soon be in the midst of chaos that seemed to express his varied interests in writing, acting and performing.

Murray and I now sat in his large basement room, surrounded by props from *Sunday Bloody Sunday*, pieces of sound equipment, Indian drapes and musical instruments. Murray's humour, in later years, was to develop a slightly warped quality, but now he was full of easy jokes and anecdotes about the film and the people he had been working with. In *Sunday Bloody Sunday*, he played the role of a bisexual. It was noted as being the first movie to show a passionate kiss between two men – Murray and Peter Finch. To the amusement of the actors, the film crew had objected strongly to this scene. The operator stepped down from his camera and asked the director, John Schlesinger, "Is this really necessary?" John screamed, "Necessary! It's the most important scene in the film!" Peter Finch was heard to say at a later date, "Murray and I did it for England." Murray had also spent a lot of time shooting a bedroom scene with Glenda Jackson. "She seemed remarkably timid, almost to the point of being a prude, for someone who in her previous film had been seen rolling around the floor of a carriage with Richard Chamberlain stark naked in *The Music Lovers*." "I was constantly aware of a lot of red, furry pubic hair," recalled Murray, laughing. "It always reminded me of a small ferret."

Eventually, the conversation turned to Murray's plans for his album, *Nigel Lived*. Murray had been signed to CBS by John Hammond Sr. (who also "discovered" Bessie Smith, Billie Holiday, Bob Dylan, Bruce Springsteen, Donovan) under the watch of Clive Davis. The idea was to record a concept album about a young man called Nigel, who to avoid small-town life, marriage, mortgage and settling down, goes to the city to find fortune and maybe fame. He lives in bedsits, goes to parties in Chelsea, smokes dope for the first time, gets laid, avoids drug busts and has his first serious love affair, all accomplished with a positive, we-can-do-anything attitude. Nigel gets a job selling clothes on Kings Road, meets the socialite Lady Sandra Coates and her friends, does well and enjoys mild success. Then comes the decline. Girlfriends, job and flat all go by the wayside and he ends up broken, on the dole, homeless and on smack.

It was an ambitious project, with the 14 songs each requiring a different approach and treatment. Some songs were straightforward love songs, including *Ruthie* and *When You Wake Up in the Morning*, while others, such as *Pity the Poor Consumer* and *Why Do We Have to Hurt Our Heads?* made political statements. This reflected Murray's strong interest in politics. Always a left-winger, he was convinced at the time that there would be a revolution within 15 years, with armed troops on the streets of UK cities. Subsequently, when riots broke out at various places in London, including Notting Hill, Brixton and the Broadwater Farm estate and during the Poll Tax Riots in the early 1990s, he took these events as evidence that insurrection had begun. Although always dubious, I was intrigued by the idea. Murray's scenario flooded into my head when driving home across Clapham Common at 3 a.m. one morning in the early 1980s (around the time of the UK miners' strike). There were tanks and Army personnel on and around the common. It looked as though manoeuvres for the sealing off of London were being practised. I was asked to keep moving, and the image was over all too quickly, but Murray would have loved the drama and spectacle.

Murray's album came at an excellent time for me in 1972, and I immediately empathised with the storyline. After many hours of listening to demos and discussing the various possibilities, I accepted the project and drove home to Sussex. The plan was to start recording at Olympic Studios in June.

There were a few "firsts" on this album for me. It was the first time I had worked as an engineer at Olympic Studios since leaving in late 1968. It was also my first experience recording out of doors and using mobiles. More importantly, it was the first time an album I had worked on changed my attitude to life, and the first time I met Steve Smith.

We started in June 1972 at Olympic's Studio Two, working on 16-track with Joe Wissert producing. Joe, a house producer from CBS in Los Angeles, had worked with many top American acts including Earth, Wind & Fire. He was then in his late 30s, balding, with a beard and moustache. He wore glasses and was dressed in the casual uniform of the day – blue jeans and a white shirt. He appeared to be a genuine guy – a quiet American with a wealth of recording experience, plus he had political views similar to Murray's. He was laidback to the point of falling over and appeared to have no interest in power or control – he just wanted to make a classic album. He arrived in London with a bunch of commercial standards and ideas for Murray to record, but after listening to Murray's demo tape for *Nigel Lived*, Joe became seriously committed to the project and threw his own material away. "Hey, man. That's beautiful. Great idea. I could work with this."

As each song needed unique treatment, we used a wide collection of musicians, including Cozy Powell and Mike Giles on drums, Clive Chaman and Phil Chen on bass, Peter Robinson on piano and organ, Fiachra Trench on piano (and musical arranger), Graham Preskett on violin, Ray Cooper, Barry DeSouza, Frank Ricotti and Chris Karan on percussion, and Mark Warner on acoustic guitar.

We squeezed the relevant musicians into Studio Two and screened them off, putting down as much as possible in live and spontaneous sessions. It was a good collection of characters and we all got on very well. There was a high level of mutual respect, and everyone was allowed to put forward ideas, as Joe had no big ego. Murray took control of the proceedings and always sang a guide vocal and banged along on an acoustic guitar during tracking. To help get everyone into the mood, he would often give an outline to the story that related to the particular song we were working on. I used my well-tried mic setups of Neumann U87s, AKG D 12s and Shure SM57s, with additional old AKG C12a valve mics.

I found it exciting being out of Basing Street and working back at Olympic and enjoyed all the different aspects of the work involved. One day might be spent in Studio Two with a rhythm section and the next day in Studio One with a steel band. I called on all my recording experience from the previous few years to deal with the vast array of instruments and ideas. We were dealing with the basic technology of the early 1970s. This meant very little outboard equipment, and we used Leslie speakers, phasing and fuzz effects to create textures, size and space, recording most of these effects directly to tape. Because we were working on 16-track it was essential to plan ahead, but we still used up tracks quickly as the process became more and more involved. Although we had about 60 percent of each song worked out before going into the studio – e.g., arrangements, sound ideas, etc. – the other 40 percent was left to take its own course once we were in the studio and working with the musicians. Joe was excellent and gave great support to Murray and me, always willing to try out any new idea that we came up with.

Murray, Joe Wissert, Peter Robinson, Mark Warner and I became a tight-knit bunch, and spent a great deal of time together when out of the studio at Toad Hall in Fulham and in various Italian restaurants around Chelsea, Kensington, Knightsbridge and Notting Hill Gate. We spent our time discussing the general plan of attack and the next day's work, devising textures and combinations of instruments, including harmonica, mandolin, brass, woodwind and strings, together with the more unusual sounds of electric harp and prepared piano.

On some weekends or days off, Murray and I would load up my Citroën 2CV with a Stellavox portable stereo tape machine, 1/4-inch tape and microphones, and drive out of town to collect a library of sound effects. Due to Murray's gregarious personality and fame, he could easily start conversations with total strangers, and it was not long before we had collected a large amount of usable material. We would go back to the Basing Street dubbing room (behind Studio One), listen to the tapes and mark down the best sections. These included the voice of a railway station guard, the sounds of rain, footsteps on gravel, passing trains and the conversations of the customers of several Fulham Road pubs. These were later flown in to mixes. All these sounds were captured secretly, with microphones hidden down my sleeves and the Stellavox strapped onto my back, covered by my coat. We found this way of working stimulating, and Murray and I got more and more into the idea of recording out-of-doors to create unusual sounds or textures.

There were two ideas of Murray's that required special planning and would involve extra cost, but they had the potential of providing some additional adventure. One was to record a male choir in a church and the other was to record a saxophone in the pedestrian subway under Centre Point, the notorious tower block in central London. We looked at a number of churches with Fiachra Trench, the pianist and arranger, before deciding on St. Paul's, Covent Garden – Inigo Jones' "elegant barn". It had a wonderful atmosphere, a great three-second reverb and easy access. We hired Pye Studio's 16-track mobile for 12 hours, and with all the required tapes loaded on board, headed for Covent Garden.

We parked the mobile in Covent Garden Market at 6 p.m. and ran cables down the side of the church and in through a window. While I plugged in four Neumann U87s and a foldback system, Murray, Joe and Fiachra explored. They found that the church had an excellent pipe organ, and Murray decided we should make use of it. He hurriedly went off in search of a telephone in order to ring Peter Robinson and ask him to come over. Within an hour, I was set up and ready with four U87s for the choir and two more for the organ.

We started by recording the pipe organ for the song *Pity the Poor Consumer*. With distant mic'ing and the three-second natural reverb, it sounded truly beautiful, and we were all happy with the results. At 9 p.m., our six-man choir arrived to work on the track *Religion*. Murray explained what he wanted, and they practised the end section for pronunciation. I then positioned them 8 feet in front of the altar, adjusted the mics and handed out headphones before returning to the mobile to sort out the recording levels. When our choir started singing, we were all stunned by the immense sound. With the natural echo and space, it sounded more like 16 singers than six. Our hot recording level created a wonderful print-through effect, an accident that proved a real bonus. With everything completed, we packed up at about midnight. As we left, the market workers were setting up for the morning.

Murray, Joe and I drove over to Oxford Street with the Pye crew and parked near Centre Point at around 1 a.m. Murray knew the owners of a nearby Italian restaurant – here we had arranged to meet Chris Mercer, a sax player. He showed up in a hassled state, and saying little, rolled a cigarette and had a glass of wine. He did not want to eat anything and seemed slightly troubled. After a while, he and Murray slid off to another table for a chat while Joe, the Pye crew and myself settled down to calamari, beautiful fresh pasta with various sauces and beers.

After an hour or so of enjoying our meal, paid for by Murray with characteristic generosity, it was time to get back to work. With permission from the restaurant owner, we plugged in one 13-amp plug and switched on the mobile. The plan was to record Chris in the subway and to capture all the wild echoes and reverbs that one heard when walking from one end of the tunnel to the other. I used three Neumann U87s positioned at strategic points (on the bends in the subway) and an AKG D12 close to the sax. The track we were working on was called *Dole*, with just piano, acoustic guitar and double bass. Chris was unhappy about playing in the subway, and he took some time being persuaded by Murray. He was considerably put out by the idea that passers-by might take him for a real busker. I guessed that this was probably what he and Murray had been talking about in the restaurant. Chris had an impressive track record, having played with John Mayall and Juicy Lucy, but gave off a very strange vibe, as though he felt he was a loser. On all the projects I had worked on with Chris, there was always something not quite right, and although I regarded him as a great sax player, at that time I found him very negative.

We finally started to record the sax at about 3 a.m., when there was little traffic noise and very few people were using the subway. Time disappeared at an alarming rate, and by the time we had a good take, we could hear the early morning traffic overhead and the echoing of footsteps as people began to use the subway. Around 5 a.m., the restaurant owner began trying to wind things up and get us to leave. He wanted to go home and sleep, as he planned to open the restaurant again at 11 a.m. Murray had managed to stall him for an hour or so by keeping him interested in what was going on and supplying him with the occasional joint, but now, with London coming back to life, it became increasingly difficult. Eventually, although we still wanted "just one final take", the restaurant owner had had enough and literally pulled the plug. All the equipment died, and Joe and I were suddenly left in darkness in the metal box of the mobile. We packed up and went home at 6 a.m.

By the middle of July, we were at Olympic Studio One working on the final overdubs. Joe brought Nick DeCaro over from Los Angeles to write string and horn arrangements, and we finished off Murray's lead vocals. After one last session at Basing Street, to record backing vocals with Sue and Sunny (Yvonne and Heather Wheatman, who'd sung on Joe Cocker's *With a Little Help from my Friends*) on the track *Party*, we were ready to mix. We had originally asked the Beverley Sisters (a vocal trio who had been popular in the '50s) to do this session, but they declined, thinking – quite rightly – that we were "sending them up".

After a three-day break, we set up in Studio Two at Basing Street on the 1st of August and started mixing. We worked during the night, starting at midnight and working through until 8 or 9 a.m. The tracks were very involved and hard to mix manually. We mixed each song in the running order of the album to help with the dynamics and to make any necessary editing easier.

We started each mix by sorting out the relevant sound effects and editing them together on 1/4-inch tape. By trial and error, we eventually found our required length of time and the corresponding multitrack cue points. Some effects turned out to be the perfect length on our first edit, such as the footsteps on gravel, trains crossing and the station master on the song *Pacing on the Station*, or the crowd of doctors and nurses in the pub that we used on *The Party*. When this happened, it made our somewhat random approach feel all the more special. Other tapes needed the odd nip and tuck until they matched the time required. All our effects had to be flown in live (either by my assistants Phil Ault and Robert Ash, Murray or myself) every time we ran a mix, because we had no spare tracks to record these sound effects to tape. The manual mixes were extremely involved, with many fader and EQ changes required. Murray, Phil and I all worked together at the Helios desk, looking after our own collection of faders and sequence of jobs. Meanwhile, Joe sat on the leather couch in front of the console, eyes closed, listening. Every now and then a hand would appear above the desk, and he would give a thumbs-up sign. When we caught a particularly good mix, perhaps with a slow, steady fade out, he would stand up and applaud.

It took 14 days to mix 14 songs and put the album together. Side one was approximately 24 minutes, while side two ran over 28 minutes. This was exceptionally long for a vinyl LP, and we knew that when cutting the master lacquer, we would be pushing the limits of the technology that was available at the time.

It was while mixing Murray's album at night in Studio Two that I met Steve Smith, a charming, good-looking musician and producer from Birmingham, Alabama. He was working upstairs in Studio One at Basing Street, recording his second album for Island Records with his group Smith Perkins Smith. He must have found Murray's project more interesting than his own, because he would come and sit in Studio Two for hours, watching and listening to us mix. He liked our energy and our attitude to the recordings and loved Murray's album. For Steve, the idea of recording on location and spinning in effects while mixing was exciting and unconventional, and our collage of different sounds, instruments and styles impressed him. On a couple of occasions, when I had time to sit and talk to Steve, we exchanged our potted histories. Steve had only been in England for a few months and he spoke with a well-defined Southern drawl.

Steve's early experiences in the recording industry had certain parallels with my own. We had both left school at a relatively early age to join a studio, although while I had served a sort of unofficial apprenticeship, Steve had virtually taught himself. He started his engineering experience at the age of 15 at Boutwell Studio in Birmingham, Alabama. It was a 2-track jingles studio, and Steve would work there during any available downtime. The owner, Ed Boutwell, had shown Steve the basics of the recording equipment, and Steve later spent weekends making gospel albums for an all-in price of $90 per album. During a two-year period, he recorded over 100 albums – all live, straight to mono or stereo. This was how he had learned the rudiments of engineering.

In 1968, he heard of a new studio in Muscle Shoals, located about 90 miles away in northwest Alabama on the Tennessee River. It had been built by a breakaway group of musicians from the well-known Fame Studios and was financed by a loan from Ahmet Ertegun and Jerry Wexler at Atlantic Records. The deal gave Atlantic a "first option" on any new artists recorded by the Muscle Shoals Sound Studio. The musicians were Roger Hawkins on drums, David Hood on bass, Barry Beckett on keyboards and Jimmy Johnson on guitar. Built in an old casket factory, on the side of Jackson Highway, the building was about 20 feet wide and 100 feet long with 12-foot-high ceilings and had been converted into offices, studio and a control room. It was a very basic setup, with egg cartons on the walls and a thick carpet on the floor. Steve remarked that, "They hit it lucky with the studio setup and it immediately gave a fabulous sound."

Steve moved to the town of Muscle Shoals and "bugged them enough" at the studio until they gave him a job as an engineer. He spent five years there, recording, on average one album a week. The huge number of artists he worked with included Percy Sledge (a local hotel bellhop), Aretha Franklin, Wilson Pickett and Sam & Dave. He met Chris Blackwell at the studio in 1970 while recording tracks with Jimmy Cliff, and this led to a long working relationship. Coincidentally, I had mixed *Going Back West* and *Many Rivers to Cross* from these same recordings the following year (March 1971) in London, also working with Chris Blackwell.

In 1970, Steve had signed a publishing deal with Muscle Shoals and planned to make his own record. This album was recorded during downtime in 1971, with his brother Tim Smith and guitarist Wayne Perkins. Island Records signed the band, and that was why, in 1972, Steve was in Basing Street Studio One. After a support slot on tour with the band Free, he was here recording the second Smith Perkins Smith album for Island. When the album was eventually finished, he did not return to America as planned, but located himself in London working as a freelance record producer.

With Murray's album completed, I made tape copies for Joe, Murray and myself, and Joe returned to the States. A week later, we discussed at length where to master the record. Although we were all happy with the final mixes, we were concerned about the length of the LP. With side two running at 28:08 it was important to achieve the very best lacquer cut available. London was not the best city in those days for mastering rooms and equipment, and anything over 23 minutes was considered long and difficult to master. We finally decided to use Bob MacLeod in Los Angeles, someone Joe was used to working with who had a good reputation. Sally and I flew out on the 1st of September with the 1/4-inch master tapes. Cozy Powell was also on the flight, heading to Los Angeles for work. It was a hell of a flight, and the plane took over 14 hours to arrive. This was only accomplished after an unscheduled landing at a small airport in Spokane, Washington, where our plane sat on the runway for two hours. We were not allowed to leave the TWA 747, although the doors were opened to combat the rising heat. Finally, one of the male passengers was handed over to the local police, but no explanation was ever given. The plane was then towed off the end of the runway, and we were told to buckle up tight. Then, with the brakes still engaged, the engines were powered up to what sounded like flat-out until the brakes were finally released. We flashed by a row of small, four-seater planes, and then – with a huge wave of relief – took off and continued our flight to Los Angeles. No explanation, no apology and no free drink.

This was my first time in Los Angeles, and there was a vast amount to take in. The city seemed huge and stretched unbroken to the horizon. We stayed with Joe Wissert and his wife Louise in their large house on Ben Lomond Drive. There was a trip to Disneyland, where Sally was refused entry due to her "indecent attire" – a rather skimpy T-shirt. I had problems due to my long hair. "We don't want no hippies in here," we were told. We finally resolved this by Joe going in and buying Sally a Mickey Mouse T-shirt while I tied my hair back with an elastic band and put on Joe's baseball hat. A fun day was had by all.

There were also car trips along Mulholland Drive at night – totally amazing views – and the occasional afternoon on the beach at Malibu. Ever since being in Canada with my brother Terry and his wife, I had found it difficult to live in other people's houses for long periods of time and much preferred the private space of a hotel. But Joe really wanted us to stay with him and to allow him to repay the hospitality he had enjoyed in London. He introduced me to friends and colleagues during trips to downtown restaurants and the dinner parties that he and Louise gave at their house. Unfortunately, I felt I wasn't good at instant repartee, and I sometimes found I had little to say to many of the people I met.

One person I did get on well with was sound engineer Robert Appere. I met him one night with Joe in a restaurant in Hollywood and we chatted away for hours. Robert did not eat a thing – he just kept snorting cocaine. He told me an amazing story about what had happened on one occasion when his work had been criticised by Lowell George, the guitarist from Little Feat. On the mixing desk lay two NAB (10.5-inch) reels of tape – these were the 1/4-inch masters of a newly completed Little Feat album. "Okay, if you don't like the mixes," Robert had said, "do them again yourself." With that, he sliced through both tapes with a razor blade and left the studio. He was a brave guy. Lowell, unable to improve on these original mixes had to call Robert back two weeks later to remix them. Robert went on to build Clover Recorders, the studio we were to use in 1976 for Robert Palmer's album *Some People Can Do What They Like*.

Joe and I mastered Murray's album in one afternoon. It went okay, although the length of side two did produce some problems – in particular the big peaks in *Religion* and the end section of *Junk*. Some distortion was noticeable, but none of us – Joe, cutting engineer Robert MacLeod or I – wanted to cut the album any quieter, and we accepted these limitations. It would have been great on CD, but that technology was years away.

California was hot, dry and sunny every day, and being at Joe's house gave a good insight into L.A. living. He drank only water from imported five-gallon glass jars, swallowed vitamin pills instead of eating breakfast, smoked neat grass and often talked long into the night. He was a great conspiracy theorist and had many crazy stories about the Kennedy deaths, Marilyn Monroe, government illegalities and President Richard Nixon's general behaviour. It sounded to me like a strange combination of ideas, facts and rumour, and some of the stories seemed too wild to be true. He was particularly worried about Nixon and often said, "He's not to be trusted, that guy. You know, there's a strong theory that he was behind the JFK murder, and he eavesdrops on everyone." This was two years before Watergate. Once that happened, I wondered what other things Joe had said might possibly turn out to be true. After our 10-day initiation into West Coast life, including the Jerry Lewis 24-hour telethon (pure emotional blackmail), Sally and I flew home via a two-day stopover in Toronto.

I made a number of new friends during the making of *Nigel Lived* – in particular, Phil Chen, Peter Robinson and Fiachra Trench, plus Phil Chapman and Rufus Cartwright, both assistants at Olympic Studios. Everyone who had either worked on or heard the album became a fan of it and thought it would be wildly successful. Murray and I thought we had "a success waiting to happen" and were truly excited when it was released in November 1972. The album cover was in the form of a book, incorporating lyrics, a collage of photographs and "Nigel's diary". However, our expectations came to nothing. The album all but disappeared without trace due to a number of factors. At the time, when they should have been promoting Murray's album, some of the head management at CBS were accused of supplying drugs to bands on their label (see Fredric Dannen's book *Hit Men*), and for a few months there was chaos within the company. Murray joked that, "Being a concept album, it was either three years too late or six years too early." He could have been right. I made tape and cassette copies and played it to as many people as possible, being obsessed with it for a couple of years. *Nigel Lived* was a milestone for me and remains one of the most imaginative projects I have ever been involved in. While working on *Nigel*, Murray was highly motivated, and I felt inspired by his creativity and enthusiasm.

I thought it was wonderful, and for me personally it was a great success. I identified strongly with the lyrics and storyline, and over the next 20 years often felt I was going through events that were similar to Nigel's fictional experience.

Because of its commercial failure, Murray regarded *Nigel* as a musical failure as well, and this adversely affected his confidence. He took the defeat of his album badly, and after a while regarded *Nigel Lived* as a write-off. He started to change his style, moving to acoustic ballads. For my part, I took a great many of Murray's ideas and approaches to recording and used them to good effect over the next 10 years. *Nigel* popped up on albums with Robert Palmer, John Martyn, Paul Kossoff, No Dice, Dana Gillespie, Talk Talk and Steve Winwood.

Murray and I worked together sporadically over the next 10 years, but never again got close to the atmosphere and energy of *Nigel Lived*. I would love to be able to remix it with the aid of a computerized desk, and see it re-released on CD. Murray and I still occasionally work together – most recently in the summer of 2007.

Postscript:

Nigel Lived was re-released on vinyl in 2017 on Intervention Records. It was a beautiful mastering job, with a double album concept – four sides at 45rpm. It finally sounded as it should have in 1972.

Chapter 9. Bob Marley & The Wailers
20 February 1973

In February 1973, Bob Marley & The Wailers were in England with 10 tracks that needed finishing off for their second album, to be released in the UK on Island Records. There were a few overdubs to do and then the mix. Tony Platt and I were both working on the project in Studio Two at Basing Street – he would do a few days, maybe a week, and then I would take over. It annoyed all of us that we could not personally see projects through to the end, but it was all part of the way the studio booker Penny Hanson "organised" the Rota system.

I was 22 years old and very white. It would take a while for me to be accepted by these guys. Most of them were older than me by about six years, except for Earl Wilberforce Lindo, the new keyboard player who was only 20. The Wailers were a heavyweight bunch of characters, obviously streetwise and at first a little intimidating. The band included Carlton Barrett on drums, Aston "Family Man" Barrett on bass and Earl on keyboards. Bunny Livingston, Peter McIntosh and Bob Marley played guitars and sang. They were all dressed in worn-looking jeans and several layers of coloured T-shirts with jackets and boots. They displayed varying lengths of dreadlocks and occasionally some wore woollen hats. With the combination of their stance, clothes, hair and attitude, they gave the impression of being tough guys who meant business. However, there was a very mellow side to their characters, and the majority of the time I found them easy to work with. While the assistant Dave Hutchins and I set up microphones, they moved around the studio slowly and determinedly, adjusting equipment, making remarks to each other, smoking and laughing.

Like me, Chris Blackwell was white, but at least he was Jamaican and could speak the patois. I missed or misunderstood a lot of what the band were saying during the first few days of recordings, and having the boss (Chris) there gave the sessions an edge.

The Wailers smoked grass all day long. This was nothing new, but these joints were big, coned, and dangerous – anything from seven to 15 inches of neat grass. Steve Smith had referred to the larger ones as "baseball bats". "They take offense if you don't smoke with them," he had once said on returning from Jamaica. It was rumoured that Bob Marley's personal roadie had a bedsit in Earls Court, London, where they stashed large amounts of marijuana. No one actually lived there – it was just safer not to carry that amount of dope around. I had been offered a joint some days earlier by one of the band, felt honoured, took a couple of healthy puffs and handed it back. "No man, that's for you," was the response. I felt it was some kind of rite of passage, to see how the young "white blood clot" could handle it. Being stoned and working was not new to the Island staff, and I got on with what I was doing, although the grass was what we would have called "serious shit".

We were now working on *I Shot the Sheriff*. Due to the way it had been recorded, it was necessary to do three edits on the 16-track master between different takes before we could continue with the overdubs. I enjoyed editing 1/4-inch tape, but 15 ips, 2-inch multitrack editing had built-in problems. Working on a master that had taken many hours to record meant particular care and attention had to be given. It was always easier if the control room was empty of people during these operations, and I asked Chris to give me 10 minutes. They all went out to the games room or the canteen so I could be left to concentrate. As they filed out, I was handed half a coned joint by Family Man. "Hey, you'll be needing this," he said, and with that I was left to it.

The first edit went okay, and I moved on to number two. Having marked it with a white chinagraph pencil, I laid out the tape in the EditAll editing block. The joint was in my mouth. Suddenly a small explosion (probably caused by popping seeds) took off the end of the joint. I watched in horror and slow motion as the glowing debris coasted down towards the editing block. Even before it touched the tape, I could tell we had a major problem. The tape op, Dave, looked at me with disbelief.

A section of the master tape had melted, reduced from 2 inches wide to about 1/2-inch. I had lost at least a 3-inch length of the section I was cutting to. I felt panic and was suddenly very stoned. "What to do?" I needed about a bar of music from somewhere to replace the one I had just destroyed! Fortunately, there were three takes of this song on the multitrack tape, and we were using different sections from different versions (hence the edits). I played some of the sections we were not using and found a similar bar. Someone put their head 'round the control room door and asked how we were doing. "Yes, a bit of a tricky one. Give me five minutes," I managed to mumble, with my head bent low over the editing block. As I worked feverishly, I tried not to think about what might happen if I failed to repair the damaged master.

Some years later, an assistant at a studio in New York ended his career with just one mistake. He was working on the album *Aja* by Steely Dan. After two years of recording, overdubbing and re-recording songs, they were finally mixing their chosen tracks. Many of the master reels looked similar, and it was later believed that a tape had been put back in the wrong box. Consequently, instead of lining up the 2" tape machine with blank tape on the "tones" reel, the assistant mistakenly used one of the final master reels. Not realizing what he had done, he replaced the tape in its box. It was only when repeated searches for the required song had been carried out that this tape was finally loaded onto the multitrack machine and played from the top. Frequency tones filled the first four and a half minutes of the tape. Just as they were about to give up and move to another reel, the last few seconds of the song they were searching for suddenly burst onto the monitors. As Walter Becker described to me at Park Gates Studios in 1984, "Man, it was crazy. Don [Donald Fagen] and I were trying to lynch the guy. He was only saved when the studio manager sacked him on the spot and escorted him from the studio. He never worked in the music business again. Man, we wanted to kill him."

It took me about 10 minutes to complete the repair and then there was still edit number three to do. In all, the editing for which I had said, "Give me 10 minutes", took about 30. I called Chris in to listen. The band followed him into the control room. I played the track and waited nervously for the verdict.

"Yeah, sounds fine," said Chris. "Now let's get on with some Hammond."

Needless to say, since that evening I have never allowed myself or any assistant to change a tape or to get within 6 feet of any tape box while smoking. Dave, the tape op, was cool and neither of us said a word about the near disaster. We continued with overdubs and then mixed the album, speeding up some of the songs to make them more acceptable to a British audience.

Some months later, The Wailers' finished album was released. It was titled *Burnin'*.

In November 1974, I began to record a live album for Bob Marley & The Wailers. It was intended that the album would consist of the best takes from recordings made at various concerts during their first English tour. The first concert to be recorded was on the 23rd of November at the Leeds Polytechnic with the Island Mobile – Ray Doyle and Phil Ault assisting. Bob Marley turned up for the sound check with the rest of The Wailers at around 4 p.m. He was 29 years old, medium height and had shoulder-length dreadlocks. His clothes reeked of ganja and he wore a red, gold and green woollen hat, a hand-embroidered jacket and a pair of denim dungarees. He spoke quietly, smiled a great deal and was sometimes referred to by his nickname "Tuff Gong" by other members of the band. The concert went well for a first night's performance, and I had no technical problems with any of the mobile gear. However, after Bob had played the gig, he came off stage, complained about the cold (the temperature was close to zero with a strong wind and rumours of snow) and went home to Jamaica. This must have been a severe blow to Chris Blackwell and the guys at Island Records – obviously the band failed to finish the tour and we were unable to record any more concerts for this album.

Eight months later, in July 1975, The Wailers came to London during another tour, and it was only then we were able to finish recording what became the *Live!* LP. Steve Smith, by now an Island Records house producer, was instrumental in organising the recording of two concerts, which took place on the 17th and 18th of July. When not working with Robert Palmer, The Allman Brothers, Clancy or Trapeze, Steve had spent some time during the previous few months in Jamaica at Chris Blackwell's request. The idea had been to meet The Wailers and record some studio tracks with them for an album. These trips, however, had all proved to be unsuccessful. "Well, I went back and forth a few times trying to have productive meetings," Steve told me later. "Finally, I booked a studio in Kingston for a week, starting on a Thursday. I think the first band member turned up on Saturday and then on the Sunday someone else turned up and said, 'No worry, man. Everybody on their way down soon.' That happened every day. At the end of the fifth day, I said, 'Wait a minute. I've got a life.' I got on the next plane out of Jamaica. We never came up with a single thing."

Steve also recounted a curious incident he had had a few months later. "I remember I was living at 434 Kings Road – one of the Island flats. It was above Smile, the hairdressers. One day, someone showed up at the front door with four 55-gallon drums – huge fucking things – and said, 'I'm supposed to deliver this.' I said, 'Well, what is it? I'm not sure I want it.' This guy says, 'It's seawater, straight out of Kingston harbour.' I said, 'I don't think I want that,' and he says, 'No, no. It's for The Wailers. They can't wash their hair unless it's out of Kingston harbour. Got to be seawater – it's religious.' I said, 'Great, bring it on in.' The Wailers were a mad bunch of fuckers."

The London concerts were an ideal opportunity for Steve to finally get the band down on tape. The Island Mobile was already busy, so Steve booked Mick McKenna and the Rolling Stones Mobile for both nights. Steve telephoned me at Basing Street after the concert on the first night. I was in Studio One making up lists of the required overdubs with Robert Palmer for the album *Pressure Drop*. "It was crazy," said Steve. "Everybody was there. I think the whole of Island turned up. I went down with Alan Callan. Due to so many people being there and the humidity, they opened the roof to let some air in. People knocked down the back doors – 30-foot metal stage doors – and gate-crashed. There were hundreds there who shouldn't have been. Blackwell asked me to check out the results in the mobile and it was a mess. Unfortunately, with the chaos and all these people on stage, microphones got moved and banged about, and basically as I told Chris, the tapes are unusable."

After agreeing on a percentage deal for Steve to produce the recording, Chris told Steve to "get in there and sort it out for tomorrow night."

The next day, Steve and I went to the Lyceum Theatre in the early afternoon and nailed every microphone stand to the stage and set up additional safety microphones. Having spent most of the afternoon setting up the stage, Steve decided he should engineer the evening's recording himself. "As I'd done all the crawling around on my hands and knees, I thought I'd have some fun," he told me later. As on the first night, there were people on stage and hanging from every vantage point, but this time Steve's careful preparations paid off. It was a great night and after the concert, Steve immediately found Chris and told him, "It's solid. We've got a good recording." Two days later, I was brought in by Chris Blackwell to mix at Basing Street Studio Two. Steve had no more involvement with the project, much to his disappointment.

On that Sunday, I first dealt with a problem caused by the microphone used by the I Threes (Marley's backing vocalists). It had not been working properly during the live recording and the signal on the tape was very weak. Sue and Sunny (see chapter 8) came to the studio to repair the backing vocals and sang with fake Jamaican accents through the entire show. That was in the afternoon. In the early evening, we began to mix the album and set up the song, *Trenchtown Rock* (somewhere near the middle of the concert). While I was working on a balance, The Wailers and Chris Blackwell were spliffing up and dancing around the control room. Chris kept asking for "more audience". This was possible, as Steve had recorded the sound from the audience microphones onto two separate tracks. David Harper's PA balance had been excellent and did not upset my levels. When Chris was happy with the sound and the overall audience level, which was now about 35 percent of the mix, he said, "Great. Let's go back to the start of the concert and run it off like that."

We played the 2-inch reels from top to bottom in order, mixing straight onto 1/4-inch tape at 15 ips. This gave us 30 minutes per reel. It felt brilliant, just like you were there at the concert, mixing the live, front-of-house sound. The entire concert recording was mixed in only three and a half hours. With the help of two crossfades and four edits, I cut the album together into Blackwell's preferred running order, and by 10:30 p.m. we were finished. At under £6,000 it was one of Island's least expensive albums to make. Because it was Sunday, I was paid time and a half and earned about £23 for the day's work. The album went on to be very successful, and the single released, *No Woman, No Cry*, was a big hit. *Live!* was described by the music press as one of the all-time best live albums. A great night had been captured, and due to the excellent PA mix and the use of the audience microphones, it sounded wonderful. As Steve said, years later, "That album cracked it for Marley. It made him accessible, especially to the American market."

Less than 18 months later, on the 3rd of December 1976 (two days before giving a free concert in Kingston), Bob, his wife Rita, the guitarist Don Kinsey and the band's manager Don Taylor were injured during a gun attack at Marley's house. The band were waiting for Chris Blackwell to arrive for a meeting when the gunmen burst in. Taylor threw himself across Bob Marley and probably saved Bob's life. Don was lucky to survive himself. At the time, various motives were put forward for the attack – either Don Taylor's gambling, Bob's affair with the "light-skinned" Miss World (Cindy Breakspeare), some local scam that had gone wrong, or party political in-fighting. I favoured the latter. A Jamaican who was there at the time alleged, "Prime Minister Michael Manley arranged it and then implicated his opponent, Edward Seaga." The incident was never officially explained.

Ray, Jody, Robert, Steve, Mobile, North Lodge, *Sneakin' Sally*

John Bindon and Angie Bowie 1975

Chapter 10. Joe Brown
4 May 1974

During the spring of 1974 at Basing Street Studios, I was on a weekend session in Studio Two with Joe Brown and his group Brown's Home Brew. The plan was to record and overdub a 7" single on Saturday and finish it off and mix it on Sunday. Joe was under some pressure from his record company to come up with the goods, and the atmosphere was tense right from the start. The more they worried about tuning, timing and sounds, the worse it appeared to get. It was not a session I really wanted to do, but I had been unable to talk Penny out of it. I had just finished working with Andy Mackay on his album *In Search of Eddie Riff*, with Amazing Blondel on their album *Mulgrave Street* and with Joni Mitchell on live recordings at the New Victoria Theatre. I was tired, having worked an average of 14 hours a day during February, March and April, and would have preferred to take a break at this point.

The band were all playing live, so I set them up with screens and close mic'ing to achieve clean sounds and as good a separation as possible. The drums were in front of the control room window, and the guitars, bass and keyboards fanned out from this point. Everyone was in their own screened-off booth. While working in the afternoon with Joe, it had been difficult getting suitable sounds, and the band were not playing well. We were making painfully slow progress. My wife, Sally, was hanging out with Vicki Brown – Joe's wife and a brilliant singer – sitting on the leather couch in front of the desk.

At 33 years old, Joe Brown was a small but intense bundle of energy, constantly telling gags and one-liners – he never stopped talking. Although born in Lincolnshire, he was an East End lad, 5 feet 6 inches tall with blonde, spiky hair, round face and mischievous eyes. He was nearly always smiling. He controlled most aspects of the session himself, including tempo, arrangement and sounds, his energy appearing endless. On this occasion, he was dressed in black boots, blue jeans and a white shirt, and I thought he had a modern-day, Artful Dodger quality about him.

Although the recording of the single was not going well, he had up until now been able to keep his sense of humour and Jack-the-lad image. He might have yelled at a musician for the occasional mistake, and sometimes he got annoyed with malfunctioning equipment or broken strings, but very soon experience would get the better of him and his charm would reappear. In the past, Joe had been very successful, especially during the late '50s and the '60s, and besides performing with Eddie Cochran, Gene Vincent and Johnny Cash, he had fronted his own bands, The Bruvvers and now Brown's Home Brew. During this period, he succeeded in having 12 Top 10 hits. Sadly, chart success would elude Joe after 1973.

At some point in the early evening, many hours into the session and still trying to put the backing track down, Joe complained about the bass sound. "It doesn't sound like that in the studio," he snapped. Musicians often say this sort of thing, but it is important to realise that it will always sound different if you close mic an instrument (for separation) and then stand 6 feet away to listen to it. Very few people put their ear 1-inch from a snare drum, for instance, but that is where most snare drum mics can be found. Close mic'ing produces an artificial result, but there are some situations when there is no other choice, and this was one such situation. I went into the studio with Joe and had a listen to the bass amp. I listened in various positions, both close to the amp and some feet away. It seemed similar to the control room sound. I headed back to the control room with Joe behind me complaining bitterly about the sound and the importance of getting it right. Now, more than ever, I did not want to be on this session.

I manoeuvred behind the desk and sat down. Most of the band were standing around in the control room.

Finally, I interrupted him, saying, "Really Joe, it sounds similar to me."

"You can't be serious. It sounds fucking awful," said Joe. "Nothing like it does out there."

"Yes, it does," I said, "and anyway we have a DI from the bass, so it's got to be close." This was an extremely inaccurate comment from me, as the DI has no real bearing on the amp sound.

"Ah, this is ridiculous," said Joe. "I want it to sound like it does in the room."

At this point, I was thinking how boring it all was. We were taking hours trying to get a sound on various instruments for a dubious song. The atmosphere was difficult and nobody appeared to be enjoying themselves – least of all me. As I was a house engineer, I should have just ridden along with it all – as usual – but on this particular day I really could not be bothered. "Look," I said, "just because you are having problems with your record company, or whatever it is, don't bring them in here."

Before I realized what was happening, Joe leaped over the Helios desk and had me pinned up against the wall. "Don't hit him Joe, don't hit him," yelled band members, "We've got enough problems already."

I heard Vicki, sitting on the leather sofa, ask Sally, "Is he always like this?"

Joe backed off and within half an hour the session had dissolved into confusion. We packed up in silence and everyone left. I drove home to Sussex, thinking of the remarks Penny would probably make on Monday morning. As it turned out, she was surprisingly moderate in her reaction to it all, although Muff Winwood, (now our studio manager), gave me one of his pep talks. I heard no more about Joe's project and never discovered whether or not it was re-recorded elsewhere.

The next summer I was working on overdubs with Robert Palmer for *Pressure Drop* at Chris Blackwell's house in Theale. Vicki Brown came out for a couple of days to do backing vocals, and I knew I recognized her from somewhere, but could not place it. After three days, it all fell into place when Joe turned up to collect her. He walked over to me and said, "How are you, you old cunt?" gave me a warm hug, and stayed to play a wonderful banjo part on the title track, *Pressure Drop*. We got on brilliantly from then on.

Chapter 11. Robert Palmer 15 May 1974

I've obtained a great deal of my studio work from meeting people by chance, either in a studio, backstage at concerts or even on the street. Sometimes, I was simply in the right place at the right time. This is how I met Robert Palmer.

On the 15th of May 1974, while I was visiting the Island Records offices in St Peter's Square for a meeting with Denise Mills, I wandered into their new studio, The Fallout Shelter. I wanted to say hello to Steve Smith. We had kept in touch and worked together in 1973 on two albums with the group Elephant's Memory and with Mick's brother, Chris Jagger.

I found Steve in the control room with Robert Palmer, sitting at the new Helios parametric desk. They were listening to backing tracks they had recorded at Sea-Saint Studios in New Orleans, Louisiana, with The Meters and Lowell George of the group Little Feat. Rhett Davies, an assistant engineer from Basing Street, was loading and unloading tapes. Over the past few weeks, Steve and Robert had recorded 23 songs in a variety of studios in New York, New Orleans and Muscle Shoals, Alabama. As Steve put it, "We were on a quest." They were now in the process of making rough mixes of selected takes. I was introduced to Robert, who was smoking a Dunhill cigarette and dressed all in white – suit, shirt and shoes. He said very little and appeared quite distant and lost in decision-making. I stayed for half an hour or so, listened to about six songs and left. Later that evening, I received a phone call from Steve asking if I would like to get involved with the overdubs, which he intended to do in the St Peter's Square rehearsal room with the Island Mobile truck. I was very pleased to be asked and immediately said yes.

Starting the 20th of May, Robert, Steve and I spent five days in the rehearsal room listening to the basic backing tracks from New Orleans and getting ideas and arrangements together for overdubbing. Steve made up a master list of things to do. We recorded a variety of guitar parts with Robert, tried out some editing and overdubbed a harmonica recorded through a Pignose amp with Steve York, of Robert's former band Vinegar Joe. We lay around on the floor smoking and listening to other people's albums – our favourite being the newly released *Paradise and Lunch* by Ry Cooder. This gave me an ideal opportunity to get to know Robert, who was amusing, friendly and not at all as he had appeared on our first meeting. He was then about 25 years old, 5 feet 10 inches tall, with dark brown hair, a warm humour and was always smartly dressed. His voice was soft, with a mixed accent, the combination of being born in Batley, West Yorkshire, and brought up in Malta. He loved reading science fiction (a big fan of Jack Vance), could be clumsy with cups of tea, and gave off a feeling of worldly experience.

Robert had been in various bands since the age of 15, including The Alan Bown Set, Dada and the successful Vinegar Joe with singer Elkie Brooks. He was very much in control, knew what he wanted and seemed to have a close working relationship with Steve. We started to get a feel for the songs as finished pieces, and worked well as a team, each of us taking care of different aspects of the sound and overall recording. The days were long, starting about 11 a.m. and working through till 2, 3 or 4 a.m. – on average 16 hours a day.

I suppose our own behaviour was a bit undisciplined, but there were also problems caused by constant interruptions from telephone calls or the staff and liggers at Island Records who "just dropped by to say, 'Hi.'" Steve wanted to get away from it all, and I suggested we could use my house in Sussex. After two phone calls (to my wife Sally and to percussionist Jody Linscott), we loaded up our tapes, guitars and rhythm box and were on our way.

The team consisted of Steve, Robert, Ray Doyle (who drove and looked after the Island Mobile) and myself. We picked up Jody and her percussion box as we left London. Jody was beautiful and enchanting. I had originally met her one evening in late 1971 when she was a member of The Monday Night Rock 'n' Roll Band – an ad hoc group of musicians brought into Basing Street Studio Two by disc jockey John Peel. Jody was about 5 feet 7 inches tall, with long, black wavy hair, dark eyes, a large mouth and a cute, upturned nose. Her skin was lightly tanned, she had small breasts and wore Indian beads, leather bracelets, jeans and soft, transparent, silk-like tops. She had an extroverted personality and was always laughing and smiling. Many men were to be captivated by this rhythmic woman – I was one of them.

We weaved through the streets of south London, taking in the delights of New Cross and Deptford, finally getting above 25 mph on the A21. I spent most of my time up front in the cab with Ray, chatting and giving directions. Ray was about 25 years old with longish brown hair and a bushy moustache. He was extremely friendly, easy-going and laid back. Ray's hobby was playing guitar – he had a passion for photography and loved a smoke. Over the previous two years, we had become good friends.

While Ray and I talked in the cab, Steve, Robert and Jody travelled in more comfort back in the "control room". The weather was beautiful, and we were traveling along at 40 mph with the windows open and the sun pouring into the truck. I had a large grass joint in my hand and John Lennon playing on the cassette machine. It promised to be an excellent adventure.

It was Sunday the 26th of May, and we set up the mobile in the woods at the top of the drive. However, we first had to manoeuvre the truck backwards through the trees. Steve and I stood on the roof of the mobile and lifted branches to make this possible – it took an hour or so before the mobile was finally nestled in amongst the trees.

The mobile was equipped in a similar way to the studios in Basing Street. There was a Helios 30-in and 24-out desk, two 3M M79 24-track tape decks, Altec speakers, an EMT 240 echo plate and a collection of UREI limiters and graphic equalizers, plus Studer stereo machines and Dolby noise reduction. All this equipment could be powered either by a generator (this was built onto a two-wheeled trailer) or, if available, a single 13-amp socket. We left the generator in the driveway and ran a power lead to the kitchen of our house.

I laid out a multi-core cable and connected up various microphones to two rooms in the house, starting with a converted bedroom, where the insulated walls were hung with coloured Hessian panels and there was a thick pile carpet on the floor. This carpet was placed on top of glass fibre and foam. There were shutters at the window, a false ceiling and a padded door. This room was acoustically dead and almost completely soundproof. In the sitting room, we connected the foldback from the mobile to my home stereo system for playbacks and communication. About 15 by 12 feet with a large carpet on the floor and two smaller rugs hanging on the walls, the sitting room was acoustically live and had a very warm sound. Here we recorded vocals and percussion and tried out ideas on guitar.

Steve and I worked in the mobile, while Robert and Jody were in either the converted bedroom or the sitting room. We recorded vocals, guitar parts, tambourines, tuned wooden percussion, rainstick and a collection of the more bizarre sounds that Jody carried with her in the percussion box. These included wind-up, plastic chattering teeth and a collection of shakers made from household plastic bottles and film canisters.

Steve and I often listened to final playbacks of recordings in the lounge on the regular stereo system. Ray and my wife Sally rolled joints, made cups of tea and prepared food. It was great fun, with everyone enjoying the peace, freedom, space, and the opportunity for uninterrupted work. I especially found it an ideal way to record. Ever since my experience with Murray Head and the Pye Mobile in the summer of 1972, I had enjoyed the possibilities of working this way, and now looked forward to the late evenings when the traffic noise subsided and recording outside in the garden became a viable proposition.

We settled into a routine of systematically going through each song, completing the necessary overdubs and crossing them off Steve's master list. Everyone took time out to walk in the woods behind the house and make shopping trips to Wadhurst, the local village. Ray set up a video camera and tuned in the relevant television channel on our monitor in the mobile. We then moved the camera to different locations in the house when recording, but most of the time we preferred the picture when it was just pointing at the house from the garden. At night, Steve slept in the bedroom/studio, Ray had a sleeping bag on cushions on the floor in the sitting room and Robert and Jody shared the spare bedroom.

After about four days, it was suggested we move location for a day or two. Through my parents, I knew the vicar at Addington's St

Margaret church in Kent, and after we had obtained permission, this became our next venue. We set off at 9 a.m. to drive the hour and a half to Addington. The mobile was compact and carried all that was needed. We reconnected the generator to the tow bar and headed northeast.

Once at Addington, we parked the generator as far away as possible to reduce the unwanted throb from the engine. Not wishing to offend the churchgoers, we laid just one multi-core cable to run microphones and foldback, and stayed well away from the churchyard. Access was very easy, and within an hour we were set up and ready to work.

After a cup of Ray's finest tea, I loaded up *Get Outside* and Robert left the mobile to have a warm up sing. This allowed me to check the microphone levels. Robert loved this approach to recording and was enthusiastic and inspired, wandering off to the Neumann U87 microphone with the customary bottle of rum in his hand and the usual cheeky smile on his face. A group of women passed by on their way to arrange flowers in the church, and we saw someone who might have been a verger come up on his bike. These people appeared to take very little interest in us, but did not look particularly pleased and said little or nothing when they passed. By contrast, we made a point of being as friendly and polite as possible as we carried on with our work.

We tried vocals inside the entrance to the church and then against the outside wall – this proving the most successful, with a self-limiting effect on the vocal. All went well during the afternoon until the vicar returned while we were doing vocals for *Hey Julia*, a track we had put together in the mobile the night before, with just a basic rhythm box and Robert on bass and guitar. We had created the track by dropping in directly onto tracks on the outro section of the master of *Sailing Shoes*. Although this is a somewhat risky thing to do (one mistake and you have lost that particular instrument on that track), Steve felt it would be an unusual way to create a cross-fade, and ultimately a good way to approach it. He was confident it would work, and with a little fine-tuning during mixing, it did.

The vicar eventually wandered over to the mobile, said hello, and asked if he could see the lyrics. He took offence to such lines as

"Your figure makes me tremble, and I sure would like to handle what's between your ears" and "You're a temptation to a man, and whatever you've injected made me feel how I felt when I sang, 'Julia you're a danger, just like giving sweets to strangers'". He then looked at other lyrics to the songs we were recording. "There's a lady in a turban, in a cocaine tree and she does a dance so rhythmically". He asked us to pack up and leave. His objections were unconvincing – perhaps he had had complaints from the people who passed us in the churchyard. However, the day had not been wasted, and we left with a couple of master vocals recorded.

So, we went back to my house (where the morality and lyric police kept a lower profile) for more percussion and vocals, finishing at 4 a.m. a 19-hour day. The next day, the 30th, was to be our last day with the mobile. After only five hours sleep, we started early at 10 a.m., with plans for a 24-track edit on *Through It All There's You*. We spent the whole day trying to get the length of the track down from nearly 13 minutes to around six minutes. We pasted a cue chart of the song around the walls of the mobile and marked it with coloured felt pens to help us identify sections and keep track of the bars. I edited out between 12 and 16 bars from each section of the song and cut the tape a total of 18 different times. Finally, at 5 a.m. – success. However, on listening to the tape the next morning before we left for London, we felt we had lost its charm, and in the end went back to the original version. This entailed another 18 edits to put the pieces back together.

We had worked an average of 16 hours a day for the five days we were in Sussex and had completed a vast amount of work. However, we had also found time to sit around for hours planning the next album and making up lists of our "perfect bands" and heroes. These were mainly musicians from our favourite records of the '60s and early '70s – Carol Kaye, James Jamerson, Ed Greene and Chuck Rainey. We also listened to records by James Brown, Ry Cooder, Little Feat, and Murray Head's "Nigel Lived" – still a favourite of Steve's. We had become a close-knit trio and got on excellently. With our positive and experimental attitude, we felt we could have accomplished anything.

We returned to London and unloaded the tapes and equipment at Basing Street. I ran Robert home to his flat in St John's Wood and met his wife, Sue. Although we had worked together for two weeks, I had not even realized he was married. Sue was petite and had short, dark hair, a great smile and was wearing a white t-shirt and blue jeans. She was amiable and relaxed.

There was now a 10-day break from Robert's sessions, but for me the work did not stop. The very next day, I was booked with the Island Mobile for a five-day stint at the Rainbow Theatre in Finsbury Park London, to record a series of In Concert programmes for American television. I was back working with Ray, and because of the scale of the project we had Phil Ault as a second assistant, plus maintenance man Paul Bennet.

We recorded five bands a night, including Focus, Alex Harvey, Foghat, The Kinks, Procol Harum, America, Roxy Music and Humble Pie. Days started at 9 a.m. at the theatre with rehearsals and soundchecks, and finished 15 hours later after the recordings. Soundchecks were done in reverse order to the evening show, so the rule was – last to soundcheck, the first to go on. We were given stage diagrams and assorted details of requirements for each band or artist and made a note of any cross-plugging.

Since changeovers were so smooth and only took about 15 minutes each, the invited audience rarely became restless. On stage, it could be loud, to say the least. After each of the Humble Pie and Focus sets, someone had to run out and paint over the cracks that had appeared in the painted black stage, and so extreme was the volume when Focus played that pieces of plaster fell from the ceiling above the band. Because television cameras are very sensitive to vibration, they were all padded out with quilt-like material to protect the picture. Although these five days were nerve-wracking and hard work, it was also immensely exciting and rewarding to be flying by the seat of my pants. I finished at the Rainbow at 2 a.m. on the 6th of June. At 1p.m. on the 7th, I began a three-day assignment with Dana Gillespie for the start of her new album *Ain't Gonna Play No Second Fiddle*. (see next chapter)

Then, without a single day off, it was back to Robert Palmer's album. I met Steve and Robert at 6 p.m. on the 10th of June at Basing Street. We sat in the dubbing room above Studio One and talked about various mixing styles and approaches. The studios were always busy, so we had to work on night-time sessions starting at 10 p.m. and finishing at 9:30 a.m. Steve, Robert and I performed the last over-dub – handclaps on *Hey Julia* in the live, tiled passageway beside the studio – and we were ready to mix.

We mixed an average of two songs a night in Studio Two – still my favourite room. The mixes were very bright, crisp and dry for their day, with almost no echo or effects. It was an unusual sound for England at that time and would probably be termed more an "American" sound. Robert wore a t-shirt that had "More Bass" printed on the front, and he would stand up occasionally and point to his chest while smiling broadly. We worked hard with no breaks, just the occasional line of cocaine and an hourly grass joint to help us cruise through the night. We were all very much aware of what we were trying to create, and all worked towards the same goal. Within five days, we had finished. I did a couple of edits, cut it all together and then made a set of 15 ips master copies for Steve, Chris Blackwell and myself, with a cassette copy for Robert.

Chris Blackwell, Robert, Steve and his friend Isaac Tigrett (founder of the Hard Rock Cafe and House of Blues) and I listened back to the final mixes at 5 a.m. on the last day of mixing. Steve turned down the lights and told assistant Barry Sage to start the tape. Steve then promptly fell asleep halfway through the first track. Steve told me later, "I didn't hear a thing except the opening few bars of *Sailing Shoes*. I was exhausted."

Chris loved the album. The whole LP, recording, overdubbing and mixing, had taken less than 27 days' worth of studio time and was spread over many weeks. Even so, the final cost of the album was £20,000 – "the most expensive Island album so far" – and a more than moderate sum in 1974. The album cover photograph was shot in the approach tunnel to Heathrow Airport at 3 a.m., with Robert and Josephine Florent, a hired model, running from one end of the tunnel to the other. The photographer, Graham Hughes, was in front of them, lying down in the back of a pickup truck with his cameras. Steve drove 50 yards behind in a '50s Chevy (these are the headlights in the photo). I thought it was a neat photograph and an unusual album cover.

Sneakin' Sally Through the Alley did not sell a large number of copies in England or America. It received poor British press but was a hit with musicians and within the music business as a whole, bringing me a great deal of work. In America, the press was positive, and it was voted "Sleeper of the Year" by Playboy Magazine. It's still one of my favourite albums.

Chapter 12. Dana Gillespie
3 July 1974

Dana Gillespie, with her entourage and band, could be described with justification as the epitome of sex, drugs and rock 'n' roll. The sessions I worked on with Dana went to further extremes than any I worked on during the whole of the 1970s.

I started Dana's second album, *Ain't Gonna Play No Second Fiddle*, at 1 p.m. on the 7th of June 1974 in Studio Two at Basing Street Studios. During the previous five years, I had become completely accustomed to having a large collection of people on sessions, either in the control room, in the studio or just hanging out in the building. For me, this way of working had begun during sessions with Traffic at Olympic Studios in 1967 and had continued in Canada during 1969 with Perth County Conspiracy – then later back in England at Island Studios with Third World War, Mott the Hoople, Murray Head and Andy Mackay. All these sessions had given me considerable experience in working through complete chaos, and now on Dana's sessions, that experience would be tested to the utmost. For sheer numbers of people present, these sessions were quite unlike anything I had ever worked on before.

The basic band consisted of Simon Phillips on drums, Robin Sylvester on bass, Dave Skinner on keyboards and John Porter on guitar. Playing on each song were different combinations of various other musicians – Phil Chen on bass, Mickey Gallagher and John "Rabbit" Bundrick on keyboards and Bob Weston and Bryn Haworth on guitars. Added to these was a large collection of musicians, actors, friends, assorted music biz personnel and various sons and daughters of the rich who comprised the celebrity circuit at the time. I had to continually step over or around most of them to get to and from the studio and to adjust microphones and such. There were often as many as 20 people in the control room, including Dana's boyfriend Leslie Spitz (an antiques dealer), his sister Barbara, their friend Sally-Anne McKelvie, John Porter's wife, Lori "Shadow" Lee, Angie Bowie, the actor John Bindon and his girlfriend Vicki Hodge, Dana and

David Bowie's manager Tony DeFries, Carol Grimes, Charlie Gillett, Lionel Bart and Suzie and Sandra from the MainMan Management's London office. It was an ever-increasing collection of characters and friends of friends. In the years to come, I would introduce Richie Hayward, Tim Renwick, Steve Smith, Alan Spenner, Tim Cross and David Malin to this circus. Dana, Bindon, Bowie, Lionel Bart and their friends all made trips to the private island of Mustique and met other inhabitants of the island, including Princess Margaret and Prince Andrew. Rumours of liaisons between Vicki Hodge and Prince Andrew were reported in the British press at the time. Even more outrageous, although it never reached the newspapers, was the alleged relationship between John Bindon and Princess Margaret.

At the age of 16, Dana had become the British Junior Water Skiing Champion. She then made a name for herself as "jailbait" for David Bowie and Bob Dylan, before signing to Tony DeFries' MainMan Management and releasing her first album on RCA in 1973. At 5 feet 8 inches tall, she was 24 years old at the time I met her, with long reddish-black hair and large breasts, a feature always mentioned in press stories. She wore short rubber skirts with stockings and suspenders and was generally flamboyant in her dress and behaviour. She had a magnetic personality, and it was difficult not to like her.

We worked for just three days – from the 7th to the 9th of June – logging 1 p.m. to 2 a.m. each night. During this time, we recorded seven backing tracks. There was a large collection of serious drugs around, and everyone appeared to smoke dope continuously. The party went on all day with a coming and going of assorted characters, but it peaked during the evenings when the full contingency was there and drug taking became an art form.

Apart from the hash and grass, there were also large amounts of cocaine, blues and a new drug called PCP. Dana often said, "It's a large intake, but the results are very positive." She had a pillbox that contained a multi-coloured assortment – Tuinal, Seconal, French blues, black bombers, DF-118 and Mandrax all nestled together. Besides this collection of uppers and downers, there was a particular yellow pill she referred to as "sideways" that kept one feeling mellow but wide awake for many hours. Taken on an empty stomach, these could sometimes produce mild visual hallucinations. I avoided most pills and kept mainly to dope, but sometimes during the late evenings I could be tempted into taking a "sideways".

After three days with Dana, I was back working with Robert Palmer and Steve Smith, mixing *Sneakin' Sally Through the Alley* during the nights in Basing Street's Studio Two. It was amazing to me that the studios and equipment could stand this continuous workload and wear and tear, not to mention the effects on the staff. The studios usually worked 24 hours a day with two sessions a day in both studios – midday till midnight, and midnight till midday. During the changeovers, the tape ops would carry out bin bags of empty vodka bottles, beer cans, razor blades and roaches. I agreed with Dana – the consumption of various narcotics was phenomenal, but the results were surprisingly creative.

On Wednesday the 26th of June, I was back with Dana, her band and attendants. We worked straight through until the 11th of July in Studio Two, overdubbing (Mel Collins on sax, Henry Lowther on trumpet, Eddie Jobson on synth and "Rabbit" on piano) and mixing. During the previous few months, I had worked with Andy Mackay, Amazing Blondel, Joni Mitchell and Robert Palmer. I felt that I was on a good run – I was pleased with my work and finally I felt I knew how to achieve the end result that I wanted.

On the evening of June the 30th, Dana handed me a white paper package of PCP, saying, "Have this later when things aren't so hectic." I slipped the paper into the back of my Marlboro cigarette packet and continued with my work. We were recording drums with Simon Phillips. He was young, only 17 years old, and new to the London session scene. He was quite brilliant and wonderful to watch. Slowly, the room filled up with even more people than usual as they heard about this new, young drummer in Studio Two. Musicians and crew from the other studio came in to listen and be inspired – they all wanted to know who this brilliant drummer was. After about 30 minutes, they headed back to their sessions and the number of visitors returned to the normal 15. A few hours later, when all was well under control, I took out the paper package and unrolled it. Inside was a glistening white powder, and assuming one snorted it, I laid it out on the edge of the desk and chopped at it with a razor blade. I made two parallel lines of the powder and snorted one up each nostril. I felt instant pain at the back of the nose and throat. The pain very rapidly spread to my head, which now began to throb violently. I was half blinded but carried on working as best I could, for as long as I could, finally telling Dana of my predicament.

"Fuck me, Phill. You're supposed to put it in orange juice and drink it," she said. "It's like a form of acid. Are you okay?"

"Well, not great," I said, "but you can try and guide me through things. How much more is there to do?"

"Not a lot," Dana said. "It's just the guitar with John we're set up for. We'll make it."

We finished at 1 a.m. that night, and I went back to Dana's flat to take painkillers and try to sleep. She wanted to keep an eye on me, and I felt pleased at her concern. In the morning, I felt fine, had a bath and returned with Dana to the studio to start another day. I never did try PCP in the recommended way.

By the end of June, we had all our backing tracks ready and were into the slower job of overdubbing lead vocals with Dana, backing vocals with the singers from Kokomo (Dyan Birch, Frank Collins and Paddy McHugh) and percussion with Jody Linscott. The group of liggers swelled in the control room and studio and spilled out into the relaxation and canteen areas. There were people everywhere in the building, including the copying rooms, empty offices and toilets, and some even escaped upstairs to Studio One. John Bindon preferred to spend nearly all his time in the control room of Studio Two, telling stories about prison and reciting monologues that often lasted an hour or so. He was an amazing guy; much more interesting than his actor/villain reputation would suggest. He could talk on any subject, and when in a pleasant mood could be wonderfully entertaining – an extraordinary man.

The first night I met John had been just a few weeks earlier on the 8th of June. It was about 9 p.m. I was working at the desk, head bent down and fiddling with some EQ pot or another. Out of the corner of my eye, I was aware of someone coming into the room, swinging something in his hand. On looking up, I just had time to glimpse what it was before he disappeared in front of the desk. He was walking across the control room swinging his rather large penis. I mused that Dana's "sideways" pills had come on a little fast and I must be hallucinating. Sadly not. I soon discovered that his party piece was to put his 12" penis through the handles of five half-pint mugs and then still be able to hold the end of it. This was usually written up inaccurately in the press as John's ability to balance a pint of beer on his erect penis. Due to the wild taste in clothes that most of the women partygoers appeared to have, there was a great deal of naked female flesh around. Perhaps John was trying to even up the balance.

We were still starting at 1 p.m. every day, but now worked through until 4 or 5 a.m. in order to get our workload completed. At 11:15 p.m. on the 3rd of July, the party was – as usual – in full swing while Dana and I were overdubbing another guitar part with John Porter. Suddenly, the red light in the ceiling began to flash. This light had been installed after the police bust in February 1971 and was intended as a warning signal. Believing it to be a possible police raid, we all immediately moved into action. There were people running in all directions, hiding drugs and disposing of roaches or other illegal substances.

I had a plan for such an emergency. By removing an EQ module in the Helios desk, I could conceal my stash inside. It took just 10 seconds to accomplish this and then replace the module. Dana went to the ladies' lavatory with her stash of drugs in a plastic bag, and searching around rapidly found that in one of the cubicles there was a piece of tiled wall that could be removed. It was two tiles wide and three tiles deep. There was a similar section in the gent's lavatory, and it gave access to the cisterns and plumbing. She hurriedly deposited her bag and came back to the control room. As the party members tried to relieve themselves of their stashes, not all the stories were as positive.

Some drugs were thrown away down the toilets while others were scattered or swallowed. After a few minutes of general panic, the telephone in the control room rang. It was the night security man, Bill Cody, who said, "Don't worry Phill. It's not a raid, just a policeman checking up on a car in the street."

"Okay guys, as you were," I said and retrieved my stash from the desk. This type of false alarm had happened to me before, and now I was always quite relaxed when the light started to flash. Many of the others were not so lucky, and for some time after this incident there was a bemoaning of their lot from party members who were annoyed that they had flushed their drugs away. Many of them left earlier than usual that night. The warning light was always causing problems, and there were many false alarms. Due to its position under the receptionist's desk, a stray knee often triggered it accidentally.

We carried on overdubbing, and by the 7th of July we were ready to mix. The mixing sessions now became even longer and sometimes we worked through till 9 a.m. – a 20-hour workday. We finally finished at 10 a.m. on the 11th of July. I had a two-day break before going to America to start Robert Palmer's 2nd album *Pressure Drop*. (see chapter 13)

On returning on the 8th of August, I went back to finishing off work with Amazing Blondel and started on an album with Joan Armatrading and producer Pete Gage. On the 24th, Dana and I got together for a 17-hour session to do a couple of remixes and cut the album into its running order. In two days time, Dana and I planned to go to New York to master *Ain't Gonna Play No Second Fiddle* with George Marino at Sterling Sound. As it was an early flight, it had been agreed that I would travel to London and stay at Dana's flat the night before. I arrived around 9 p.m. and joined the small gathering of friends – Dana, Leslie, Barbara, John and Shadow, Suzie, and John Hawken – the keyboard player from Renaissance and The Nashville Teens. They were all happily enjoying an acid trip.

Within five minutes of arriving, I was given a drink of orange juice laced with the drug and I joined them. Instead of the early night I had planned, we sat up all night listening to music, smoking grass and talking. It was a large basement room, wonderfully decked out with Indian sheets, bedspreads, tapestries, and a large collection of brass ornaments, including hookahs and snakes. The floor was strewn with cushions and a couple of mattresses – it was an extremely comfortable room for hanging out.

At 7 a.m., a limo collected Dana and myself and we were driven to Heathrow Airport to catch our flight, TWA 705, leaving at 10:30 a.m. Once out in the daylight and dealing with crowds of people, it became obvious that we were both still tripping wildly. Somehow, we managed to check in our bags and make our way through emigration and aboard the plane. MainMan liked to do things in style, so we travelled first class. The acid still had a firm hold.

I discovered that first class is a great way to travel. After we had found our seats and got comfortable, we were watered and fed with champagne and roast beef. Due to the state we were in, the flight appeared to go by very quickly, and very soon we landed at JFK International Airport and made our way through customs. In those days, I was always anxious about entering America, as I only ever had a visitor's visa and no work permit. It was far cheaper for the record companies not to get involved with formalities such as these. On this occasion, as with Robert Palmer just a few weeks earlier, I had no trouble with immigration and was soon through the barriers with various 1/4-inch stereo master tapes. Dana, however, was taken apart at customs. All her bags were searched, and she was detained for 45 minutes and asked many questions. Nevertheless, within an hour and a half of landing, we were in another limo driving towards Manhattan and the Sherry Netherland Hotel, where David and Angie Bowie had an apartment overlooking Central Park. We had been invited to stay there by Angie, who was an old friend of Dana's.

David was out of town, but we were met by a completely naked Angie. Opening the door, she immediately said, "Good flight? Right then, what's it to be – a cup of tea, a line of coke or a joint?" We had all three. I was relieved to notice that the acid was finally beginning to wear off. Angie, still naked, showed us around the many rooms of the apartment, including four bedrooms, a very large lounge and dining room and a beautiful bathroom. She pointed out the bedrooms we could sleep in and said, "Make yourselves at home while I put something on."

I think this was a strange period for Angie. She told us crazy stories about the changes David was going through due to fame, success, and cocaine abuse, and what it was like living in a hotel in

New York and the sexually charged atmosphere of the times. It appeared they had an open marriage. It was obvious that Angie had been very beautiful. She was now quite thin but with beautiful long legs, a cute bottom, almost no breasts and a wonderfully soft, pale-white skin. She had a pretty face, short, mousy-coloured hair and large dark eyes. I thought she looked lost and sad.

Dana particularly wanted to meet Mick Jagger, who was a good friend of Angie's, and he came over in the early evening. He didn't seem to have changed much from the time I had worked with him on *Beggars Banquet*. He still appeared to have a huge ego and to be a control freak. Tony DeFries also turned up in the evening, and we all ate in the apartment on room service. The five of us sat at a dining table that could seat about 12 people. We ate an assortment of food, including caviar, oysters, steak and pasta, and drank several bottles of wine chosen by Tony. Jagger's chameleon-like qualities came into full use as he switched effortlessly between rock 'n' roll banter with Dana, innuendoes with Angie, and heavy-duty management speak with Tony. I felt that Mick and Tony were at the top echelons of the music business and were way out of my league. By mid-evening, I was feeling tired, a little drunk and stoned, and having been up for about 42 hours, I was not in sync with much of the conversation or the antics going on around me. This was high rolling rock 'n' roll, and I didn't feel up to it, so I decided to go to bed. In the morning, Angie, amused by my behaviour the evening before said, "God, Phill. That's the first time anyone has slept in that room alone. Are you religious or something?" Exactly whom I was supposed to sleep with I never found out.

Dana and I spent the next day at Sterling with George Marino and mastered *Ain't Gonna Play No Second Fiddle*. It all went very smoothly. The evening was spent with Angie at the hotel. She and Dana chattered away for hours. There were rumours at the time that they were having some kind of lesbian affair, but in fact they were simply close, supportive friends. I spent my time watching television and blue movies and listening to music.

The next day, I was back with George at Sterling to master another album. This was an LP I had mixed some weeks before for the band Hustler. By 4:30 p.m., I was back at the hotel planning what to do in the evening. The remainder of the four-day trip disappeared in a haze of drugs, while I listened to Angie and Dana continuously talking about music and sex. Dana's boyfriend, Leslie, turned up briefly from out of the blue, and the third evening just disappeared.

On the last day, I spent most of my time walking around Fifth Avenue and window-shopping. In the evening, the three of us – Dana, Angie and I – planned to go out on the town. I showered and got dressed in my usual shirt and jeans and then sat in the lounge listening to an album by John Lennon. Dana and Angie spent a great deal of time getting ready in Angie's bedroom and would appear from time to time to have a line of coke or a toke on a joint before disappearing again to their inner sanctum. After a few hours, they emerged, giggling, from Angie's bedroom and pirouetted in front of me. They were dressed to kill, in tight dresses (Angie in red, Dana in dark blue), suspenders and high-heels – the lot. I thought they both looked like high-class hookers (probably the idea) and could not believe I was about to spend a night on the town with these two – they looked fantastic. Although I was impressed by their appearance, I felt removed from the situation. I could deal with them looking outrageous in the studio in London, where I just carried on working. But this was different – I was on their turf now.

A black stretch limo picked us up from outside the hotel foyer and we first went to a bar for something to eat and drink. Behind the blacked-out windows and the glass partition between the driver and us, we smoked joints and laid out lines of coke as we were driven 'round New York, sightseeing. After a few small snacks and a couple of margaritas, we moved on. By 8 p.m., we were at the Shubert Theatre to watch the two surviving Andrews Sisters in the musical *Over Here*. John Travolta was also in the cast. It was an excellent show, and already being a fan of the Andrews sisters, I really enjoyed it.

After more coke and joints in our living room on wheels, we went to a cinema for a midnight showing of the movie *Flesh Gordon* – a sex spoof of the famous science fiction character Flash Gordon. More naked flesh.

We walked through Times Square and stopped at the occasional bar for a drink, using the women's lavatories to snort more coke. We must have looked amazing – this young guy in jeans with these two beautiful women – immaculate from head to foot. To walk through the Times Square area amongst the collection of tramps, dealers, pimps, stray businessmen and others who are still around at 2 or 3 a.m. might sound risky, but we were never hassled, and our driver was never far away. Finally, we climbed back into the limo and were returned to the Sherry Netherland Hotel at 4 a.m. It had been a wonderful night.

We flew back to London the next day, on the 31st. As we got comfortable in our first class seats, intending to sleep our way home, Dana said, "You know, Phill, in the madness of party time in the studio every night and the whole MainMan thing, you always seem to me to stay the comparatively calm one through all this swirling mayhem and madness. Even when people freaked out in the studio, or while Bindon was telling stories, you always kept working – under duress. My God, I don't know how you did it – but thanks."

We arrived back on the 1st of September, and after a day to sleep I was at work in The Fallout Shelter, Hammersmith, with Jess Roden, and Dana took off to Spain with Leslie. We later found out that the limousines, first class air travel and New York expenses (including the Jagger/DeFries meal) were all charged to us against royalties. We were both so naïve that we thought everything had been paid for by MainMan. *Ain't Gonna Play No Second Fiddle* was released and sold moderately well, but never enough to make any real money.

Over the next two years, Dana moved from rock into blues and signed to Ted Carroll's Ace Records. Shadow left John and married the Hon. James Lascelles (a relative of the Queen). Sally-Anne McKelvie became a missionary in South Africa (her mother was a Shand Kydd). John Porter moved to Los Angeles and went on to produce The Smiths and Buddy Guy. Dave Skinner moved to Sydney. John Bindon was involved in a stabbing in Putney and fled to Ireland, later dying in London. Sandra married manager Kenny Smith (Eurythmics, Annie Lennox).

I worked with Dana many times over the following 15 years on blues albums and her Indian LPs of the 1980s. She won half a dozen awards during this time, including Top British Female Blues Vocalist. She now shares her time between London, Vienna, Italy and Sai Baba in India. She recently told me, "When I look back at the things I was doing then, I feel weak at the thought of it. So much traveling, studios and things to do – I can't ever remember being bored or having long periods when there was nothing to do. I was over the top in those days."

I did not disagree, but it had been brilliant fun.

Phill and Dana – Studio Two, Island, 1975

Chapter 13. Robert Palmer
18 March 1975

In May 1974, while tracking overdubs for *Sneakin' Sally Through the Alley* at my house in Sussex, Robert Palmer and I devised the "favourite musician game", where we would make lists of our favourite musicians and heroes. One of the bands on our list was Little Feat. Earlier that year, when recording backing tracks in New Orleans for *Sneakin' Sally*..., Robert had played with Lowell George of Little Feat. He'd said how much he would love to work with the entire band. To my surprise, Steve Smith had immediately followed up this idea and arranged for Robert to record with them, for a week, later that summer. "I just got on the phone to Lowell," said Steve. "You know me. I'll phone the record companies, the managers – whatever it takes."

Only one month after finishing *Sneakin' Sally Through the Alley*, we found ourselves in Baltimore working on Robert's second album, *Pressure Drop*, with our heroes Little Feat.

The "favourite musician game" would be played many times during the next three years and resulted in some great combinations of musicians and sessions. Fifteen years later, I would play a variation of this game with Mark Hollis and Tim Friese-Greene of Talk Talk. This version – thankfully it only existed in our imagination – was nicknamed the "band from hell" and included Phil Collins on drums, Paul McCartney on bass, Keith Emerson on keyboards, Roger Daltrey on vocals, with Dave Stewart, Alvin Lee and Mark Knopfler on guitars. Usually, the producer of this horror super group would be Chris Hughes.

On the morning of the 14th of July 1974, I took a cab to Heathrow Airport where I had arranged to meet Steve Smith. As soon as I saw his bloodshot eyes and unshaven face, I knew that he had been up for most of the night. We were about to fly to New York to master *Sneakin' Sally*... with George Marino at Sterling Sound, after which we planned to move on to Baltimore to start Robert's new album. We checked in our baggage at the airline desk and headed for the bar and a few brandies. Steve took a couple of downers to help him sleep, and we boarded the plane. We settled in for the seven-hour flight. I took out my portable cassette tape recorder to record some of the sounds of the aircraft, such as the take off and the general hum when flying at 30,000 feet. These sounds were used later on the track *Off the Bone* from Palmer's album *Some People Can do What They Like* in 1976, and on *Christians who Kill* – one of the SPA recordings of 1993. Under the influence of a mixture of Mandrax and alcohol, Steve, who was smoking a cigarette, almost immediately fell asleep across the centre section of the 747. Some minutes later, he woke up violently. A stewardess was beating out a fire on his jacket lapel – he had set himself alight.

We spent the 14th to 16th of July in a hot and humid New York City, mastering *Sneakin' Sally Through the Alley* and taking in the nightlife of the city. Steve made some telephone calls to confirm our arrangements with Little Feat, who were finishing off their album *Feats Don't Fail Me Now* at the Blue Seas Recording Studios in Hunt Valley near Baltimore, Maryland. They had agreed to stay on for a further five days and record album tracks with Robert. Before this session we took a few days off, flying to Toronto, Canada, on the 17th to see my brother and a few old friends for the evening. This was only the second time I had been back to Toronto since leaving Canada in June 1970, and it was not a long enough visit for more than a polite drink with Terry. We got on fine during this brief encounter, and Steve and Terry chatted away for hours.

After being refused check-in at The Hilton under the names of Smith and Brown, Steve was pissed-off with Toronto and keen to show me America. We travelled to Atlanta on the 18th to stay the night at the wonderful Hyatt Hotel, complete with fully-grown trees in the foyer and glass "pod" lifts on the outside of the building. Steve was on the phone at every opportunity, still finalizing plans. With another whirlwind tour of the city of Atlanta behind us, we flew north to Washington for a day's sightseeing before meeting Robert on the 21st in Baltimore to start work.

Robert and I had a quick conversation about sound and approach. "I don't want to tell the guys what to play," he said. "What the song requires should be shown by the way I sing it. The volume and tempo of my voice and the phrasing – that's what determines the music that goes with it. We're going for a certain atmosphere

here, and if we don't reach it in three takes, then we should leave it and move on to something else. Help me to keep things moving fast."

Blue Seas Recording Studios was on an industrial estate and featured a 20-channel ITI desk with parametric EQ, limited outboard equipment and a 3M 24-track machine. All the band members of Little Feat were there: Lowell George on guitar, Richie Hayward on drums, Kenny Gradney on bass, Bill Payne on keyboards, Sam Clayton on percussion and Paul Barrere on guitar.

I set everyone up in a small, tight semicircle, only using screens between drums and keyboards. They were all very friendly to me and had a sharp wit and humour. While I was positioning a drum mic, Richie said, "So, we're expecting this jive limey. Have you seen him?" Robert walked in at that moment and said, "No, he couldn't make it. I've come instead," and everyone cracked up laughing. There was an immediate, positive feeling, and we spent five days cutting basic tracks, with Robert in the studio singing live vocals and helping the vibe, and the band in this half circle in front of him. I used Neumann U67s and Electro-Voice RE20s for most instruments, with a Sennheiser on Robert's vocal. I had to concentrate on getting to grips with a new desk and monitors, but nevertheless it was a sheer delight. The band loved Robert and the sound we had created, and I got on well with everyone, especially Richie Hayward and Bill Payne. Watching Richie play was fascinating, as he always looked as though he might collapse and stop drumming at any moment. Little Feat had just finished *Feats Don't Fail Me Now* and were happy and relaxed, so it was "eyes down, music and party", all live – a storming band.

I was in awe of these guys and loved their playing and style. Lowell appeared more distant than the others, but that could have been just my anxiety – I was recording Little Feat! There were no outside distractions, and we rehearsed and recorded several songs each day. Besides Robert's collection of song demos, we recorded tracks by Allen Toussaint and Lowell George. This was one of the most enjoyable five days I had ever spent recording.

Steve, Robert and I left on the morning of the 27th of July with six songs recorded and moved back to our base in Washington, D.C., for a couple of days' rest. Steve had a friend named George who was the marketing director of Head, a sportswear manufacturer. George had been promising Steve a trip on his boat for some time. This weekend break seemed an ideal opportunity to take him up on his offer.

The boat was a 40-foot, ocean-going yacht and could berth six. It was cramped below deck but had all the necessary requirements for the sort of sailing we had in mind – fridge, cooker, loo, and sound system. After loading onboard supplies of grass, beer, food and Slivovice (plum brandy), we headed out to sea. We sailed for five or six hours and then anchored out of sight of the mainland about a mile from a bay, made some food, and after a quiet evening chatting and listening to James Brown, we slept.

The next day was already hot early in the morning, so we decided to stay where we were and head back in the evening when it was cool. We got stoned, sunbathed, swam, drank beer and listened to our rough mixes, all feeling really pleased with the results. George was the perfect host – probably in his early 40s, with sun-bleached, blonde hair, tanned skin, blue eyes and an infectious smile. He was affable and courteous and wanted us to enjoy the sailing experience, even when anchored. He gave the impression of a successful businessman who was laidback and happy with his life.

While we were having lunch, there was no other boat in the vicinity except for a small speedboat circling about 300 yards away. Onboard were three women who were intermittently taking turns to try to water ski. We waved and cheered every time they hit the water. After we had watched them for a while, Robert signalled that he would like to have a go at water skiing too and beckoned them to come closer. They were all in their early 20s and bronzed, wearing bikinis and baseball hats. Two had long, brown hair and could have been sisters; the third was shorthaired and blonde. We talked for a while, boat to boat, and they asked a million questions – "Are you musicians?", "What are two English guys doing out here?", "Have you got any grass?" Robert asked to have a go and was duly picked up and decked out with the necessary gear – this amounted to just a pair of skis.

Robert appeared to be a confident swimmer, and unlike me would dive over the edge of the boat at any opportunity. We watched at a hundred yards distance as he tried a few times to ski with little success, although sometimes he stayed upright for a minute or so. Unfortunately, as he revealed later, he also received several unpleasant rope burns across his back and chest. Within 25 minutes he was tired, in pain and seemed to be in some difficulty. He was waving his arms and calling out, although we could not hear what he was saying. George dived in carrying a lifebuoy support ring, and one of the women in the speedboat also swam to him. They supported him on either side and he was guided back to our boat. He was lucky – it was a close call and he had nearly drowned. While he got warm, rested and spat out salt water, the woman who helped save him invited herself and her friends to dinner and then swam back to the dinghy to tell the others. Robert was obviously shaken by the experience and mumbled, "Jesus, that was close." Two hours later, the women joined us on the yacht for pasta, wine, and of course, James Brown on the stereo.

We partied into the evening, and then with music blaring headed back to port in the dark, late at night with everyone suffering from an excess of Slivovice, wine and beer. We tied the women's dinghy to the stern of the yacht and secured their oars and outboard motor on our foredeck. We were still out in the open sea and there was no moon, so apart from the shore lights in the distance we could see nothing but pitch black. Everyone was completely wasted, tripping over ropes and falling about on deck. It was probably very dangerous. I had almost forgotten that we were on a boat and had completely forgotten about George who – in the same state as the rest of us – was trying to steer us all home.

Suddenly, with absolutely no warning, we lurched forward and stopped. "Strange," I thought, "I did not know boats could stop so quickly." We had run aground on a sandbank. I suddenly realized that this time we were all in danger of drowning, and I sobered up surprisingly quickly. George moved the women to the stern of the boat while Steve, Robert and I took the oars and a long pole from the bow and tried to push the boat backwards off the sand. This proved to be difficult because the yacht had stuck amidships at a part of the hull out of reach of our poles. However, by moving everyone aft, we eventually coaxed it off the sand. Fortunately, there was no damage to the yacht, and we finally reached land. We moored at the dock, and after saying goodnight to the women we went to our bunks and slept, exhausted.

On the 29th, Robert went off on tour with Little Feat for six days down the East Coast of America, having been asked by Lowell to join them after such a successful time in the studio. Although he did not say much, Robert must have been delighted to be performing with one of his all-time favourite bands and left for the tour with a huge grin on his face. Back at our hotel, while I watched and recorded the Watergate trials from the television, Steve made phone calls to set up the next phase of recording. This was to be overdubs at the celebrated Muscle Shoals Sound Studio, with its rhythm section. As this could not happen until the 5th of August and as Robert was still away on tour, Steve and I decided to drive there and see some more of the country.

We hired a big Pontiac and headed south. I drove, as Steve had no licence. We travelled through the Blue Ridge Mountains of Virginia, North and South Carolina, Georgia, Alabama and Tennessee, staying in motels, drinking in bars, enjoying wonderful Southern cooking, and because of Steve's gregarious nature, we met a large assortment of musicians, singers, dealers and amusing characters on the way. These included Barbara Cusack, who roller skated around her house, Nashville clothing store owners Danny and Marcia, fire-eating Hilga, and Pete the "rock man". Steve and I got on very well. We had developed a great deal of respect for each other, and over the years he became like a brother to me.

As we drove through amazing scenery, we told each other our life stories and talked of current and future projects. Steve had, at the age of 26, achieved a great deal. He had been studio engineer at Muscle Shoals in the late 1960s, and then was singer, guitarist and keyboard player for the Island Records' band, Smith Perkins Smith. Later, he had been house producer for Island Records in both the UK and the USA, producing albums for Palmer, Jim Capaldi and Bob Marley, amongst others.

We spent some time in Nashville with J.C., an old girlfriend of Steve's, and visited the Grand Ole Opry and the well-known Exit/In club, where we heard a set by Chick Corea. It all went by very quickly, and soon it was time to pick up Robert from the airport, drive to Alabama and start work at Muscle Shoals.

Muscle Shoals Sound Studio was a shack on the edge of the Jackson Highway, number 3614, a few miles out of town. It was permanently set up for the Muscle Shoals rhythm section. The band consisted of Roger Hawkins on drums, David Hood on bass, Barry Beckett on keyboards and Jimmy Johnson on guitar. The microphones were fixed permanently in place, so I just used whatever mics were plugged in and adapted. Part of the reason for coming to this studio was to obtain the "Muscle Shoals' sound", so I felt it would be frivolous of me to start changing things. Besides, we were only here for two days and needed to work fast.

The first day was spent with the full band. The intention was to record new alternate versions of songs we had already recorded with Little Feat, and we ran through these plus the ballad *Give Me an Inch*. Although we kept a master take on three of the songs, we did not improve on our earlier Little Feat versions, and after 14 hours called it a day. This was a typical way of working for Robert and Steve in the mid-1970s, in that although a satisfactory master version of a song had been recorded, they would still try for an alternative.

The fact that we failed to improve on our Little Feat version was not a problem and did not dampen events. The next day, the 6th of August, we changed tack and overdubbed keyboards with Barry Beckett and added the Muscle Shoals Horns to *Here with You Tonight*. In the evening, we tried out some new vocal and harmony ideas and then packed up our tapes and drove to the Huntsville Airport. Unfortunately, we were well behind schedule, so we missed our flight to Washington and had to spend the night sleeping at the airport on plastic chairs. This was a small-town airport, devoid of bars, convenience foods or any form of distraction or entertainment. As usual, we took it in our stride and settled down to an uncomfortable night. The next day, after just a few hours' sleep, we flew to New York via Atlanta.

On the 10th of August, we were all on a plane back to England, with over half an album recorded and a holiday adventure behind us. Having dropped off the tapes at Basing Street, we were suddenly met by reality – I was booked to record an album with the rock band Hustler starting in three days' time. I had time to absorb this information as I was driven home to Sussex in a taxi, which was just as well, as a further surprise lay in wait. It was late afternoon by the time I arrived home. After a real cup of tea, I unpacked and caught up on the local news. "By the way," said Sally after a while, "I'm pregnant – due in March."

As there was no rush to finish Robert's second LP and we had no more "favourite band" sessions arranged, we took a break from this project and had to wait several months before we could continue with round two. Again, I would have to obtain permission from Penny Hanson and Muff Winwood (both of whom worked for Chris Blackwell and Island) to take time off and be away from house engineering at Basing Street. I was not paid when I was not working at Basing Street, so I could see no real problem, plus I always brought these freelance projects back to Studio Two to mix. Although I had to go through this procedure, I was always given permission, and saw it as simply part of the hierarchy and politics of Basing Street Studios – and of Muff Winwood in particular. Hanson and Winwood eventually cleared it, and I arranged payment direct with Island. I would be paid £1,000 for the whole album – a reasonable sum for the time – plus a 1/2 percent royalty (given to me by Palmer "for input") – an unexpected but very welcome bonus.

In the meantime, I settled back into the studio and worked on sessions for Joan Armatrading, Stomu Yamashta and Dana Gillespie. (see chapters 12 and 15)

On the 18th of March 1975, our daughter Rebecca Jane Brown was born in Crowborough Hospital. Just six weeks later, on the 7th of May, Steve Smith and I flew to New York and spent a couple of hours mastering a Paul Kossoff single, *All the Girls Are Crazy*, with George Marino at Sterling Sound. We then met Robert Palmer to begin the second phase of his album. While Steve telephoned L.A. to make final arrangements, Robert and I hung out in the hotel room playing music and working on the demos. We had fallen into a way of working since *Sneakin' Sally...*, whereby Robert would play me various records and point out what he liked about them – the hi-hat on this track, maybe the bass from that. Over a period of a couple of days, I would get a feel and background for the sounds he wanted on his songs. Once we were working, he would very rarely mention or refer to these records again.

We moved on to L.A. on the 9th, and booked into the Sunset Marquis Hotel on Sunset Boulevard. I spent a couple of days relaxing by the pool, although I did take some time out to do a mix for Del Shannon at Kendun Recorders. This was one of a number of studios with acoustic design by the Eastlake Audio company (their studios on the West Coast were referred to as Westlake). The walls of the control room were lined with volcanic rock. I was never a big fan of this type of studio, as to me the rooms always felt lifeless. Robert got out his little black book of addresses and disappeared. As usual, Steve spent most of his time on the phone.

Robert had said some months earlier that he felt that the new songs we were about to record were very different to the previous work and required a whole new band. "Something smoother but very tight." He had wanted a Barry White/Gene Page approach (lush string arrangements and tight bass and drums), and thanks to Steve, our new band was Ed Greene on drums, James Jamerson on bass, Paul Barrere on guitar, Jean Rousseau and Gordon Dewitte on keyboards, with arranger Gene Page himself doing the string arrangements.

"You know what we're trying to do on this trip," said Steve on the eve of recording. "It's to try and put together the right combination of musicians and then let Robert drive the outcome. You know – this calibre and collection of musicians playing live in a room. There's big egos between them and it makes their playing better."

We started on the 12th of May at Nashville West. The studio had a small live recording room and a very basic, tatty-looking control room. There were wires spewing chaotically from the desk and some of the EQ modules crackled intermittently. However, the sound was excellent in both the recording room and the control room, and after playing our rough mixes back from the Blue Seas recordings we started work.

The sessions were straighter than the ones we had done with Little Feat, with a more session musician feel – very slick and professional. As usual, Robert was in the main room with the musicians, singing live vocals and controlling events. With a band of this quality, recording was easy and a great deal of fun. Once the sound and levels of instruments were sorted out, they changed very little throughout the day. It was relaxed, there was complete mutual respect within the studio, and everyone felt free to contribute musical parts and ideas.

On one take of *Work to Make it Work*, James Jamerson suddenly took off on an excellent bass solo and on reaching the end of the track, put his hands up to the sky, and said, "That's for you Lord." We played back the take to check for mistakes and kept it as our master. James was in good form, having recently given up alcohol and other "demon food". Robert and I felt honoured to be there working with him. We left on the evening of the 16th with five tracks mastered and went to a party held in Robert's honour by Island Records.

This party was held in a house owned by Jeffrey Dengrove, on Sunswept Drive in Studio City. Apart from the Island staff, there were musicians, producers and engineers and a collection of liggers and loonies. After an hour or two of heavy techno-chatter, I slid out of the main room and settled on the floor in one of the bedrooms, hoping for a quiet smoke. Some spaced, hippie-looking lady in her mid-twenties sat down on the bed and started reciting her own poetry. "My God," I was thinking after just a few minutes, "is it really a choice between dealing with all the business talk out there or having to put up with this space cadet's poetry?"

I made some excuse and left the room, bumping into Jeffrey on my way out. "Hey Phill, I was looking for you. You may find this interesting. Come in here." I followed him into another bedroom. Jeffrey went to a small trap door in the centre of the room and opened it. "Down you go," he ordered. I climbed down the five or six steps and found myself in a wonderful 24-track recording studio that had been built in the basement of the house. It was compact, but still big enough to have a medium-sized control room and separate live area for recording. The window partition was built as an aquarium, with fish swimming around between the panes of glass. The lighting was soft and subdued – a calm environment. "Jeffrey, this is great," I said. "We could have recorded Robert's album here. Can we play something and check out the monitors?"

We spent the next hour listening to rough mixes of Robert's album and various other tapes of Jeffrey's in his studio – Sunswept Sound. One by one, as people heard the music and tracked it down, the room began to fill up, spoiling the moment. I made my excuses and left, heading back to room 101 at the Sunset Marquis.

On this trip, we were working in short bursts, recording different songs with different bands, and we found it easier to book studios at the last minute. This caused problems with studio availability, so we had to keep moving around. We spent the weekend of the 17th and 18th at The Village Recorder, working on vocals and keyboards and tidying up the tracks. We then spent some time recording a clavinet overdub performed by Jean Rousseau, who also added some clavinet parts to the Trapeze album that Steve and I had been working on in England. Steve had brought the multitrack tape with him with this in mind.

It was time for another break. I drove Robert out to the desert for an afternoon, and we walked and chatted while searching for lizards in the scrub. We talked about how well the album was going and how enjoyable it had been – a change from the old Vinegar Joe days. From the little Robert said on the matter, I had a picture of group indecision ("Too many cooks") and fallouts with his co-singer Elkie Brooks, who had been married to Pete Gage (another Vinegar Joe member). I had met Elkie a few months before, during a difficult time recording an album with Joan Armatrading. On that occasion, and later at a charity gig at the Hard Rock Cafe, Elkie had appeared loud and aggressive, and I could see how Robert may have had problems with her.

On the 20th, we moved over to Whitney Recording Studios and the first of two string sessions with Gene Page – all very efficient and smooth. The day after – the 21st of May – we flew to San Francisco and booked into the Hyatt Regency Hotel.

This was an extremely bad flight. It reminded me of dubious Notting Hill Gate mini cab journeys across London and helped to put me off the idea of internal flying in America. The take-off was astoundingly bad, and the plane lurched sideways to the left when just a few feet off the ground. The aircrew were offhand, the food inedible and the overhead storage sections rattled with a scary consistency. The flight only lasted an hour, and it was the quietest that Steve, Robert and myself had been for days. "This is worse than your 2CV," quipped Steve, but his complexion was dead white. We all believed it was the pilot's first passenger flight. I thought it could be our last. We did finally walk away from the aeroplane, relieved and happy after it had landed heavily and braked violently to a halt. We caught a cab to the hotel and went straight to the bar.

We continued to enjoy a rather luxurious lifestyle, and not for the first time I was thankful that Island had given Steve a gold credit card. We did a quick tourist trip around the city and went out to the Golden Gate Bridge. The city was beautiful, and with its steeply built streets and cable cars, appeared just as I remembered it from seeing the film *Bullitt*. Unfortunately, the trip was only fleeting, and by the 23rd of May we were back in Los Angeles, ready to record our second string session with Gene Page at Whitney Recording Studios. This session ran like clockwork, and eight hours later we had finished recording, packed up our tapes and were listening to the rough mixes in the car as we drove back to the Sunset Marquis Hotel, detouring through the Hollywood Hills.

Parts of Los Angeles can be interesting and beautiful, but with the combination of clouds of nicotine-coloured smog, massive, sprawling suburbs, congested downtown business centres, more loonies per square mile than anywhere I have ever been, rumours of police brutality and the process of having to drive everywhere, I can't imagine anyone choosing to live there. San Francisco, yes – L.A., definitely not. I was ready to leave.

We spent a few hours back at Whitney Recording Studios the next day, just cleaning up some tracks, making final checks and up-to-date rough mixes.

Steve and I flew home to London on the 25th of May. We were booked to continue working on the album for Trapeze on the 26th, so I planned to stay at Steve's flat for the night. There was one small problem – Steve had lost the band's multitrack tape during the flight.

Being naturally cautious, I had carried all six of Robert Palmer's 2-inch tape masters, with some difficulty, in the cabin during our flight home. I had lived with Robert's tapes for weeks, carrying them to hotels and studios, in and out of taxis and cars, around the southern states, aboard planes and through customs, and I wasn't going to let them out of my sight at this late stage. Steve, however, had checked in his Trapeze tapes with the rest of his luggage, and it had supposedly been put in the hold.

We waited by the baggage carousel until every last bag, suitcase and folded pushchair had been removed. The conveyor belt stopped. Soon, we were the only passengers still waiting by the carousel, but there was no sign of the blue and white plastic Ampex container, so carefully labelled by Steve the night before. The necessary forms for lost baggage were all filled in and an hour later we left.

The next day, still buzzing from our time in Los Angeles, Steve and I explained to Mel Galley and the band what had happened, and after they recovered from the shock, we started work on overdubs for the songs we did have. I thought we had lost the tape for good, but Steve was his usual laid back, optimistic self and carried on working, showing only little concern. Three days later, our tape arrived by Securicor – it had been flown to Paris. Big smiles all round. We worked straight through until the 20th of June and did the overdubs and mixing all in one go. I continued to stay at Steve's flat on Southwick Street.

I had not been home or seen Sally and my daughter Becca for seven weeks. Becca was now three months old. Sally accepted this very well at the time, although it transpired later, she was suffering from postnatal depression. As usual, I felt I had little choice.

Overdubs for Robert began six weeks later on the 18th of August, with the Island Mobile at Chris Blackwell's house in Theale. This was a rebuilt, 300-year-old farmhouse surrounded by water from a disused, flooded gravel pit. I made use of this water two years later for John Martyn's album, *One World*.

Completing Robert's album became a family affair, with Sally, our daughter Becca – now 5 months old – Robert's wife Sue, and Ray Doyle and Barry Sage, good friends and work colleagues, there to help with the mobile. We spent the first two days checking out our tapes and updating the list of final overdubs that Robert and I had begun at Basing Street the previous month. We then recorded Robert's multitrack vocals for *Work to Make It Work* and a repair to the vocal on *Here with You Tonight*. The majority of these vocals were recorded outdoors against the stable block wall. We then set up mics in the barn and recorded percussion, guitar and harmonica.

From time to time, a guest musician would come out from London for the day, Martin Frye on tuba, Mongezi Feza on flageolet and sax, David Snell on harp, Mel Collins and Ray Allen on saxophones, and Vicki Brown (see chapter 10) on vocals. We were very productive and worked 13 hours a day, with plenty of time out to listen to other artists' projects and to take our evening meals together. Chris Blackwell occasionally called in to the mobile to see how things were going and to offer encouragement, but these visits were rare due to his heavy workload in London.

When we were out of the mobile, James Brown was still played a lot of the time and would always blast from Sue and Robert's self-contained flat first thing in the morning. Within 10 days, we had recorded and finished our overdubs, and after having taken three days off we moved into Studio Two at Basing Street on the 1st of September to mix. Although the American studios had been excellent, and an exciting new experience, it was great to be back at the wonderful Helios desk with the Tannoy monitors that I knew so well.

Working at a leisurely pace, we mixed two tracks per day for five days. Due to the care we had taken selecting the right musicians and capturing the best performances, each track sounded great as soon as I brought up the faders, and mixing was a thrill. Steve helped me by taking care of some of the manual mixing cues, while I looked after riding the vocals, cuts and fade outs. I recall my left hand shaking furiously at the very end of the fade to the master mix of *Fine Time* due to a combination of adrenaline, nerves and cocaine. Steve and Robert applauded enthusiastically. "Yes, we got it!" yelled Steve. We worked hard but had a great deal of fun. The whole project had been a treat – working with our musical heroes, driving through the stunning southern American states' countryside, mobile recording and even the running aground and near drowning.

Pressure Drop was released in October 1975. As with the first album, *Sneakin' Sally...*, the reviews in the British press were mixed.

One said, "Sounds like this man means business," while another read, "Every other week you read about yet another British musician who's gone to America to record a 'funky' album, mistakenly assuming that if you travel to New Orleans you can automatically attain that very special groove. Creating an atmosphere, however, has more to do with emotion and feel, than local producers, musicians and studios."

That's exactly what we thought we had captured – emotion and feel – while using some of the best players around. But even music critics are entitled to opinions, I suppose.

Phill and Robert at sea, 1975, *Pressure Drop*

Robert Overdubs at Chris Blackwell's House, *Pressure Drop*

Chapter 14. Pink Floyd 15 November 1974

This was to be my first day off for months, the beginning of a four-day break at home in Sussex. I had worked almost solidly since the 26th of June, 14 hours a day and seven days a week, on a number of projects with Robert Palmer, the band Hustler's debut album, Dana Gillespie, Jess Roden, Amazing Blondel, Joan Armatrading and Clancy. This was all in addition to the six albums I had already completed between January and June of that year. Most of the time, I was away from my home in Sussex. Rather than taking the long drive home (and back the next day) I spent many nights sleeping in the spare rooms of either Steve Smith or Dana Gillespie's places when working in London.

It was 10:15 a.m. and I was sleeping in. The phone rang and I immediately recognized the commanding voice of studio booker Penny Hanson, "You're recording Pink Floyd at Wembley Arena tonight. Come up immediately. It's for BBC Radio 1. You'll be recording tonight and tomorrow night."

I was not at all happy about this and said so. I had other plans – mainly to sleep in and then to go out for a meal with Sally. Penny ignored my objections, and added, "Brian Humphries had planned to do it, but there have been problems with the PA. Brian thinks he should now do the PA mix and you can record in the mobile. Brian has set it all up. He did that last night, so all you have to do is watch the levels."

I tried to explain that it wasn't quite as easy as that, and that Pink Floyd live set ups were always involved, and it was my day off, but Penny would not budge. It was always difficult to get Penny to change her mind, or to understand a situation from an engineer's viewpoint.

Rhett Davies, Phil Ault, Tony Platt and I were always having heated discussions with Penny over which particular sessions we should work on and what type of music and sessions we were best suited for. Most important of all, it seemed difficult to convince Penny that we took our work very seriously. We felt the office staff did not know what really went on in a recording session. This was in stark contrast to the early days at Basing Street Studios when sound engineer Frank Owen had been studio manager and Sally Wightman was the studio booker. They had welcomed the opinions of the engineers, assistants and maintenance personnel and we had had easy, open discussions.

Had I known beforehand I was to record Pink Floyd I would have spent the previous day at Wembley setting up and getting a feel for the scale of things – choosing microphones, setting up the desk and devising some kind of contingency backup for any breakdown of machines. There was more to it than just to "watch the levels".

"If it's that easy," I said, "why don't you give it to someone else?"

"It's you Brian wants," she replied. "There will be a cab waiting for you."

I got up, got dressed and drove my Citroën 2CV the two hours to Basing Street, angry as hell, arriving around 1 p.m. There was enough time to take the cab to Wembley, to be there for the soundcheck and to acclimatize myself with this huge project and the 30 inputs (the maximum the desk could handle at this time). However, there was one thing I had to do first.

I went down to the kitchen, filled a bucket with cold water and carried it into Penny's office. She was sitting at her desk, as usual looking very smart in a cream skirt and white blouse with a silk scarf round her neck. Her hair was perfect. She glanced in my direction, and it was clear from her manner that she either hadn't realized she had given me a problem, or she had forgotten all about it. Annie, her assistant, was also there and both were getting ready to go out for lunch.

I made a direct hit from head to toe, taking Penny completely by surprise. She sat there, drenched, with a stunned look on her face. "I hope this inconveniences you, the way you have just inconvenienced me," I said, and left in my cab for Wembley.

The concert went well, and I had no major problems with the equipment. From the moment the solitary bass drum and sound effects started until 10 minutes later when the band started playing, I felt relaxed and comfortable. All mics were working, and levels were still correct from those of the soundcheck. We overlapped our recording of multitrack tapes every 25 minutes and basically "watched the levels". I sat back, enjoyed a great concert, made a live rough mix of the proceedings and ended the night feeling pleased that I had been there.

On the 19th of November, I was back at Basing Street working on some demos with Robert Palmer when studio manager Muff Winwood called me into his office and threatened to sack me. True to form, he did not see the funny side of what I had done and had no idea of the injustice I had felt from Penny's actions. To make matters worse, I had to apologise to Penny.

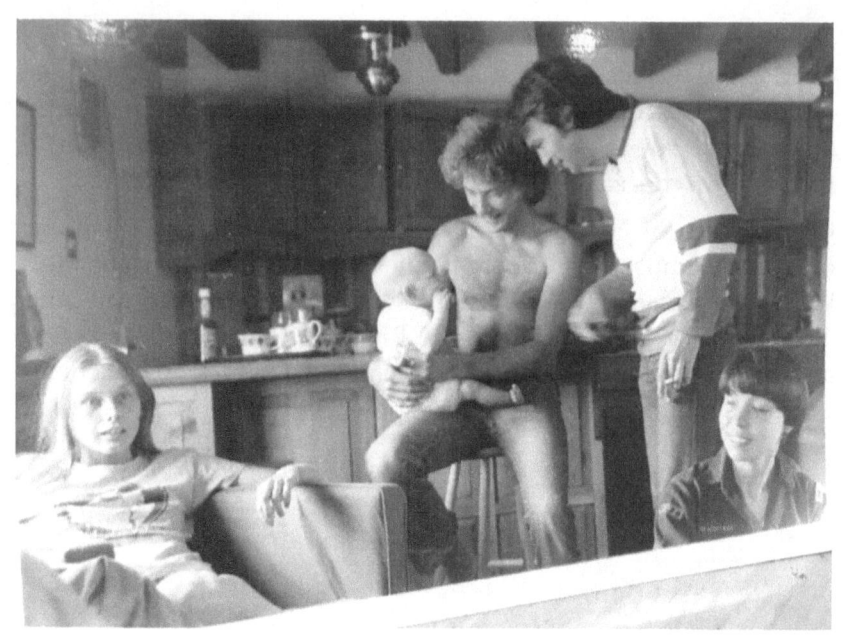

Sally, Rebecca, Steve, Sue, 1975, *Pressure Drop*

New Helios Desk, Island, Studio Two, 1976

Chapter 15. Stomu Yamashta and Rock Follies
16 February 1976

Months of continuous work that began in November 1975 now peaked during February 1976, when I found myself working on two albums at once. During the day, from 11 a.m. to 7 p.m., I was mixing *Rock Follies*, while at night – from 8 p.m. to 5 a.m.– I was recording Stomu Yamashta and his *Go* project.

Rock Follies was a television show comedy/musical/drama (and corresponding soundtrack album) based on the music business, co-written and produced by Andy Mackay (Roxy Music) and Howard Schuman. I had started working on it in late January, after back-to-back sessions with Amazing Blondel and Jim Capaldi. The *Rock Follies* recording sessions were long and manic, as there was a total of only 15 days available to record and mix all the music – not only for the television show, but for the album as well.

There were about 15 people on the sessions, and most were from the television company – producers, directors, writers and those in charge of the script. We worked so fast that the whole project was plagued by musical and technical mistakes. However, the sessions were made easier by the humour of Ray Russell, who was the guitarist and arranger. Andy's laidback attitude also helped, as did the game of matching up the television story with real-life studio events. Of the three actresses portraying the fictional group, The Little Ladies, Charlotte Cornwall appeared nervous and neurotic and took a daily Valium to help her deal with the stress, while Rula Lenska seemed to be out of her depth, very detached and had difficulty singing in tune. Julie Covington, unlike her television character, was totally professional, and I thought she was the only real singer. The sessions were constantly interrupted by emotional outbursts, musical mistakes and demands to be taken seriously. There were many occasions when Andy, Ray and I would hide behind the desk, laughing hysterically, trying not to be seen by the singers and musicians.

On the 4th of February, we finished recording and moved into Studio Two to mix. The crowd of people was now reduced to six. Up to this point, I had been working an average of 14 hours a day with no real breaks, trying to finish each day's workload before driving home to Sussex at night. However, things were about to get even worse.

Stomu's album was very different in content and approach and included a band of name musicians. It was labelled a "rock/classical concept album" but turned out much better than this description might suggest. I had worked with Stomu the year before on the album *Raindog*. This had been recorded and mixed in Studio One in just two weeks, during which I had struck up a good relationship with Stomu. That was the first time I had any working experience with a Japanese artist. He seemed very straight and honest in his dealings with people. Eighteen years later, while working with Fusanosuke Kondo on an album in London and touring in Japan, I discovered that such straightforwardness and honesty is perfectly normal behaviour in Japan.

Stomu had built up a reputation in both the classical and jazz fields as being a genuinely experimental percussionist. With justification, he was described in his own publicity material as "an artist who really does succeed in breaking down barriers." Stomu was now in his late 20s, with long, straight, black hair, thin face and sinewy body. He appeared very centred, and through patience, stamina and determination usually achieved what he set out to do. He could be very single-minded in his working approach, and at times gave off a feeling of intransigence. He had released two previous "rock" albums on Island Records, *The Man from the East* in 1972 and the aforementioned *Raindog* in 1975, in which many western musicians had been involved, including Morris Pert, Peter Robinson, Gary Boyle and Maxine Nightingale. Both albums had received excellent reviews. His music had been used in the films *The Devils* and *The Man Who Fell to Earth*, and he had worked with the British Royal Ballet on the more classical-orientated *Shukumei*. His beautiful wife Hisako, a leading classical violinist and very successful in her own right, was also a guest on these albums.

On *Raindog*, Stomu had welcomed my comments and suggestions, and I had brought in my old friend Murray Head to help write lyrics and perform the lead vocals. Stomu had been impressed. The sessions had gone smoothly, and partly because of this he was back at Basing Street wanting me to record with him again.

To fit in with the schedule of some of Stomu's musicians and allow enough time to record all the backing tracks with this particular band, the album had to start on the 6th of February and be finished by the 27th. Meanwhile, Andy was due to finish the *Rock Follies* project on the 11th, and as we had built up a good friendship over the previous three years, I did not want to let him down by pulling out. Penny appeared unconcerned about my feelings for the artists or their preferences, and said to me, "Decide which one you want to do. I can always get Brian [Humphries] to do Stomu." I decided that rather than lose either album, I would work on both sessions at once during the five days that they clashed. At this time, I did not realise how vast the scale of Stomu's project was.

Stomu's band consisted of Steve Winwood on keyboards, Michael Shrieve on drums, Klaus Schulze on synthesisers, Al DiMeola on guitar, Rosko Gee on bass, Pat Thrall and Junior Marvin on guitars, Brother James and Stomu on percussion, and Paul Buckmaster with string and brass arrangements. Among the instruments that Klaus Schulze was using was an original Moog synthesizer. Subsequent models were made more compact, but at that time, the Moog was an enormous device consisting of four or five separate units, bristling with oscillators and dials. Each sound had to be individually patched before being played, and a number of patchbays were provided for this purpose.

I set up Klaus in the 8-by-6 vocal booth where the Moog occupied the entire space. The rest of the musicians were set up in a large circle in Studio One. I felt that this was the best way to achieve optimum visual contact between the musicians while allowing a certain amount of acoustic separation, plus I liked the idea of recording them with an orchestral or classical approach. This was a topic that had come up in conversation with Paul Buckmaster, Stomu and myself on their arrival, when they had briefed me as to what they were trying to do.

"We want to get a very sophisticated, rich sound," said Paul, "controlled, but at the same time fluid."

"Yes, and please I want to work with everyone live," added Stomu. "We should treat it just like orchestra. Although we have the songs arranged, with this quality of musicians I expect one-off performances during takes. We need plenty of freedom, and I must have much space for percussion."

"Yeah, and plenty of control," Paul reminded me.

During this 15-minute discussion, I had formulated a possible plan and placed percussion in front of the control room window, with (anti-clockwise) booths for drums, bass, guitars, additional percussion, piano and organ. Assisted by Robert Ash, I plugged up microphones while six Japanese guys unloaded cameras, slide and movie projectors and various stands and lights. It was planned that while we were working, NASA films of the 1969 moon landing would be shown on the full-sized projection screen on the far wall and slides would be projected onto the ceiling. Candles were used for illumination and to help the vibe. The plan was to try to make it feel like real time, and it would take at least four nights to reach the moon, most of the time just drifting through space.

Down the centre of the studio was a collection of musical sculptures from Instruments Sonores des Freres Baschet in France, a phenomenon Stomu had tracked down during his months of touring. These instruments consisted of 16-foot springs that could be made to vibrate when struck and glass tubes of varying length that, when stroked, gave off sounds similar to using a moistened finger on the rim of a wine glass. All the sculptures could be played or gave off a sound. Having all the percussion instruments (in the form of a wide "H") running down the centre of the studio allowed Stomu a clear passage and easy access to all these devices. He was flamboyant in his approach to playing, and great to watch as he ran about wildly with sticks and beaters, hitting various pieces of percussion.

The theme of *Go* was change and polarity, fantasy and reality, death and rebirth.

There were three main producers – Dennis McKay, Stomu Yamashta and Paul Buckmaster, with additional help from Steve Winwood and Michael Shrieve. This presented some problems with individual sounds, particularly the drums and the overall monitor mix, as there were (including myself) six different opinions on offer. Because they had the loudest voices, Paul and Michael usually won.

We recorded with very few acoustic screens, and in employing a classical approach, there was a large amount of leakage. I used Neumann U87 mics on the drums and piano, with AKG D12s on all the bass and guitar amps and Hammond. There was an assortment of U87s, Neumann KM 84s and AKG D 224s on the percussion. In all, I used 22 mics and eight DI boxes on the collection of instruments. All 32 inputs on the Helios desk were being used, and I recorded onto a 3M 24-track machine, including two ambient room microphones onto tracks 23 and 24. With the large number of microphones, leads and headphones used, and the outboard equipment of compressors and limiters, we were technically pushed to the limit. Unusually, the studio was on a 24-hour lockout due to the large number of instruments, film gear and all the plugging and desk settings involved. The studio would stay permanently set up like this until the end of the album.

When Stomu's album started on the 6th of February, I moved into Chris Blackwell's old flat in the roof of the church above Studio One. He had lived here when he was in London, during 1970 to '74, but it was now empty most of the time. A door at the top of the rear spiral stairway led straight into the flat. There was a large main living room with a 15-foot ceiling and two round windows set high on the walls. The room contained a leather couch and two chairs, a low glass table and a collection of modern lamps and spotlights. Along the rear wall was an open-plan kitchen, and a door to the right gave access to a mosaic-tiled bathroom with a sunken bath. In the middle of the main room, there was a spiral staircase leading up to a gallery area and a large double bed. This whole area was fashioned in a similar way to the studios, with the same brown carpet on the walls, floor and ceiling. From the bed it was possible to glimpse the rooftops opposite by looking out of either of the two high windows; otherwise, it was generally a dark room. It was well equipped with a television, a stereo system and air conditioning.

I had spoken to Penny about the possibility of using the flat for a week or two due to the heavy schedule, and she had arranged it with Chris. Originally, I had felt excited and privileged to be staying in CB's flat during the breaks between sessions. However, as time progressed, and I failed to leave the building for even a short walk, I began to wonder if it had been such a great idea.

My routine was:

11 a.m. – *Rock Follies* in Studio Two, cup of tea and a jam donut. Start mixing with Andy Mackay, Ray Russell and Howard Schuman. Cocaine at hourly intervals throughout the day, and with luck we would get three songs mixed. Finish around 7 p.m., back to the flat for a shower and a light meal or just to sit quietly.

8 p.m. – Stomu in Studio One, line of cocaine with Robert Ash, fire up the machines and get ready. A great deal of a spliff to keep calm and help the effects of too much cocaine. Finish anytime between 5 and 8 a.m., up to the flat and a couple of Valium to help me sleep. Three to five hours later, the whole cycle repeated.

I did not leave the building for eight days. Important things like cigarettes, food and drugs were all either supplied or obtainable from within the studio. This way of life was obviously not good for the health of my body or mind, and slowly it began to take its toll. Stomu sessions were intense and became more difficult as the days progressed. This was mainly due to the combination of technical requirements, the number of producers and musicians, the use of large amounts of cocaine by almost all involved and the clash of various musical egos.

While Steve, Al and Brother James were quiet and relaxed and just went with the flow, Michael, Paul and Stomu displayed determined and temperamental personalities. From the moment the session started, I would be required to work at maximum pace, both physically and mentally, while I looked after 32 microphone and line inputs, attended to the requirements of six musicians and five producers, and operated the desk and tape machines. Robert Ash was an excellent asset on these sessions and followed my every move, while keeping an attentive eye on the tape machines and making sure no microphones were accidentally moved by a musician. By contrast, mixing in Studio Two for *Rock Follies* was much easier to handle and the daytime sessions became a break from the intense stress of the nights in Studio One. Robert had opted to join me on my sessions in Studio Two and now logged the various takes of *Rock Follies* mixes during the day.

On Stomu's project, Robert and I were pushing the equipment and our concentration to the limit. Although the finished album was planned to sound as a more or less continuous piece, it would be made up of 14 different sections or songs. The usual procedure was to choose one and play it repeatedly until we had a master. The music was spacious, atmospheric and gentle. The delicate fade in of instruments over a backdrop of Moog synthesizer would permeate Studio One for hour after hour as we floated through our projected space films.

One night, we were working on the first six-minute section of side one (*Solitude, Nature,* and *Air Over*). We had recorded a couple of run-throughs and were now on take three. It started off with wind, intergalactic sounds and a haunting, discordant percussion sound from Stomu before building with piano, bass and drums. This take unfortunately broke down before the last chorus section. There was easily enough tape left for one more version of this six-minute piece, and I left the machine in record and said, "Okay, we're still rolling. Take four." The Moog drifted in with the wind and we were off again. I looked down into the studio and nine guys were playing, heads bowed. I looked up to the far wall and saw the Apollo lunar module disconnecting from the command module in preparation for the moon landing. The version of the piece they were playing had a fluid, ethereal quality from beginning to end.

As it reached what should have been the end, Klaus unexpectedly went into the next track, *Crossing the Line*. This was a beautiful track and became my favourite song of the album, but right now we had a problem. Robert and I immediately found ourselves at the beginning of a five-minute song with only about two minutes of tape left. I felt reluctant to stop them for two reasons. Firstly, I didn't want a technical problem to stop or interrupt this excellent atmosphere, and secondly, this was a heavy bunch of musicians, and the thought of having to say down the talkback system, "Sorry guys, we ran out of tape," was horrendous. I moved into "live mobile recording mode" and realised we could use the other multitrack machine, a 16-track. Luckily, on this song we were only recording to 18 tracks of the 24-track machine. Two of the 18 were recording the signal from our ambient mics, which I thought we could probably manage without.

We loaded up the 16-track machine with new tape and got ready. Due to the way the Dolby noise reduction was wired up, the signal could be sent either to the 16-track or to the 24-track machine, but not to both at once, so it would be necessary to switch between them on the fly. I had never found a need to do this before and did not know if it would work at all, or if it did work, whether or not there would be any clicks. The familiar Moog wind and intergalactic atmospherics were floating through the speakers and the lunar module was getting ever closer to the moon's surface. I checked all the levels reading at the desk on the first 16 tracks.

"God, Robert," I said, moving over to him at the tape machines. "You realise that wherever we switch – that will have to be my edit point? How quick do you think this switching works?" The Moog continued to build in dynamics and power. "Maybe we could crossfade over the Moog section," I said.

"I don't know," said Robert, "but I think you should pick your spot and count me in, and pretty quick." Just at that moment, Michael Shrieve played the drum entry and everyone picked up the new song.

"Scrap that crossfade idea," I said. Our remaining length of tape on the 24-track machine was getting shorter. Robert put the 16-track machine into record.

"I've got the rhythm of the song," said Robert. "Let's go, in two bars."

"Okay, but switch just before the snare beat... one bar." I took a deep breath and counted "One... two... three and..."

Robert switched, and the meters immediately began to read. The only tracks we did not have were those on channels 23 and 24, our ambient mics. We did not know whether it had worked or not and would only find out on playback. I settled back at the desk and followed proceedings. Below me, in the studio, unaware of our activities, the band was already building the track with percussion, timpani and piano to Winwood's fragile vocal entry. "When you're caught, the other side..." sang Winwood as he played along on piano, "...possibilities aren't always what they seem, reject them and all your choices will be free, crossing the line."

"These lyrics seem strangely relevant," I thought.

We were flying in more ways than one. In the studio, through dull lighting and flickering candles, I could just make out the musicians playing with their heads bowed or eyes half-closed. On the screen, walls and ceiling, a projected backdrop of stars and planets mingled with the lunar module skimming over the moon's surface. In the vocal booth adjacent to the control room, Klaus moved furiously around the wall of pots, patches and parameters that made up the Moog. I was taking all this in, plus watching the record levels on the 16 VU meters, keeping an eye on the limiters, compressors and echo sends, and worrying if we would be able to salvage this take. At the same time, I was feeling euphoric and increasingly removed from proceedings, just watching it all going on around me. Robert brought over a joint and chopped out a line of coke on the edge of the desk. "Well, I think we deserve these," he said, lighting the joint and handing me a hollow plastic tube, "I don't know if it will work, but at least we didn't panic or stop them – and if it does work, it was a great idea."

As luck would have it, both these songs became our masters. It was almost impossible to play them back-to-back in the way they had been recorded, so while the band took a break, I copied the 16-track over to fresh tape on the 24-track machine and then edited them together. This was carried out with no problems. Robert and I loaded up the finished version, and with fingers crossed, hit the play button. Surprisingly, it had worked, with only a slight variation in hiss level. I felt it had been a complete accident, as it could so easily have gone either way. "Well done, Robert," I said, "a perfect switch." We were both grinning broadly. The ambient mics were lost, but this was not thought to be a problem. Dennis McKay, one of the three producers, planned to "sort it out in the mix." Unfortunately, he achieved this by gating every instrument and losing our natural room sound, then replacing it with artificial echo. This treatment was eventually used for the whole album, much to my disappointment.

I finished mixing *Rock Follies* on the 12th and tried to catch up on some sleep. This proved difficult, as I was always so wired by 5 a.m. The night sessions continued to be long, intense and mentally hard work. As the days progressed, I began crossing a line of my own. On the 14th of February, Sally was taken into hospital with problems over her three-month pregnancy. She arranged for our daughter Becca to be looked after by our close friends and neighbours, Angie and Duncan Campbell. I stayed in London, working, feeling that I could not let everyone down now by leaving the project. When I phoned Sally at the hospital to talk to her, she appeared okay with this decision, adding, "There's not much you can do here, really."

I carried on working as best I could. My body and brain were trying to deal with the difficult and intense sessions, the build-up of weeks of cocaine abuse, too little sleep and now a major family crisis. As I engineered the sessions, looking through the window of Control Room One and floating through space, I felt I had reached a ravine and was looking over the edge. I felt insanity or something very dark lurked down there, and at all costs I must not fall. The sessions, technical problems, sleep deprivation, cocaine, Sally, guilt were all whirling around in my head, and I felt it was all becoming too much to deal with. I was aware of being very near to some form of emotional or physical breakdown. Despite all this, I still felt that I could not pull out of the sessions. We now had eight out of 14 masters completed.

On the morning of Monday the 16th of February, at around 1 a.m., Duncan (who was looking after Becca) turned up. We were right in the middle of working on *Ghost Machine* and were close to a final take. We had just been playing back a previous take as Duncan had arrived, and now everyone was wandering into the studio for another run-through of the song. I was really surprised to see him, but welcomed Duncan and told him to sit at the back of the control room while I asked Robert to make him a mug of tea. He put his arms around me and said, "No, that's okay, Phill. I won't have any tea. Sally has lost the baby. It's time to go home."

I realized then that it was all over and spoke to Stomu and Paul. Although they accepted that it was the only thing I could do, they somehow managed to give me the feeling that I was letting the band down, which of course is exactly what I had been trying to avoid. Everyone, including myself, was so wired and spaced that it was all very dreamlike. Michael Shrieve, in particular, did not want to see me go and told me, "There's not much you can do about it now." Rosko, Steve and Brother James appeared indifferent. I don't think it really clicked with any of them that I really had to go.

Duncan led me out of the studio, put me in his Renault 4 and drove me home. He said very little about Sally, just the basic facts. I spent the first half-hour in the car going on about the Stomu sessions but then became very quiet and we drove in silence. He dropped me off at home at about 3 a.m., and the next day I visited Sally in hospital. We were both upset by the miscarriage, but as Sally said, "It must be for the best. We have to accept it and look forward." I made sure she was okay before collecting Becca from Angie's on my way home. I decided belatedly that it was time to take on my responsibilities at home and have a three-week break. Robert Ash took over recording. I never went back to the sessions. The album was later mixed by Dennis McKay at Trident Studios.

My attitude towards work was never quite the same again after the Stomu sessions. For 10 years, I had felt 101 percent connected with the process of work – mic positioning, adjusting level gains and EQ and the hours of intense listening. I had always felt locked into the job – just an extension of the desk. From that point on, however, that feeling of total commitment and "living" the session fell to about 80 percent. Instead of working intuitively, I now felt more conscious of what was happening as my hands moved about the desk, making adjustments. I now regarded the whole recording process as more of a job.

There had been previous albums that had affected me on a personal level, but never to this degree. All the recent events – working 20 hours a day, the cocaine, the Valium, my fear of impending madness, Sally's miscarriage, my feelings of guilt for not being there and my subsequent shift of attitude to work – seemed to echo Stomu's themes of change and polarity, fantasy and reality, death and rebirth.

Chapter 16. Robert Palmer 12 June 1976

I left Basing Street Studios and my job as a house engineer on the 12th of June 1976. During my six years at Island, there had been many changes. Staff members had come and gone, and there had been innumerable innovations in both studio equipment and recording techniques. The only problems for me had been during the final 18 months, when the office politics with Muff Winwood and Penny Hanson had peaked. I felt it was time to leave the safety of being the house engineer; it was time for more freedom to work with artists and projects that I chose. Tony Platt had already left Basing Street the year before and initially ran into problems with a lack of work. I hoped that my six years at Island and my track record would put me in a better position.

In theory, I could now choose which sessions I wanted to do, but in practice not a lot changed. First, I finished off the projects that I had started, or those that were already booked in for me. These were with Trapeze, Moon and The Hollies. Then, over the following 12 months working as a freelance engineer, I recorded four albums for Island Records. The first was *Some People Can Do What They Like*, Robert Palmer's third solo album, with Steve Smith again producing. Robert Palmer had left England at the end of the last album, *Pressure Drop*, and was now living in Nassau in the Bahamas. He had taken the flooding of his flat in St John's Wood to be a final omen and left London for sunnier climates – and reviews.

During June, there were discussions about the budget for his new album project. Robert, Steve and I had, as usual, discussed musicians and a possible sound approach. We were still planning to record live band tracks with little treatment. It was thought that since the majority of the musicians we wanted to record with on this album all lived in Los Angeles, it would save money to record the entire album in that city. Steve spent a few days in meetings with Island Records fine-tuning the budget and approach for the album, after which he flew to L.A. and negotiated a favourable deal with Clover Recorders in Hollywood. We were all set for adventure number three.

Having finished The Hollies on the 23rd of July, I spent the morning of the 24th with manager John Glover mastering an album for Back Street Crawler (ex-Free guitarist Paul Kossoff's band) at Island's Cutting Room in Hammersmith with John Dent at the controls. Back home in Sussex that evening (before flying to L.A.), Sally, some friends and I walked the quarter mile up the road to Frankham – Susannah York's house – to see a play written by her husband, Michael Wells. The play was to be performed by Susannah in a Roman theatre in their garden. It was all about the breakdown of a marriage, but despite the subject matter it was very funny. They made great use of the surrounding woods and fields, as well as the large stage area. During the interval, we wandered to the drinks tent for refreshments and had a look around the grounds. Although we enjoyed ourselves, the most memorable thing about the evening for me was that while in the refreshments tent, I sneezed, which caused a severe nosebleed. I had to spend the second half stemming the flow with a wad of tissues. Sally, believing this to be caused by cocaine, began to worry about my forthcoming L.A. trip.

The next morning, I flew to New York and on to New Orleans to meet Robert Palmer and Steve Smith. I found them in the courtyard of an old Colonial hotel in the French Quarter, drinking champagne and looking very jet set-ish. Steve was with his new girlfriend, Stephanie, the daughter of a Texan oil baron, and Robert was with a beautiful Asian Playboy Bunny – business as usual. I had been traveling for about 12 hours, so after we had all eaten at a restaurant off Bourbon Street, I went to bed early, planning to catch up on the news the following day.

During the morning of the 26th, Robert and I spent several hours listening to records and demos and continued to discuss sounds and the general approach to the album. It was to be a collection of rock and mid-tempo tracks with a couple of ballads – similar to *Pressure Drop*, but with more sophisticated arrangements. Robert's new songs – in demo form – were honed down to the bare bones, but still sounded slick and polished.

It had been decided that the core of the L.A. band would again be Little Feat. They were still the best musicians for the sound and style we required. However, Steve had arranged a day in New Orleans with the Meters, remarking, "We'll use this day for arrangement ideas, and you never know, we might get lucky." We spent from 2 p.m. 'til late recording at Sea-Saint Studios but did not get anything we could call a master. The Meters had just finished a tour supporting The Rolling Stones and were not in "studio" mode. All they seemed to want to do was play Keith Richard's riffs, and I thought they sounded a little too loose. Compared with their playing two years earlier on tracks for *Sneakin' Sally Through the Alley*, they were not on form. Nonetheless, it was a fun day, and Robert had an opportunity to warm up his voice.

On the 29th, Robert, Steve and I flew to L.A. without the women and moved into a lavish house on Mulholland Drive, rented by a friend of Steve's named Lee. On the ground floor, there was a kitchen and breakfast room, bathroom, bedroom and two large main reception rooms – one housing a full-sized snooker table. On the second floor were four bedrooms, another bathroom and access to an attic den. We moved our bags into the house, convinced that it would be more comfortable than hotel life at The Sunset Marquis (although that was one of my favourite hotels).

We started work at Clover Recorders, a 16-track recording studio at 6232 Santa Monica Boulevard in Hollywood. The studio had been set up by Robert Appere, an American engineer I had met on my first visit to L.A. in 1972. Appere was a speedy, intense man with an aggressive sense of humour. He had recorded Little Feat's *Dixie Chicken* album and always had his fingers in various pies. The studio was neat, compact and a similar size and layout to Basing Street's Studio Two. The control room housed an excellent API desk, UREI compressors and a few effects, including the usual 1970's equipment of ADT machines and harmonisers. The monitors felt accurate, and it appeared to be an easy room to work in. The studio room was moderately live and could comfortably accommodate about 10 musicians. There was also a collection of offices, a games room and a corridor with drink machines and telephones. The small staff was friendly and relaxed, and I immediately felt at home.

We started work on the 2nd of August with Richie Hayward on drums, James Jamerson on bass, Paul Barrere and Steve Cropper on guitars, Bill Payne on keyboards, and Jody Linscott on percussion. For some of the tracks we used various combinations of other musicians – Michael "Spider" Webb and Jeff Porcaro on drums, Pierre Brock, Carol Kaye and Chuck Rainey on bass and James Alan Smith and William D. "Smitty" Smith on keyboards. As usual, we worked quickly, with Robert in the studio doing live vocals and directing the band. For the first eight days, we started at 7 p.m. and worked through until about 4 a.m. This gave me plenty of time off in the mornings to swim, sunbathe and adjust to L.A. time.

We then moved to 2 p.m. starts with a slightly different band – we now had the combination of Jeff Porcaro, Paul Barrere, Smitty, Bill Payne, Pierre Brock and Jody. This became a favourite combination of mine, both for the playing and for the characters themselves, but the discipline was loose, and it could be difficult to get everyone together in the studio at the same time to start work. The days were always slow to get started, and there was always somebody missing – usually to be found on the telephone.

About 10 days in, we all gathered one day at 2 p.m. in the control room for another day's recording. We were discussing what song to record next, as all our selected demo songs now had master takes that we were happy with. Paul was chopping out lines of coke on an empty 2-inch tape spool, and as usual there was a relaxed, non-working atmosphere. I loaded up the 16-track tape machine with fresh tape and powered up various compressors and outboard equipment. Robert went to the mic and started singing the opening lines to the Lowell George song *Spanish Moon*. Bill Payne joined in on electric piano. Slowly, one by one, the rest of the band joined in, and they soon settled on an even tempo. When Jeff Porcaro started playing harder, I thought we could be onto something, so I put the 16-track machine into record, re-checked my levels and signalled to Robert that we were rolling. A minute later Robert yelled, "Okay. From the top," and Jeff counted in. They were off. Six minutes later we had a complete take. Jeff's drum stool had broken after a drum fill, but he kept on playing, half standing and with a large grin on his face.

An excited and noisy band came into the control room for a playback – they knew it was a good take. It had a neat, sneaky intro and settled into a great feel between bass and drums – steady and tight. The track started to build and soon the whole band was flying, Hammond organ, electric piano and guitar all spiralling around each other. Everyone listened with their eyes closed and big grins on their faces. The track continued to play, featuring Smitty on organ and then stripping down to basic instrumentation. It was a great take, and Steve said what we were all thinking, "Fucking great, guys. That's our master." It was now 2:45 p.m. Steve said, "Okay guys. What song are we gonna do next?" – déjà vu. We overdubbed and mixed *Spanish Moon* later that evening. A finished track recorded, overdubbed and mixed in a day – so easy.

Originally, staying in the house on Mulholland Drive had seemed a good idea, but Lee entertained a great deal and threw around three parties a week, which often carried on all night. We would come back from the studio tired at 2 or 3 a.m. to be met by the Hollywood cool (and on one occasion Michael Shrieve and Joni Mitchell). We would feel obliged to be sociable and stay up drinking beer, playing pool and taking coke from a large pile in the middle of a glass table, snorting it through a rolled up $1,000 bill.

We also had to listen to a vast collection of L.A. space cadets who recited poetry, told stories about extra-terrestrials or tried to impress us enough to get a gig with us. After a couple of weeks, we'd all had enough. The final decider for me came when I returned home one night and found some guy with a blonde in my room – not only in my room, but also in my bed, screwing. I crashed in Jody's room, and in the morning Robert and I checked into apartments at the Sunset Marquis. Steve and Jody followed two days later, and we all stayed there for the rest of the album.

It was good for all of us to be back at the Sunset Marquis again, and to be able to enjoy some privacy. Steve's girlfriend Stephanie turned up, and little was seen of either of them outside of studio hours. Robert still disappeared into the night after sessions for unknown activities. One night, he rang my doorbell at 5 a.m. "I was looking for something to smoke, and, well, look... I've got a double act happening. Why don't you come along and join in?" he slurred. Realising with some surprise that Robert had brought two women home to his bedroom, I replied, "Er... here's some hash. Probably not, but I'll think about it." I went to bed. Robert's next album was called *Double Fun*, but there was probably no connection. Sally arrived from England on the 12th and settled into the lifestyle of swimming in the mornings, reading or hanging out with Jody in the afternoons, and spending the evenings and nights at Clover Recording.

We had recorded masters for all our songs within the first four weeks and now began to work on overdubs. The instruments being recorded ranged from steel pans to penny whistle and included Greg Carroll on harmonica. Robert had heard Greg playing in an L.A. gay club one night after a session and had invited him down to the studio.

Steve was noticeably less involved with the day-to-day running of the sessions than he had been on the previous two albums, leaving it to Robert to guide people through. This felt very natural at the time, and I did not read anything into it regarding Robert and Steve's friendship, although in retrospect this was the beginning of the end of their working relationship. He later told me on the flight home, "Yeah, well, you know it's a difference of opinion on the songs between Robert and me, and that difference has led us into different directions. I hate self-indulgence and feel that some of the songs are very laboured. I think we've done everything we can do with this approach. This is what I think – Robert would probably say something different... but the thing about truth is, there's my version, your version and then there's the truth."

Needing more tracks for overdubs on some of the songs, we brought in another 16-track tape machine and synchronized them together. This was the first time Steve and I had ever done this, and it was a bit touch and go, the machines sometimes slewing around for about 25 seconds before locking together. To allow us to work faster we recorded a stereo mix of our main 16-track masters onto tracks 1 and 2 of the second 16-track machine. Now we could work with just this second machine and continued overdubbing, only needing to sync the two machines together again to retrieve our original backing track during the final mix.

Robert's wife Sue flew over from England to join the fun as we went into the final days of overdubbing and mixing at Clover. Sue was small, with shortish, dark brown hair and facial features similar to Robert's. She was good at anything artistic – album covers, photography, paintings and cutting hair. There was now Steve, Stephanie, Robert, Sue, Sally, Jody and me as the hardcore group. We spent most of our time off resting and taking care of mundane jobs, including visiting the hotel launderette. Sometimes, in the evenings, we would take a two-hour break from recording, and all go out for a meal together – Dar Maghreb on Sunset Strip being a favourite restaurant. After sessions, we had a choice of one of the many parties to which we were now being invited. I found dealing with the L.A. loonies at these parties hard work after a day in the studio. As these became more and more of an ordeal, I preferred to spend my spare time with Sally; just the two of us.

Around the 18th of August, the singer/songwriter Joe South and his bass player Tommy Dean turned up in L.A. and came to the studio to meet Steve. At the time, Steve was in discussion with Island about recording an album with Joe back at Basing Street Studios in London. Joe appeared very cool and friendly and loved what we were working on. He liked Steve's general approach and spoke positively about recording in England. I would engineer, and if Richie Hayward was in agreement, he would come over and play drums. (see chapter 17)

It was also about this time that Robert's Playboy Bunny arrived back on the scene for the album cover photo shoot. This was photographed one night in Beverley Hills, with Robert and his Bunny sitting on a grass embankment playing strip poker.

We started to mix on the 24th. I was becoming a little concerned about the fact that my U.S. visitor's visa would run out on the 31st and was pleased to be getting on with this last phase of the project. As with all the previous albums with Robert, we mixed manually, Steve and I manoeuvring at the desk while Robert sat in front listening. While the mixing was going on, Robert had definite ideas about the production and he became heavily involved with the approach for each song. On *Hard Head*, he asked for the bass, the machine bass drum, tambourine, harmonica, guitar and organ to be treated as what he called "a mixture of The Wailers and King

Tubby", while the percussion, drums, timbale and steel drums were to sound like a "Brazilian/Trinidadian/African carnival" or "Fonk". Everything else that was left out of these two lists was to be treated as "Joni Mitchell meets Aretha Franklin". Although these descriptions were far from technical, I understood the basic feel of Robert's suggestions. They were usually based on the sound of instruments or a particular groove or atmosphere and not some fluffy, esoteric idea.

I grouped the three separate lists of instruments to three sub-groups and interpreted Robert's ideas as best I could. This was a simple process when compared to what was to occur two months later on Steve Winwood's project, when I was asked to "make the toms sound like blancmange". (see chapter 18)

Even with both 16-track machines operating together, we mixed quickly – at least two songs a day. Within six days, we had finished. On the 31st, I cut the album together into its final running order and made safety copies. The album included *Off the Bone*, a dub version from the treated overdubs of the song *Pressure Drop*, mixed by me at North Lodge in Sussex on the mobile in May. Robert gave me half the publishing royalty for this song, but when Steve intervened, we all three took a third. That was fine by me as Robert had again given me a 1/2 percent production royalty too.

As we finished the album, the whole subject of the budget became a bit of a sore point. Despite the early attempts to keep costs under control, *Some People Can Do What They Like* turned out to be the most expensive album so far for Robert, at about $75,000 [USD]. We had used 28 days of studio time for tracking, overdubbing and mixing, 22 reels of 2-inch multitrack tape, 10 reels of 1/4-inch mixing tape, and an unknown number of boxes of cassettes and razor blades. Twenty-three musicians, two engineers, three assistants, one producer and one model had been employed, not to mention Robert himself. Then there were fees for house rental, cars, hotel accommodation, flights, meals, hire equipment and per diems. Oh... and a cocaine bill for Robert of $10,000.

Chapter 17. Joe South
5 October 1976

In 1976, Joe South had the appearance of being in his mid-40s, with long brown hair and the dress sense of an ageing hippie. He was, in fact, 34 years old. He gave off a shy but friendly vibe. During the final few days of mixing Robert Palmer's third album, *Some People Can Do What They Like*, at Clover Recorders in Hollywood, we had played Joe some of the songs from the album. He appeared to enjoy the sound, production and performances. While I was busy mixing, Joe and bass player Tommy Dean spent most of their time in a lounge area with Steve Smith, discussing plans for a new Joe South album to be recorded in London during September.

Joe had been signed by Charlie Nuccio at Island Records' L.A. branch a year earlier and had released the album *Midnight Rainbows* in 1975. In retrospect, it seems possible that – for some reason – Chris Blackwell was not keen to have Joe South on his label. However, CB had given Charlie a large amount of freedom (and rope – there was always a risk of failure) with which to sign acts. It had been Charlie who first introduced Steve to Joe, and they had a couple of meetings at Joe's house. Steve told me later, "I went over to his place and there were about a dozen Grammy awards, plaques and trophies for BMI Songwriter of the Year, and five million performances of this song and that song. His place is amazing. However, I feel Joe's the kind of guy who meets the record company and says, 'Oh yes, sure. I'll do whatever the record company wants me to do. Yeah, I'll work with you.'" Steve added that he felt Joe could turn out to be indecisive and inconsistent in the studio.

These meetings had given Steve the impression that Joe was somewhat lost, both musically and spiritually. Joe's manager was Bill Lowery, a well-known character who'd been in the music business for years. Steve made a trip to Atlanta to meet Bill, to get the background story. "I asked him if there was any problem with Joe," said Steve, "and was given the entire tragic story of his background. He'd lost his brother, he'd lost his woman, he'd lost his this and he'd lost his that. I think he's probably done a few too many drugs and is almost shell-shocked – worst of all he's lost his confidence. This is the guy who has written some of the best songs in rock 'n' roll. An incredible songwriter, but now basically a rehab."

Steve planned a fresh approach for Joe, and for this reason had suggested recording in England with a combination of English and American musicians.

With Robert's album finished and delivered, Steve Smith and I flew back to England on the 1st of September along with Sally, Jody Linscott, and Richie Hayward. Richie came and spent three days cooling out at our house in Sussex before we regrouped at Basing Street's Studio One on the evening of the 3rd. Richie and I had struck up a good friendship during the past two years, and we enjoyed each other's company. With walks in the woods during the day and the evenings spent at the local pub talking, we had a pleasant break and arrived at Basing Street refreshed and ready to work. Joe's album promised to be an interesting project and would involve three of my favourite people (Jody, Richie and Steve). The basic band was a trio – Richie on drums, Tommy Dean on bass and Joe South on electric and acoustic guitars, with Steve playing some keyboard parts. We planned to overdub Jody on percussion and Neil Hubbard on rhythm and lead electric guitars.

I set up Richie's drum kit in front of the control room window, facing into the studio. I used my usual drum mics – Neumann U87s, AKG D 12 and Shure SM57s. In front and to the right of Richie was Tommy's bass, boothed off for separation with DI boxes and an AKG D 12 microphone. On Richie's left was a screened-off area for Joe's guitars and vocal. I set up a selection of microphones – Neumann, Shure, AKG and Sennheiser – because I had yet to discover which ones would prove to be successful. We slowly settled into the session, and after setting up, the musicians ran through some of the songs we were going to record. Joe was quiet and seemed relaxed. "We're gonna start slow and taper off," he said from his booth. How right he was. We finished at 8 p.m. "Okay, that's great for today," said Steve. "Let's leave it there, have an early night and come in tomorrow and cut an album." Steve went off with Joe and Tommy, while Richie and I went for a meal.

During the short period I worked with Joe South, he never complained or let on to any of us that he was not happy. However, to my amazement, we later discovered that Joe was having all sorts of problems. In a letter he subsequently wrote to the record company, these problems were itemized in a long list that was, to me, totally baffling.

Most of Joe and Tommy's equipment was built for standard American 110-volt power and had to be connected to heavy duty transformers that would allow us to plug into the 240-volt main electricity supply. The maintenance staff and I had done this many times before for American artists with few problems. Surprisingly, in view of what he wrote in his letter, on this occasion we received no complaint from Joe or from Tommy and we truly believed that everything was okay. There was a slow start to the proceedings, but neither Steve nor I were concerned. We both felt that once the musicians had settled in, we would be able to record at least three songs each day.

Steve and I often took a day or two to set up for the start of an album, and we were not concerned by the initial lack of progress. Joe, however, found fault with this schedule and did not appreciate the fact that he had been given a day or two to recover from jet lag before starting work. Again, this was not mentioned at the time – if Joe was concerned about studio time and the money being spent, he did little to alleviate the problem. He had what appeared to be some great songs but had difficulty performing any of them through to the end or to the standard required. Richie was playing well, and Tommy seemed to be enjoying himself, but Joe was very quiet and distant. He spent most of day two sitting in his booth running through songs.

At the beginning of the session on the third day, I was in the studio with Richie and Steve. Dave, the assistant, was lining up the tape machines and getting ready to start recording when the phone rang in Control Room One. I picked up the receiver. It was Tommy, sounding speedy and breathless. He asked to speak to Steve.

"Look Steve, Joe is in the hospital and today's session is off. I've got to go." With that, he hung up the phone.

"Surprise, surprise," said Steve, "Joe's ill. He's in hospital."

This sounded a bit far-fetched. However, I reflected that if something goes seriously wrong, it's not always possible to continue with a recording session. Only a few months before, I had left Stomu's session because of Sally's miscarriage. I went and made tea for everyone.

There was obviously little that Steve, Richie or I could do without Joe. Steve phoned the Island offices in St Peter's Square and tried to get more news. At first, we were informed that Joe was a diabetic and had forgotten his medication. News then came through that Joe really was in hospital because he had had a heart attack. This was difficult for the three of us to believe – he had looked fine the night before. Richie Hayward, Steve Smith, myself (and the studio time) were all booked for the next 10 days – an expensive commitment for the record company – but now with no artist. We began to realize the magnitude of the problem. We sat on the floor of Studio One, reviewing events and trying to decide what to do.

"Well, there are some people who are uncomfortable in any unfamiliar situation and are better off at home," said Steve. "I think – judging by the lack of progress during the past few days – that Joe is one of those. He doesn't like change or working in a strange environment, plus his confidence is at a low level... but he just hasn't come up with the goods. You know, we've been really accommodating. I've already got him a doctor and yesterday I met him before the session and took him down the local market near his apartment to show him what to buy. I think he is a guy who has not recovered well from his experiences over the last three years. It appears that he has now become conveniently ill. What are we going to do with our time?"

We agreed that we had to do something, and soon. We began to discuss the possibility of recording something different, using the time and the musicians that were already booked.

"Well, there's always Murray Head," I said. "I could check what he's up to." Murray Head was an Island artist with whom Steve had wanted to work since 1972, when they met during the mixing of *Nigel Lived*.

"Yes," said Steve. "Great idea. How soon can you find out?"

I went off to ring Toad Hall. An answering machine said, "Can't talk now. Ring after 7." Returning to the control room, I told Steve, "He's not around right now. I'll give him a ring in a couple of hours. What do you want to do now?"

"Okay. You and Richie take the evening off but ring me later."

Around 5 p.m., Richie and I left Basing Street's Studio One, drove down the road and scored a gram of cocaine. We snorted a couple of tracks, and just after 7 p.m. we drove over to The World's End pub on The Kings Road. We drank three shots of tequila, shared a beer and talked quietly about the day's events and life generally. "Life's a bitch and then you die," said Richie. "What a fuck up. I hope he'll be okay. What do you do for excitement in this town?"

At about 9:30, we drove over to Dana Gillespie's flat in South Kensington. I wanted to introduce Richie to Dana. They got on well immediately and we sat around with the coke, some grass and Dana's pillbox. After ringing Murray Head from Dana's at 10 p.m., I left Richie in her care. I drove the few hundred yards to Murray's flat on Neville Street and explained the situation. Fortunately, Murray was available for at least seven days, and as I had hoped, was excited by the possibility of working in the studio and getting the chance of playing with Richie Hayward. I rang two other musicians, Alan Spenner and John Porter, while Murray got in touch with Bryn Haworth and BJ Cole. I then telephoned Steve, gave him the good news, and arranged to drive over and stay at his flat off Sussex Gardens. I said goodnight to Murray and added, "Bring everything with you tomorrow – demos, guitars, strings, batteries – everything."

At 3 a.m., sitting at his kitchen table, Steve and I quickly made alternative plans for the next day. Steve decided to cancel all the studio time booked after the first eight days. He would not be charged for this, as he would have complied with studio rules by giving seven days' notice. Meanwhile, we would complete the task of putting together a band for Murray and see what happened.

During the late morning, Steve rang around various people – Penny at Basing Street, Denise at Island Records and an assortment of musicians including Neal Hubbard and Rabbit. About 12:30 p.m., I left for the studio to meet Murray. There was a certain amount of excitement amongst the studio staff due to the various rumours that were circulating, and Penny wanted to know all the details on Joe.

While Murray changed his guitar strings and distributed clutter all over the place in his usual manner, I began stripping down the Joe South setup and arranging a new, more flexible one. I did not know at this point how many musicians we might end up with. By 3 p.m., Steve and Richie had arrived, and most of the musicians we had contacted had returned our calls. We aimed to start recording at 7 p.m., so Richie went for a walk on Portobello Road, while Steve went back to the phone. Around 5:30 p.m., I nipped up the road to the Anglo-Yugoslav restaurant and had a large mixed grill. It would probably be a long night.

The band finally consisted of John Porter, the guitarist and all-rounder from Dana Gillespie's band, Alan Spenner and Neal Hubbard, the bass player and guitarist from Kokomo and Joe Cocker's Grease Band, along with Bryn Haworth also on guitar, pianist Rabbit, Murray and Richie. We screened off all the instruments and recorded our "instant" seven-piece band live – acoustic guitar, drums, bass, rhythm and lead guitars, mandolin and grand piano. Both Steve and I just wanted to let these guys loose on the songs, the arrangements and the feel and see what happened. However, it was obvious from the outset that Murray's approach to the recordings was going to be quite different. He had very set ideas about the end result of each song, and this inevitably slowed things down. Instead of inspiring this impressive collection of musicians with his enthusiasm as we had hoped, he began to discuss every last detail with everyone. I was surprised, but I had enough to do sorting out the technical side of the recordings and left him to it. We finished our first day's recording at 3 a.m. with two masters in the can.

During the next six days, we cut about 14 songs, mostly written by Murray, including *How Many Ways*, *Affair Across a Crowded Room* and *Rubbernecker*. We also took the opportunity to record other songs. The band delighted in playing Ry Cooder tracks, mastering *How Can a Poor Man Stand Such Times and Live?* Steve felt there were enough basic tracks for a complete album, so towards the end of the week we recorded a few vocal repairs and made rough mixes.

Richie went home to Los Angeles on the 17th of September, and we sent a copy of our rough mixes to Island. There may not have been a masterpiece amongst these tapes, but it was a solid follow-up to his successful album *Say It Ain't So* (which was written about Joe Wissert, see chapter 8), produced by Paul Samwell-Smith and released on Island in 1975. We obviously still needed to decide which of the tracks worked and which songs needed to be re-done or thrown out. These were early days in the recording of the album and involved relatively little expense, as we had spent only eight days in the studio – six recording and two over-dubbing. However, for reasons I never found out, there was a distinct lack of enthusiasm from Island, and nothing became of the tapes. I think Steve would have been happy to go either way – he would willingly have taken the tapes and made a good album (he was particularly sold on the reggae version of *Rubbernecker*), but he was also surprised at Murray's fussing and said so to me at the end of our initial recording.

"He brings it on himself. I think with Murray you have the reverse of the Midas touch. Everything he touches turns to shit."

Steve's disillusionment and the lack of enthusiasm from Island did nothing to improve my relationship with Murray. It seemed like another nail in the coffin. I had hoped that using the Joe South studio time might be fun as well as helpful for Murray – but for him it was just another failure – and I was there again.

Steve went off with Stephanie for a break, and I went back to looking for work, trying to get used to my new position of being self-employed. Within a month, I was working with Steve Winwood on his first solo album. (see chapter 18)

Meanwhile, Joe South recovered and returned to America, and on the 5th of October wrote a letter to Charlie Nuccio at Island Records in L.A. In the letter, he offered to make an album himself using the remainder of the budget from the aborted project, after which he asked to be released from his contract with Island Records. The accompanying litany of complaints and disasters shows a staggering lack of meaningful communication between Joe and almost everyone he came into contact with while in London. Complaints about "bad second and third harmonics" in the control room, getting shocked from the amp's voltage-converting transformers and a (fictional) ruinous 70 Hz signal going to tape were brought up. Steve and I had no idea of the grief Joe had obviously been going through – at the time, there had been no mention of the problems with transport, hotels, Island Records, electric shocks, food or telephones. His comments about equipment and technical facilities made very little sense and came as a complete surprise, as he had never mentioned a word about any of this to either me or Steve.

Later, Steve referred to this time as "The Rehab Period". "You know, you come across a fair number of people who have been really successful in the past, and now ask for help to revive their careers," he said. "Back in the early to mid-1970s I had Lesley Gore, David Byron [ex-Uriah Heep] and Del Shannon. I learnt a great deal from this period, but I don't think you can say it was a great experience. A large part of making records is learning about human nature, and I think sometimes you find out that your view of what's going on and theirs differ quite a lot – so much so that their reality seems somewhat scary. You're there with your honest, workman-like method, trying to get somebody to do their best work, while all the time they're dealing with all sorts of unseen demons..."

Steve and I never saw or heard from Joe South again. Maybe Steve was right. Some people's reality is rather scary.

Chapter 18. Steve Winwood
31 October 1976

"Can you make the tom toms sound like blancmange?"

I was working with Steve Winwood at Chipping Norton Studios in Oxfordshire. Mark Miller Mundy was there to "help" with production, although he had never made a professional record before. It was he who had asked for this unusual drum sound, and I did my best to interpret what I thought he meant. After all, Steve had invited Mark to be an associate producer, and he appeared to listen to what Mark had to say.

Mark and I had met earlier in the month at Island's Fallout Shelter studio in St Peter's Square, Hammersmith. Within weeks of finishing with Joe South, I had received a phone call from Denise Mills, Chris Blackwell's personal assistant at Island Records, who also looked after Winwood and Bob Marley. "I want to know if you'll do a couple of days with Winwood," she said. "I've no idea what he is up to, but evidently he would like to record a track called *Walk Me to the Lilies* with a friend of his called Mark Miller Mundy – a neighbour I think. It's Mark who has suggested this song – he describes it as an "old country song". Mark will be there himself, by the way, to help out."

Denise knew Steve Winwood well. He had not worked on his own material for the past three years, and she was worried that he might not even show up. "But I'm not paying you those Robert Palmer rates, you know," she continued. "I'm not even paying you a daily rate, because I don't know how long this idea might last. I'll pay you by the hour – let's say £6.50 an hour."

As usual, I accepted Denise's offer. Denise Mills was one of the "strong women" of Island. These had included Sally Wightman (now my wife), Elsa Peters and Penny Hanson. Denise was tall and thin, small-framed, intimidating and did not suffer fools gladly. I learnt early on at Island to be polite and careful with my dealings with her. I liked Denise, and generally we got on well. She could be difficult at times and had a similar offhand manner to that of Penny, but she was straight and forthright, and I always knew where I stood. That usually meant I just had to say, "Yes, Denise."

I turned up at The Fallout Shelter, as instructed, on Monday the 11th of October, at about 2 p.m. Steve and Mark arrived and we set up piano, Hammond, a guitar amp and a basic rhythm box. Steve then played around with the song – mainly on piano – for about eight hours, and we packed up at about 11 p.m. That accounted for the first day, during which Steve had hardly said a word. I was used to some sessions taking a while to get going and was not surprised at Steve's seeming lack of enthusiasm.

The next day passed in more or less the same way, although we did get as far as putting a couple of ideas to tape, and Mark had some comments to make. Mark seemed pleasant enough and had that over-politeness and "English camp" of the born rich. He asked many questions about the desk and studio equipment and was friendly and flattering. By contrast, Steve was very quiet – perhaps he didn't want to be in London, didn't like the studio or was not keen on the song, but he never said. He was, as usual, very shy. Steve tried out Mark's ideas, exhibiting very little personal opinion, and again we finished at about 11 p.m. We took a day off, meeting at 3 p.m. on the 14th to continue. We spent another day trying different arrangements and approaches to *Walk Me to the Lilies*, but nothing special appeared, and by 11:30 p.m. the session had ground to a halt. Maybe Denise had been right.

Just before leaving for the night, Steve said quietly, "*Walk Me to the Lilies* isn't really for me, but I do have a bunch of ideas that I've been working on. How do you feel about moving out to my home studio or the studio at Chipping Norton to try them out?" Mark and I nodded in agreement with this suggestion, and after a short discussion decided to use Chipping Norton Studios. As a residential studio, it could provide everything necessary to accommodate any other musicians that might become involved. I had worked there before and liked the layout and sound.

Two weeks later, on the 27th, we were in Chipping Norton, working five-day weeks from 2 p.m. to 3 a.m. each day with a congenial band, consisting of John Susswell on drums, Alan Spenner on bass, Brother James on percussion and Junior Marvin (soon to join Bob Marley) on guitar. I was still being paid by Denise on an hourly basis.

The studio was built in an old school house and had a large, rectangular studio area, which gave a good live sound. Above, and built parallel to the live room, was a small, compact control room and various small rooms and offices. There was a maze of corridors that ran the full length of the building and connected two stairwells, and ultimately, the studio to the control room. At the far end of the building there was a large kitchen where the band and staff would eat in the evenings. Outside, there was a group of buildings that had been converted into apartments. These, along with the bedrooms in the main building, could accommodate about 10 people. We were well looked after by the friendly studio staff, and it was an easy and relaxed place to work.

As the band started to run through Steve's songs and ideas, the ambience was good and at times quite magical. While we were recording, Steve said little to anyone and just played, hunched over the Hammond, Fender Rhodes or piano, often wearing a dark blue duffle coat with the hood up. This seemed to accentuate his isolation and made it difficult for the musicians to make any eye contact with him. I had known Steve for almost 10 years, and we had worked on many sessions together, including Traffic, Amazing Blondel and more recently, Stomu Yamashta's *Go* project. I had become used to Steve's withdrawn and shy manner (although, this time, he appeared to be more so than usual) and always enjoyed working with him. I regarded him as a very talented musician and singer, and for a long time he had been a hero of mine.

While we were working on these sessions, Steve had invited me to stay at his imposing stone manor house (Lower Dean Manor) in the hamlet of Turkdean, about 20 miles away. The main living room of the house was a 30-by-30, old-style stone hall. There was also a cosy sitting room, a small study, a well-equipped kitchen, bathroom, two utility areas and a large access hall. On the first floor, there were four or five bedrooms, some en-suite. During my time here, I only saw two bedrooms and the main stone room. The house was large and had apartments for live-in staff. Outside, in the extensive grounds, there was a collection of timber buildings, including sheds and greenhouses and two large barns. In one of the barns, an impressive home studio had been built, while the other housed Steve's splendid collection of cars – a 1930s Fleetwood Cadillac, two Ferraris, four French sports cars from the '60s, a Mercedes saloon and a Lancia fastback.

Each day, Steve would roll out his valuable-but-delicate Ferrari Dino, and after coaxing it to start in the damp and misty Gloucestershire mornings, we would drive the half hour to Chipping Norton. We travelled down narrow country lanes, barely 4 inches off the ground, at speeds of over 100 mph. I was sure I was going to die, but my ego consoled me with the thought that at least I would be remembered as the engineer who crashed with Steve Winwood. We never spoke on these journeys, which was hardly surprising. When we arrived, I always needed a cup of tea and a joint with Alan Spenner before I felt calm and ready for work.

At night, after sessions and an equally scary drive home, Steve and I would sit in the vast stone room at his manor with a blazing fire until 5 or 6 a.m., smoking ourselves into a stupor. The room was built from large, stone blocks and incorporated massive, 7-foot-high leaded windows, heavy oak doors, a carved Inglenook fireplace and a 12-foot-high ceiling. Fanning out from the fireplace were three large armchairs, a dining table (capable of seating 10), an old sofa and a couple of wooden pews. The wood fire appeared to be going continuously, and by the time we arrived home each night it would be stacked with wood and giving off maximum heat. There were four or five large wall hangings and portraits on the walls and several rugs on the stone floor to try to make it feel warm and home-like. This had worked to some degree, but near to the outside walls and windows, the room could still feel cold and damp.

We would slump into the vast armchairs with cups of tea and vaguely discuss the day's events, with Steve fading to an inaudible mumbling after about 30 minutes. Steve's appearance was that of an 18th-century street urchin, in faded, creased, camel-coloured trousers and a thick shirt with a pullover. Although we spoke very little on these occasions, this did not feel awkward or embarrassing – just very laid back and surprisingly comfortable. The only light in the room came from the fire and a candle or two. There was always a strong smell of wood smoke. We would sit quietly, taking it in turns to roll joints and feed the fire in almost total silence – no music, radio or television – only the occasional noise from the Gloucestershire wildlife to interrupt a fleeting train of thought.

Back at the studio in Chipping Norton, we ran through songs and ideas, and on the whole, the atmosphere was calm, friendly and relaxed. I had worked with most of the musicians before and we had always got on well; Brother James was humorous and friendly, John Susswell was efficient and sharp-edged, Junior Marvin was cool and in control, and as always, Spenner was amusing, mellow, on form and easy-going. In contrast, Mark Miller Mundy could be quite trying in the control room with his constant stream of questions, and he tested my patience on many occasions. He had a bizarre way of describing sounds or giving directions to the musicians and came out with a few wonderful requests. On the evening of the 31st of October, while recording the song *Vacant Chair* (with its chorus of "O-ku nsu-kun no-ko" – African for "only the dead weep for the dead") in all seriousness he asked me to "make the tom toms sound like blancmange".

A few years later, I was working with Marianne Faithfull, also at Chipping Norton, with Mark Miller Mundy producing. During the previous week's recording, Mark had confused the band with his inane comments and contradictory requests. One evening, while the band took a break, Mark had inexplicably retuned the drums and fiddled with equipment, causing anger and chaos within the band. Morale was low. Late the following night, after another day of mayhem, Marianne and I spent a couple of hours discussing Mark – what he was like to work with, his attitude and unusual approach. I thought Mark was nervous and self-indulgent; Marianne thought he was a bit of an idiot. She had known and worked with him for far longer than I had, and I took her word for it. "You know," she said, "last week he asked the band to play like lemmings falling over a cliff. Where's that at?"

By the 12th of November 1976, we had 10 tracks recorded. Some – like *Vacant Chair* and *Time is Running Out* – were almost complete, while others, including *Hotel Blues* and *Luck's In*, remained unfinished ideas. There was easily enough material for an album, and many of the songs had that fragile, Traffic feel to them. Then, one morning, we got a call from Denise, "Hi Phill, Chris Blackwell's in town. He just got in from the States. He wants to come out and listen to what you're doing. Can we arrange it for later today?"

I ran off some rough stereo mixes in the afternoon, and that evening after a supper of pasta, a few bottles of red wine and mountains of garlic bread, we had a playback for Chris in the control room. Some of the band – along with Steve, Mark and myself – now squeezed into this small room, and giving CB the only comfortable chair and the best audio position in the house, we played the results of our two or three weeks' work. At the end of the playback, the band members left for last orders at the pub. This left just Steve, Mark, Chris and myself in a haze of blue cigarette smoke that the air conditioning was frantically trying to deal with. Chris turned to Steve and said, "I think it's great," and added after a long pause, "You should re-record it with Andy Newmark and Willie Weeks."

"How do you mean?" asked Steve defensively.

"Well, you know," said Chris, pushing forward as usual, "the songs are really good, and I think that the rhythm section of Willie Weeks and Andy Newmark would be excellent. Just what the tracks need."

"Oh... well... okay," said Steve, with a surprising lack of emotion. "We can give it a try."

As usual, very little was discussed about the situation, although later that evening, after Chris had left, someone did remark, "If it's so great, why do we have to do it all again?" I, for one, felt a little fazed, but this feeling of slight resentment soon faded, and we all accepted the idea. Chris had a good feel for music and his ideas were usually successful, and after all, he was the boss. Chris had seemed genuinely pleased that Steve was working again on his own material.

We packed up at Chipping Norton and headed home, taking a few weeks off to allow Denise time to arrange the new sessions. By the 15th of December, with a couple of days rehearsing at St Peter's Square behind us, we were at Basing Street's Studio Two with Winwood and the new band. This was now a trio, with Andy Newmark on drums, Willie Weeks on bass and Steve on the usual assortment of keyboards.

Andy was set up in the studio with his back against the control room window. His kit was mic'ed with four Neumann U87s, an AKG D 12, an AKG D 224 and a Shure SM57. Against the wall on the right sat Willie and his bass amp with another AKG D12 and DI. This left Steve in the middle of the room with his Rhodes, piano and Hammond facing the control room window and the other two musicians. I used a collection of microphones for Steve's equipment, including U87s, D12s, D224s and four DI boxes. Dealing with just three musicians made a pleasant change for me, and it took very little time to set up and get ready. Andy was a confident but polite New Yorker, around 30 years old and very successful. He had originally made his name in the early 1970s drumming for Sly Stone. There's little I can say about Willie. He sat quietly, bent over his bass guitar playing beautifully and staring at the drums – polite and friendly, but not particularly sociable.

The sessions started at 6 p.m. and continued through the night until 8 or 9 a.m. Although the hours were long and tiring, the combination of large amounts of adrenaline, excellent musicianship and the pleasant atmosphere made the sessions fast and enjoyable. Mark Miller Mundy was still around, but Chris Blackwell was also on the sessions, which made me feel happier. Chris always made efficient use of studio time, so I knew I would not have to worry about trying to make the tom toms sound like 'blancmange', the Hammond mimic a 'jet engine' or make the bass 'liquid lava'.

Steve, Andy and Willie were very relaxed and played each song until we had a master that everyone was pleased with. Then, they played them again. The sessions were enormously productive with an almost session musician approach – no five- or six-piece band playing in a studio in the country; instead, it was eyes down and concentrate. As Steve Smith would say, "Guys of this calibre playing together – it makes their game get better." In this creative atmosphere, even Winwood became more accessible, and with the new setup, eye contact was now possible between the musicians. He even left his duffle coat in the control room. The tracks we recorded were tight and sparse. I was particularly impressed by Andy's style, accuracy and busy hi-hat patterns.

At the end of the five days, we called a halt and picked the versions we thought were the best. Only one recording from Chipping Norton survived and made it onto the list – this being *Vacant Chair*, co-written by Vivian Stanshall, an old friend of Steve's and an ex-member of The Bonzo Dog Doo-Dah Band. The rest of the songs, now whittled down to four, came from the Basing Street sessions. We finished at 9 a.m. on December the 20th and took a break for Christmas, planning to meet in the New Year for overdubs.

Steve, Mark and I re-grouped without Chris on the 3rd of January 1977 at Basing Street's Studio One and began overdubbing. Again, we worked night sessions, beginning at 7 p.m. and finally leaving most mornings at 8 a.m. Progress now became slow, and Steve appeared unsettled and reverted to being very quiet. This could not be said of Mark, whom I was finding increasingly tiresome.

We worked for eight days before Steve explained that he preferred the sound of his own Hammond at home in Turkdean. This was a slight blow for me as I was set up and very comfortable in Studio One, but Mark and I again adjusted to another new idea, and in the end felt it was no great problem. Besides, using the Island Mobile truck was always an adventure. Steve was adamant that his Hammond sounded best, and I had to agree that he had always had a unique sound on record. Damage caused some years before, while he was on the road with Traffic, had made the Leslie run slow. He had preferred this broken sound of the Leslie, at both high and low speeds, and had it fixed permanently in these positions. Again, there would be a few days' break while Denise arranged the mobile and cancelled our time at Basing Street. Obviously, we could have brought the Turkdean Hammond up to London, but this was not discussed at the time, and I can only assume that Steve had other reasons for preferring to be at home.

We loaded the tapes, and taking Ray Doyle and the Island mobile, we relocated at Steve's house on the 20th of January. I settled into my old bedroom, and Ray had a room somewhere in the attic. We still worked during the nights, starting around 4 p.m. and working through until about 6 or 7 a.m. There remained one track –

Midland Maniac – to record as a master, and then at last we would be able to concentrate on the final overdubs. We had recorded, with just piano, various versions of this song at Chipping Norton, Basing Street and at Turkdean, but Steve was not entirely happy with any of them.

One evening, when we were listening to takes and discussing what to do about this problem, Steve said, "Look, we've got a version from Basing Street that had a good first half and a good end, but I'm not pleased with the middle section. And we have that great take from last night that has a brilliant middle but a duff end, and there are a couple of others I quite like the intros from..." I knew what Steve was going to suggest. "Phill, any chance of editing these together? 'Cause otherwise this could go on forever."

"We can give it a try," I said, thinking that pianos are never easy to edit between. Without a click track, there could be problems with differing tempos.

I spent the early hours of the morning in the mobile with Ray, trying to get the 24-track edits to feel right, and eventually I called Steve and Mark in from the house to listen. After checking the edited piano track through twice, Steve said, "It's good and bad. The edits work fine, but our three different piano sections are out of tune with each other. I don't know if that will cause problems. Let me try some drums, just to see how it all feels." This struck me as an unusual approach – to record the drums to a free-tempo piano track with no click. Usually, the drums would be recorded first.

We set up four mics on the kit and got a quick, basic drum sound. Steve's home studio was potentially excellent, with a Helios desk, 3M 24-track tape machine and a large live area for recording. However, we were using none of this equipment and ran two multi-core cables from the mobile to the studio live area. I used the foldback system to feed the piano down the headphones, and within a couple of takes Steve had played drums through all eight minutes, to just the piano. Although I knew he could sing, play guitar, bass and keyboards, I was impressed that he could also play drums – particularly to just a piano track, with no click. "We'll leave it there for now and come back and listen tomorrow," he said. "It's 7:30 [a.m.]. Let's call it a night."

We ended up keeping the edited track and the drum take, but from then on, every instrument we overdubbed on *Midland Maniac* had to be retuned for each section. This was achieved much of the time by vari-speeding the 24-track tape machine and making a small, final correction on the instrument itself. It occurred to me then that if anyone was a midland maniac, it was Winwood himself.

Winwood had many strings to his bow. He had perfect pitch and could play most instruments – extremely useful during this overdub stage of the recordings. We worked for four days recording guitar and keyboard ideas and then took an eight-day break, returning on the 1st of February for another four days. We then took a further break, this time for six days. I did not consider this way of working to be very productive, and progress was slow. Steve was still somewhat distant and difficult to communicate with, and I was becoming bored with the slow progress of overdubbing. Mark still described sounds in a very bizarre way, but appeared happy with my interpretations and results. I felt there was no overall plan, and this added to my frustrations. At the time, the idea of trying out every possible variation of every overdub was quite alien to me, although 10 years later – when I was working on the Talk Talk albums – I would become quite used to this approach.

Some evenings, we would take a two-hour break and have friends over for a meal. Steve employed domestic staff – a housekeeper, a cook, a car mechanic and a guy who did the garden, looked after the horses and brought in logs for the fire. Sitting down to venison with all the trimmings, we would be entertained by Steve's American wife, Nicole Tacot Winwood, who appeared to me at first to be a typical L.A. groupie and the complete opposite of Steve. However, the more I came to know her, the more I felt she was a sweet but troubled woman. During these dinners, I would say little and just listen to the general chatter, sometimes picking up pieces of information about our guests. Most of the conversation was local and countrified, covering such information as whose land the next hunt would meet on, where the next hare-coursing event would take place and who was screwing whom, where and why. Mark, with his camp humour, was amusing and acted as the perfect country gentleman at these functions.

Although I found him confusing and pedantic in the studio, I grew to like him in this environment. It appeared that Mark's father owned half of Gloucestershire.

By February 1977, things began to get hectic for me with other work coming in, but as Winwood's sessions were still five days on and then about seven days off, I found I could work them into the schedule without too much difficulty. Sessions with Paul Kossoff's Back Street Crawler and Eddie Baird (ex-Amazing Blondel) went ahead at Basing Street, and there were rehearsals for an album with the band No Dice (producer Steve Smith), due to start at Olympic Studios in April.

Meanwhile, Winwood's recordings still continued at Turkdean with just Steve, Mark, Ray and myself. All overdubs were played by Steve, including piano, Hammond, drums, guitars, some bass and Fender Rhodes. It was wonderful watching these performances and the control he maintained on various instruments. However, during Steve's vocal overdubs I became a little disappointed. I was a huge fan of both the sound of his voice and his vocal style – these were two qualities that I had always loved about him. For me, it went back to the songs of the Spencer Davis Group – especially *I'm A Man* and *Gimme Some Loving*. For some reason, he no longer appeared to have the vocal quality, sound or stamina of previous recordings. I have no idea why – he had sounded wonderful on Stomu's *Go* album, recorded just nine months before. Because of the general lack of communication from Steve over the previous few months, I had no knowledge of the difficult times he may or may not have been going through, and I had gained no further insight into him. All I could do, along with Mark, was to record his vocals when he requested and keep any of these takes he might be happy with. I did just that while hoping the sound, performance and general vibe would improve.

By March, we were nearly finished and moved back to Basing Street for the final overdubs and mixing. We recorded percussion with Reebop Kwaku Baah and Brother James, and backing vocals with Jim Capaldi and Nicole Winwood. This was a particularly "up" period, and having Capaldi and Brother James around gave a boost to the energy and atmosphere of the sessions. Steve completed the final overdub, a guitar solo on *Luck's In*, and by the end of March we had our six songs ready to mix.

From April 3rd to the 7th, on night-time sessions in Studio Two, Mark, Steve and I worked together on the mixes. During the previous five months, we had listened to a wide variety of monitor mixes while overdubbing an assortment of instruments and sounds. This had led each of us to a very different approach to how the desired sound, balance and atmosphere could be achieved, and consequently the mixing became involved and confused. As ever, I found Mark's descriptions of sounds hard to understand and never quite knew what he wanted. Back in December, when we were laying down all those wonderful backing tracks at Chipping Norton, and then with Andy Newmark at Basing Street, we had hardly talked at all. Now all three of us were politely arguing our separate corners.

We finished this first run of mixes, and I made tape copies for Steve, Mark and me to take away and listen to. I also made a set for Chris Blackwell. As we were packing up, I said, "You know Steve, I find it difficult to work like this, with everyone wanting different things and no real direction... and this kind of aggressive vibe in the studio..." "A little aggression in the studio can be a good thing," he replied.

Two weeks later, on the 21st of April, we were back in Studio Two at Basing Street and re-mixing. Chris Blackwell, in London for a few days, came to the sessions. Within minutes of arriving, CB said to me, "I'm giving you a 1 percent royalty on Steve's album as a thank you and for sticking with it." This is something I can't imagine the record company accountants and lawyers doing today. I was pleased and honoured by Chris' actions.

We remixed the album in three days, and I made four more sets of safety copies. It had taken almost six months to record, overdub and finish the album – the longest time I had ever spent on a project. A few days after finishing the mixing, I mastered the album at the Trident cutting rooms and then joined Steve Smith at Olympic Studios for the start of the No Dice project.

Winwood's album was called simply *Steve Winwood* and was released at the peak of the punk movement in the summer of 1977. Some leading critics dismissed Winwood as "a tired survivor of the psychedelic 1960s". The album achieved moderate success however, especially in the USA. Winwood later said of the album, "I felt it was a strong album, but somehow I still felt as if I was on the treadmill – making records because I was under contract to do so." I wondered if this might be an explanation as to why he had appeared so distant.

Mark briefly became an in-house producer for Island Records and went on to record Marianne Faithfull's excellent album *Broken English* – with much assistance, no doubt, from ex-Island engineer Bob Potter.

Steve Winwood disappeared to his home studio and worked alone on his follow up album, *Arc of a Diver*, released three years later. This time, he not only played all the instruments on the album himself, but also engineered and produced it. As a result, I think the album has more of that old Winwood magic.

For the majority of the time, engineering Steve's first solo album had been an enjoyable experience for me. This was especially true of the days spent recording Hammond and piano, or listening to a particular performance that would make the hairs on the back of my neck stand up – as on *Vacant Chair* and *Let me Make Something in Your Life*. It was also a lucky career move and helped to promote my name up the record company lists of freelance engineers. Winwood's album helped me to obtain work with John Martyn, Roxy Music, Jim Capaldi, Dire Straits and – 20 years later – Talk Talk. All this initiated from a couple of days trying to record the song *Walk Me to the Lilies* – a track we never mastered.

Chapter 19. John Martyn
11 November 1977

During my first 12 months as a freelance engineer, I had recorded and mixed two significant albums for Island Records. The first was Robert Palmer's third album, *Some People Can Do What They Like*, and the second was Steve Winwood's first self-titled solo album. In the summer of 1977, Chris Blackwell asked me to work with him on John Martyn's new LP, *One World*.

Chris planned to use the Island Mobile and record for three weeks at his house in Theale. This is where I had recorded overdubs for Robert Palmer's *Pressure Drop* album two years earlier, and Chris liked the idea of recording outside. He had been impressed by the apparent ease of working this way, the great sound and ambience of vocals and instruments and the extra freedom when working from home. The house was almost totally surrounded by a flooded, disused gravel pit – a large lake with a house in the middle. The three-storey detached house had wooden beams, leaded windows, giant chimneystacks and a beautiful stable courtyard.

On Saturday the 16th of July 1977, we set up the Island Mobile in the courtyard, from where we had easy access to the barn and to the converted stable block. While we were working on the album, Ray Doyle (mobile), Barry Sage (assistant), John Martyn and I all lived in this stable block, which had four bedrooms, a kitchen and a bathroom. There was also a large, self-contained flat at the far end. This we used as our main studio, and I put John, effects pedals, drum machine, amplifiers and guitars in the main 15-by-12 room. I took direct injection feeds from the guitar and after every effects pedal, as well as mic'ing up the amplifier. Ray, Barry and I spent a great deal of time making sure the feeds were as clean as possible. Hutch (an Island Roadie) turned up on his way back from the west country to see Chris, and left a huge PA rig. We set the PA stack up on the far side of the stables pointing out across the lake. I used two Neumann U87s on the opposite side of the house to mic up the outdoor PA sound coming back off the lake. A further two Neumann U87s were placed close to the water's edge, as far away as our leads would allow. These picked up the sound of the water lapping and a distant, "strangled" sound on the guitar, which was perfect for lead guitar solos. We tried to protect the microphones from the damp night air using polythene, with limited success. When they went down on particularly wet nights or because of a heavy dew, we replaced them and then dried out the originals on the Aga. Between 3 a.m. and 6 a.m. was the toughest time on the mics, but these quiet hours before dawn created the most magical atmosphere for recording, resulting in two of our classic masters – the title track, *One World* and my favourite, *Small Hours*.

On the second day, while we were still settling in, Mark Sugden, an old friend and drummer, rang up with a problem. He had an ounce of opium he did not really like. "It keeps making me throw up. Do you want to buy it for £25?" He came over that afternoon and we sat in the sunshine with cups of tea talking over the past. Mark was then 26, about 5 feet 8 inches tall and lightweight, with blonde hair trailing down his back, but cut short and spiky on the top of his head. He had a twinkle in his eye, an infectious laugh, an easy-going personality and natural humour.

Mark's group, 25 Views of Worthing, had been signed to Island Publishing by Lionel Conway in the spring of 1972. Lionel and Muff Winwood, now an Island Records A&R man, wanted me to record four masters with the hope of signing the band to Island. I was busy recording tracks with them in Studio One at Basing Street when Chris returned to London for a visit. He wanted to check any new signings, see how things were running and to listen to all the new tapes. The Worthings were not his kind of music, and during a "night of the long knives" the band was dropped rather suddenly, along with some Island office personnel. One day you almost have a record deal, and the next day you don't.

It took everyone involved some time to get over the loss of the deal, and it probably hit Mark the hardest. I was all too accustomed to projects failing – my success rate averaged about 20 percent. But hey, that was five years ago, and now there were other things to chat about – girlfriends, wives and house repairs. Although there were often huge breaks between the times I saw Mark, I always enjoyed it when we did see each other, and he made me smile. We had a very pleasant couple of hours, and Mark departed close to 5 p.m., leaving the ounce of opium with us.

I informed John of our acquisition and he laughed, took the opium, rolled a joint and opened a bottle of whisky. His actions immediately stamped a particular attitude on the recording of the whole album. Soon, the five of us (John, Chris, Ray, Barry and myself), under John's guidance, were mellow and laid back. John played a cassette of some of the demos on a portable player, and it was not long before we had a good idea of the approach to the songs we were about to put down. Every two or three hours, we would eat a small ball of opium or roll a joint. It was a very enjoyable state, although unfortunately within five days we were all addicted. Waking on the fifth day, we felt slightly hungover, tired, lacking in energy and not really on top of things. After eating a small ball, the body and brain returned to working order and all the wonders of life flooded back.

Feeling like Winnie-the-Pooh with his pots of honey, and unknown to each other at the time, John and I both secretly hid a few small balls of opium in the barn for emergencies and rainy days. During the first six days, whenever we had tea, we had the additional pleasure of a small ball of opium. Chris said he'd always known there would be one drug that was "more interesting" than any other. Towards the end, we went on half rations for a couple of days, but when the supply eventually ran out, we substituted large quantities of grass and hash joints and the occasional hit of brandy. Within two weeks, it was just a memory. I had no contacts for opium normally, and did not try to get any more.

We fell into a routine, starting at about 2 p.m. and working through until 5 a.m. Chris would spend the mornings on the phone, taking care of any business or betting on the horses. Ray and I would check the equipment (especially the outside microphones), line up the tape machines, lie in the sun or row the rubber dinghy out on the lake, taking photographs. It was idyllic.

I used six tracks for the guitar, two for the outdoor returns and two more for vocal and basic drum machine. I had control over the blend of the six main guitar sounds because of our separate DI feeds. These included one feed straight out of John's guitar, another after his compressor, one each post-effects and echoes, and finally one with everything but preamplifier. Some of the songs, like *Dealer* and *Certain Surprise*, were arranged and recorded quickly and easily. Others, such as *One World* and *Small Hours*, were played repeatedly for many hours. Chris and I would then edit the multitrack into an arrangement of verse, chorus and instrumentals, from time to time taking bets on which bar we were on.

Chris had always been a gambler, taking chances on building the studios at Basing Street, the signing of bands, his involvement in different styles of music and his choice of personnel. Over the previous seven years, I had gambled with him on electronic stopwatches, table football, different takes of the same song, bar numbers and – within a few months – I would gamble with my career. But right now, this *One World* album was one of the most exciting projects I had ever worked on – the location was excellent, the sounds were beautiful, the sky was clear and late at night or early in the morning it was truly magical. The outside mics not only picked up the guitar coming back across the lake, but also recorded scurrying animals, birds and the sound of water lapping at the lake's edge. John worked in the self-contained flat, and Ray, Barry, Chris and myself were in the mobile. We changed the reels of tape every half-hour (we were recording at 15 ips) and took breaks every three or four hours for tea.

After seven days, we had six tracks down and took two days off. I drove John back to his house in Heathfield with his guitars. I had first met John back in 1971 at Basing Street. Like Alan Spenner and Paul Kossoff, John was difficult to get to know at first, and would conceal his true feelings with a sharp tongue or within an alcohol-induced haze. John also gave off a strong impression that he could be physically aggressive if pushed, although this may have been self-preservation and merely a bluff, as in the case of Alan Spenner. I liked John and had always got on well with him, never having had any real trouble with his behaviour. He was 5 feet 10 inches tall, then close to 30 years old, with a mass of curly dark hair, a beard and a round, boyish face. He lived in blue jeans, shirt, a scarf tied round his neck and a black jacket or waistcoat. If he was sober and in a good mood, he would be mellow, laid back, charming, inventive, verbally amusing and spiritually alive. When dark, drunk or angry, he managed to reverse all these attributes and could become difficult, aggressive, loud and obnoxious, or alternatively very quiet and depressed.

On Monday the 25th, I picked John and his gear up from his house and we were soon back at Theale ready to record more backing tracks and start overdubs. Lee "Scratch" Perry came out to the house to see Chris, loved what we were doing and hung around for the day. Lee, a highly successful Jamaican record producer, had worked with The Upsetters, The Heptones, Junior Byles, and Bob Marley & The Wailers. Short, stocky and then about 45 years old, Lee was extremely sharp and entertaining. These attributes were topped off by an infectious schoolboy humour. He giggled a lot, reeked of grass and was rarely seen without a half-smoked joint – the old 7-inch baseball bat.

Lee was fascinated by John's effects pedals and thought naming a fuzz box "Big Muff" was hilarious. He could not grasp that it was the manufacturer's product name and not some coarse in-joke of John's. I don't think we ever convinced him otherwise, and he and John, inspired by the effects box, wrote and recorded the track *Big Muff* in a day. Lee's lyrical ideas for the song all had sexual connotations, while John's appeared to be about Muff Winwood and the layout of Basing Street Studios. When working, Lee was wonderful to watch, dancing round the room triggering echoes and phasing effects. We recorded 80 percent of the finished song during that day. After this whirlwind of activity, Lee left and we resumed working with John on his own, with the occasional guest.

Andy Newmark came out for a day and played drums on *Dealer*, *Smiling Stranger*, *Certain Surprise* and *Big Muff*. We set him up in the barn, giving him plenty of drum machine click track in the headphones to help him stay in time with John's original performances. There were only two takes per song from Andy. He was really on form – a wonderful day. I loved the performances from Andy, but was later disappointed to discover that most of his work had been replaced by further overdubs at Basing Street with Bruce Rowland and John Stevens. Only Andy's drums on *Dealer* survived on the finished album. Steve Winwood and Danny Thompson also came out for a couple of days and tried out ideas on most of the songs. They were set up in the self-contained flat with electric piano, Moog and bass. Although we recorded many ideas and parts, we kept only the Moog on *Small Hours* and *Dealer* and the acoustic bass on *Couldn't Love You More* and *Certain Surprise*. Because of the delightful location and the amiable characters involved, everything was light and easy. Well, almost everything.

One morning, John overheard a conversation between Chris and myself. Unbeknown to Chris and I, John was leaning against the outside of the Island Mobile while we were talking. We were discussing our schedule, how much time we could allow for certain overdubs and how we thought John was coping. He could be tricky to handle sometimes, and I had just said so to Chris.

As I stepped out of the mobile, John, who was toying with a small knife, said, "So I'm tricky am I?"

"Pardon?" I said.

"So, still talking about me, eh Phill?" answered John.

"I'm sorry?" I said.

"You and Chris – have you sorted me out, made all the right decisions?"

"No, we're just going over schedules and takes," I said, feeling embarrassed that he had overheard our conversation.

"Well, I'm glad you don't bother asking me. Just talk behind my back," continued John.

"Look John, it's not like that," I said. "We're just sorting out what still needs to be done. Speak to Chris if you're unhappy about anything. Really, it's okay."

The situation was almost humorous, but I could not quite grasp what mood John was in that morning. However, if I was going to be knifed, I wanted it to be about more than schedules and my opinion of John's ability to deal with hard work. "I guess you haven't had your coffee and opium, have you Mr. Martyn? Would you care to join me?" I said in a very "British hospital" voice. "I happen to have a very small piece left that I've hidden in the Space Echo unit."

"You bastard," replied John.

We wandered off and sat in the kitchen for half an hour. I reassured him I was on his side, which was perfectly true. I think he was nervous about having "the boss" controlling his record.

Two small balls, a cup of tea and a joint of grass, and it was all resolved and forgotten. I returned to Chris in the mobile and we started the day's work.

John really should not have been worried or in doubt. We had captured hours of great takes on a number of brilliant songs: the edgy, nervous *Dealer*, the haunting, womb-like throb of *One World*, the dark psychedelia of *Smiling Stranger*, the fresh celebration of *Dancing*, and the magic, hypnotic *Small Hours*. Many of the songs recorded included live mastered vocals from John, who at one moment might be sounding warm, mellow and easily in control, and at the next would travel to a place of uncomfortable darkness, becoming someone obviously on the edge of his emotions. It was going to be a great album.

Then disaster struck for me. Having now recorded most of the album tracks, we had started overdubbing. Quite out of the blue, on the 4th of August, Chris asked me to go to New York to work with Robert Palmer, who was having a tough time trying to record his fourth album. There was not a great deal of information, just that he was not getting sounds he was happy with, there were problems with the band, and he was having difficulty capturing masters. I was very reluctant to leave John's project and I put up various objections.

Chris said, "Look, we're due to finish in a couple of days for a month's break anyway. You've recorded the basic tracks and some of the vocals. I'll finish it at Basing Street with Frank Owen, and you can remix any of the tracks you're not happy with when you get back. It's the perfect time to leave. Besides, Robert really needs you and you know how to give him what he wants. I'll give you a 1 percent royalty for co-production and $5,000 [USD] advance for Robert's album. Phill, you're now much more useful to me in New York than here."

I reluctantly agreed, confirming the proviso that I would be allowed to remix any of John's album tracks on my return if I thought it necessary. We finished as much work as we could with John and two days later, on August the 6th, the Island Mobile was packed up and Ray and Barry drove back to London. I drove John home to Heathfield. Throughout the journey, there was an awkward atmosphere. I was feeling guilty about leaving John's album, and he behaved as though he thought I had a choice in the matter, which of course I didn't.

I flew to New York on the 17th of August and settled into a room on the 47th floor of the Essex House Hotel, near Fifth Avenue. This was my fourth album with Robert, but it turned out to be by far the most arduous one to record. I put this down to the New York session scene, with difficult musicians and excessive charges. When talking to Steve Smith about the "joys" of recording in New York, sometime later, he said, "Ah, the New York session syndrome. Yep, 'I'm going to muscle in, make my money and get out of Dodge.'"

I'm not going to get into details of the personnel or recording process, suffice it to say it was slow, tough and somewhat unrewarding. The most enjoyable time was spent mixing at The Hit Factory. I returned to London in mid-October with a set of 15 ips copies for Chris to listen to. Chris phoned a week later, saying he was not 100 percent happy with the results. He thought we had six great tracks but did not think the track *Let Me Feel Your Thing* could be included due to its sexual content. He wanted to record extra material, and also thought that some of the songs needed to be remixed. He was particularly surprised with our mix of *Every Kinda People* – Robert and I had dropped the drums out on the chorus.

"That's the hook," said Chris. "You can't take the drums out on the hook. Anyway, Robert will be over in a few weeks' time to continue working, as soon as Denise can arrange it all. We'll sort it all out then."

I thought most of his comments were fair judgment, and I looked forward to finishing the album at Basing Street's Studio Two – although I did like our mix of *Every Kinda People*.

On Friday the 11th of November, my son James Rupert Brown was born at Pembury Hospital. Sally had a rough time giving birth and haemorrhaged. Fortunately, everything was quickly sorted out, and she was fine within a couple of days. I was at home for the rest of the month. Sally, Becca (now 2½ years old), James and I had a few weeks to adjust to our new roles.

By the end of November, I was remixing some of John Martyn's album tracks at Basing Street's Studio Two. *One World* had changed from the simplicity of the Theale masters, but it still sounded beautiful.

Towards the middle of December, I received a phone call in Sussex from Chris Blackwell. There were the usual pleasantries and updates, and then he said, "I really wanted to speak to you about the John Martyn deal. As you didn't finish the project, I thought we should adjust things with the deal. And now with Palmer?"

This took me by surprise and I didn't handle it at all well, or get a chance to slowly think things through. All I could remember was that at one moment I was recording John Martyn's *One World* album, which was going well, and the next I was sent to New York to work with Robert Palmer. This turned out to be two long, hard months on a difficult album that was still unfinished. After that, I had mixed and completed John's album. I thought the deal should remain intact.

"Well, I didn't finish it because you sent me to the States to work with Robert," I said. "You know the fight I put up? I really wanted to finish John's album. I know initially you didn't think Robert's album was up to par, but I could only work within the situations that were given to me at the time. I didn't know anything until I arrived in New York, and we made the best of a difficult situation. You heard the tracks in New York when you came to the studio with Grace [Jones] and you liked them. I think we should leave the deal as it is."

For the first time in my life, I stood up to Chris, calling his bluff and sticking to the deal, gambling – possibly not the best move. Finally, he said, "Okay, fine..." and ended the call.

I immediately felt I had made a big mistake by not agreeing with Chris, but still hoped everything would work itself out if given some time. This was not to be. I was paid any monies due for Robert Palmer and John Martyn, and contracts came through for signing – 1 percent royalty on each album. But I was never directly employed by Island Records again.

Over the next few months, I slowly adjusted to this new situation. Obviously, I was a little shocked by the rapid departure and sad to be no longer involved with Island. Only six months earlier, Chris had thanked me for my work on Steve Winwood's album. Now, it appeared I had made a faux pas and pissed Chris off. Although the outcome was not what I had expected, over the next few months I slowly began to feel that I had been right to stand up to Chris for what I thought was fair. Here ended a 10-year relationship, first as assistant (Olympic), house engineer (Island), and then as a freelancer. However, I couldn't be mad at Chris; he had given me a great break in 1970 by employing me as an engineer. Whenever I had come up with the goods and agreed to the Island deals, everything had been fine, but I had failed with Robert's album and gone against Chris on John's deal. It was time for me to step completely out of the Island umbrella, and for Chris and Island to embrace some new engineers. My last album (and session) for Island Records had been mixing John Martyn's *One World*. It's still one of my all-time favourite LPs – especially for atmosphere.

At the beginning of March 1978, I received the following letter from Robert Palmer:

Hi Phill, Sally, Rebecca and James,

Well, as I said, I was home watching the television when the phone rings and Denise (drunk) says how she's looking forward to seeing me the next day and my ticket's ready to pick up at the airport, will I mind sharing a flat with Grace Jones and aren't I bored living in the boring Bahamas (she says she's in the studio at Basing Street, picking the album to pieces with Chris). So I say I thought she said it was boring in the Bahamas and that I have no intention of foregoing my ennui for impractical whims, and what's all this about anyway when "the team" cannot be assembled for a week. Silence. Chris, "Hi, err... a friend of mine just mixed a couple of tracks of yours and they're rather good." "Oh," I say, silence.

Chris: "Well this is what I think you should do. He lives in New York and commutes to Philadelphia, so maybe you should arrange to meet him and see how you get on, with a view to working together and re-cutting some tracks." (Apparently he thinks five are classics and the others disposable.)

"What's his number?"

Two days later I'm in his apartment in the old part of New York. Tom Moulton: disco mix master. Well the man is charming, gifted and gay. He plays the mixes he's done and so are they. Home again. A week later I'm at Sigma Sound Studios in Philadelphia with a five-piece rhythm section, ready to cut "Love Can Run Faster", "Best of Both Worlds", "You Really Got Me" (Kinks tune) and the ballad we'd had a go at previously. Two days later and they're cut - great rhythm section - very flexible and clean and directable. Tom slows and speeds up the proceedings very effectively and I'm inspired. The Brecker Brothers come up for the day to do "You Really Got Me" and overcharge me, but they do a great job and leave with promises. All the overdubs are finished within three days and Tom sets to mixing "You Overwhelm Me" - (he's gone on that one).

His engineer (a Polish/Chinese sweetheart) gets all the sounds set on everything, limiting the guitars and doing lots of things I couldn't keep up with, but certainly coming up with them. Then Tom has a little box with five faders on it, which he puts all the parts through one at a time, following the levels and the ins and outs. When he's satisfied with all the parts he listens through again and makes final adjustments in "update" and then when he's done - voila! - it's done.

Then he takes a cassette, which he listens to in his car while he's commuting and has a disc cut as soon as he gets back to New York. He lives with it for a week or so and then goes back to update (if he has to) and finishes it off. They do sound good. Not homogenised (the ingredients preclude that). So I suppose a fresh ear increases the dynamics. All's well that ends well... well... well... He's going to lengthen "Come Over" (hot) and it should all be ready by the 9th. When there's something to listen to I'll try and get it to you. "Let Me Feel Your Thing" has been censored.

In the meantime, I flew to L.A. for a couple of days to be in the finale of the Sgt. Pepper's film, where I met lots of expatriates, including George Martin who was very nice. It was a Robert Stigwood/Dee Anthony do, so everybody else was very gay. Fascinating. Mostly lots of money and no taste, but I got my Christmas shopping done, exquisitely, on a low budget. My New Year's resolution is not to be so clumsy. So far I haven't spilt a thing.

Try to organise a trip for the four of you between now and May. Happy days. Lots of love from me and Sue and whatever it will be.

Robert

Postscript:

Production credits on the album went to Robert Palmer and Tom Moulton, with "Executive Production by Chris Blackwell and Dave Harper". Dave Harper? I was disappointed that I had not been credited as co-producer on four of the finished songs. Robert had his first real hit from this album with the Andy Fraser song *Every Kinda People*, (with the drums reinstated) reaching the Top 10 in America, but only #53 in the UK. Although this LP helped to achieve a much wider audience for Robert, I never felt it was as good as his previous three albums. I may have been biased by the New York experience.

As for John Martyn's *One World* album, production credits went to Chris Blackwell.

Sadly, Robert Palmer died of a massive heart attack in 2003, aged 53. John Martyn passed away six years later, in 2009.

During Island 50, the Island Records 50th Anniversary celebration in 2009, and at meetings to discuss artists on his (and Tricky's) new record label, Brown Punk, I met up and chatted with Chris Blackwell on a few occasions. As usual, he was laid back, charming and looking great for 72. We got on well and warmly remembered the early years of Island Studios, Basing Street and artists Robert Palmer and John Martyn. "That was the era for running a studio," said Chris. "I always thought you could only succeed with a label if you had a studio too. Crazy days."

Chapter 20. Shakin' Stevens 12 January 1978

On Friday the 2nd of December 1977, John Fenton telephoned me at my house in Sussex and invited me to the theatre. John had been the producer of my first engineering session at Basing Street Studios in 1970, with the band Third World War. (see chapter 5) We had always got on well and developed a good relationship, and although I had not seen him for about four years, we had kept vaguely in touch. John explained that he had been to see the West End show *Elvis!* the previous week and was convinced that the singer, Shakin' Stevens, could be a big star. Stevens played Elvis Presley in his 20s, and P. J. Proby was Elvis in his Las Vegas years.

I met John at his flat in Knightsbridge the following week to go and see the show and catch up on the past. A lot had changed during the past four years, but you would not have known it from John's appearance – that was the same as ever. He still looked like an East End barrow boy, in jeans and T-shirt and no hair. However, his weathered face did give some hint of recent troubles. He still pinned me with the very centre of his eyes, spoke excitedly and took control of the situation. This had always been followed through by his wealth of ideas and opinions, and by a genuine power to make others feel as enthusiastic as he did. Over a cup of tea, he told me his story:

He had had a turbulent psychiatric history from the age of seven and suffered various mild nervous breakdowns during the 1960s. In the early 1970s, both his Seltaeb company and Third World War folded, one after the other, and he found himself in a very bad financial situation. This rebounded into his personal life – he was at the time supporting his second wife and two children. Half of the now disbanded Third World War were living at his Knightsbridge flat, and his wife had finally had enough. She said that having a rock band living in the house made it impossible to bring up two young children properly and left for the country.

As John explained, "It had been rough for weeks, and climaxed after some crazy experience I had coming back from the Isle of Wight with Vivian Stanshall and a piranha fish – but that's another story – and ended up with me chasing her, stark naked, out into the street at 2 a.m. during a thunderstorm, with a long wooden pole. She had attacked me with a piece of the four-poster bed. Two little old ladies wrapped her in a blanket and took her over to her cousin's. Anyway, a divorce was decided on and the lawyers moved in. The fact that her father was Lord Lieutenant of Somerset and a circuit judge at the time did not help to make it an easy ride."

John described how he had dealt with both financial and emotional problems and the resulting stress. It became difficult to deal with day-to-day events, and sleeping was impossible. After a particularly bad 10-day period with little sleep, John went on a three-day bender. This resulted in his apparent drinking of three bottles of brandy and taking 60 Tuinal sleeping pills – all during a 67-hour period. Not surprisingly, he collapsed and was taken, unconscious, to the St. Stephen's Hospital on Fulham Road, where he was pronounced dead on arrival. He was revived (obviously) and connected to a life support machine "with tubes and wires protruding from every orifice" as John put it. "They phoned my wife and said I was dead.

"I lay recovering in a tent for hours. And then, just as I'm regaining consciousness with all the resulting euphoria attached to that, suddenly a zipper comes down the side of the tent and two little blue-pointed heads poke through and say, "'Ere, 'ere, 'ere – you've been a naughty boy. Would you like to make a statement?' So I ripped out all these tubes, knocked one of the policemen unconscious and then was on the other one with my hands 'round his throat. Just as he was turning the same shade of colour as his uniform, I felt a jab in my backside. I woke up in an ambulance with six men in white coats taking me to Banstead Mental Hospital."

John had been "sectioned" under Section 25 of the Mental Health Act. He was certified insane, and spent the next three months locked up, being given a wide variety of treatment, including tranquiliser drugs and six courses of ECT (electroconvulsive therapy). However, he had a wide range of friends and acquaintances, both business and personal, and with their help he managed to create quite a stir. To keep himself "sane" he tried to smuggle out a daily account to friends, directors and producers – "In fact, anyone who would listen or could help me and keep my profile high." He also made circuit diagrams of the ECT machines and broke into the safe, retrieving his and other patients' medical notes, to which he set fire.

"Occasionally, in moments of madness," said John, without a trace of irony, "I even escaped. It was just like... *Cuckoo's Nest*. There were people being murdered in there."

The final straw for Banstead Hospital came when a BBC film crew arrived to film his seventh ECT treatment. He was finally thrown out of the hospital, and then spent many months as an outpatient.

"They'd had enough of me. I have the distinction of probably being the only mental patient who's been thrown out of a mental home while under the certification of insanity."

Over the following years, John became addicted to drugs and alcohol, cleaned up, re-married and sorted out his life. He was now back with renewed energy and ideas and was ready to work. I sat in John's living room, somewhat stunned at this barrage of crazy information, all delivered while chain smoking roll-ups. John talked rapidly and moved about the flat, taking time out to laugh heartily through his congested chest. "God, he's a great character," I thought. "A one-off. Few would have survived... I wonder what the story with the piranha fish was?"

John and I went to see the *Elvis!* musical. The show was excellent, and Shaky was great in the role of the 24-year-old singer. After the performance, John and I went back to his Knightsbridge flat and talked late into the night. The flat had not changed much during the last four years, and there were still books, boxes, amplifiers, papers and tapes scattered liberally throughout the rooms. However, the hallway, which was still papered with news cuttings, headlines and photographs from floor to ceiling, was beginning to show signs of wear.

John suggested that we record an album of old 1950's-style rock 'n' roll numbers with Shaky, "to make the most of the publicity from the *Elvis!* show." We discussed the many ways this could be done, bearing in mind that it must be inexpensive, as there was no record company involvement. It was important to John that the record should capture the high energy of the music and of Shaky's stage performance. After much discussion concerning live gigs verses the studio approach, John and I decided it would be best to try to record the LP in a controlled, "live" environment in order to get the best from Shaky. It was decided to use Studio One at Basing Street and to try and make it feel like a club date by inviting an audience of friends to be there during the recordings. We worked out a budget of £4,000. The money was divided approximately along the following lines: Basing Street Studios recording time, £750; Advision Studios mixing time, £1,000; tape, £750; musicians, £800; food and drink, £400. This left about £250 for equipment hire and any other miscellaneous items. Although there were no fees organized for engineer, arranger, or producer, we planned to take payment in the form of a percentage of the album sales.

Mike Shaw, an old friend of John's and company secretary at Track Records (the record label formed by Chris and Kit Lambert in 1967 to release records by Jimi Hendrix and The Who), personally put up the £4,000 required for the project. It was hoped that when it was completed Track would pick up the album and release it. Track was distributed through Polydor, and due to a previous arrangement owed them two albums. *L.A.M.F.* by The Heartbreakers (with Johnny Thunders) had been the first of these remaining albums to be delivered. We hoped to be the second.

I set up in Basing Street's Studio One at 2 p.m. on December 18th. Being near to Christmas, there was an energised party vibe among the staff. The studio, however, was beginning to show severe signs of wear and tear by late 1977. The brown and cream-coloured surfaces were tatty and the floor was beginning to feel like the old Marquee Club – somewhat sticky underfoot. All the equipment and fittings in the control room had been through seven years of intense hard work and abuse. It was probably time for a facelift.

Drums, bass, guitars, piano and sax were all arranged in a semicircle in front of the control room window. This had become one of my favourite setups in Studio One, and I had used this layout since 1971 with Jeff Beck. I started working with the band at 4 p.m., finding sounds and a balance and sorting out headphones for those who wanted to use them. The band was made up of Ace Skudder and the Sunsets, with the addition of Alan Holmes on sax (from Sounds Incorporated).

At 8 p.m., our invited guests started to arrive. Quite soon, the large studio space was completely filled with the band, equipment, Shaky, an invited audience, tables and chairs and food and drink. The band played through some songs and warmed up while the audience ate, drank and smoked and responded with whoops and applause.

In the control room, John chopped out two lines of coke (this came under "miscellaneous items" in the budget) on the edge of the Helios desk and rolled up a joint. Concealed by the relative darkness of Control Room One, we shared these substances and then moved into action. I put the 3M 24-track into record, and John yelled down the talkback, "Okay guys, we're rolling. Let's go."

The band then played two sets of rock 'n' roll numbers, including all the songs we wanted to record. It was close to the edge and anarchic – the perfect situation for John, who divided his time between the control room, where he would check out the sound of the instruments with me, and the studio where he would "vibe" the band, Shaky and the audience. We changed reels every 30 minutes (about seven songs per reel) and succeeded in recording over 20 songs, including *Justine, Let's Dance, Till I Waltz With You Again, Such a Night* and *So Glad You're Mine*. The band played well and it was a great evening, with everyone working hard to achieve the desired results. The recordings had a small-club feel to them, and I was pleased with the way our ideas had turned into reality. We ended up with enough tracks for two albums.

The next day, we moved our tapes to Advision Studios on Gosfield Street and overdubbed saxophones and some vocals. In the evening, I made quick rough mixes and copies of all the songs, and we took them away over Christmas to have a good listen. Up until this point, everything had been fine and a great deal of fun.

On the 12th of January 1978, we regrouped at Advision and mixed the 12 tracks selected for the album and a couple of alternate versions of songs that might be suitable for singles. All this was achieved in two days. Shaky was worried that certain "sexual sounds" he had made during the vocal performances might upset his mother and wanted them pulled back in the mix. John convinced him (at length) that these sounds were necessary and eventually we left them in and moved on. John and I were both amazed by Shaky's remarks and began to feel he must be lacking in intelligence. I had only met Shakin' Stevens a few weeks before the sessions and since then had spent just three days in the studio with him. I did not really know him. Unlike John, Shaky did not look me in the eye when talking to me, but instead glanced nervously to the floor or to some distant object of intense interest just over my left shoulder. Most of the time he was very quiet and just nodded in agreement, but when his mind was fixed on something he was difficult to divert and had strong opinions on how it should end up. Interestingly, he began to have more to say as the album progressed, and during mixing appeared to be trying slowly to move to the fore. His method of control seemed to waver from being quiet, indecisive and shy, to becoming argumentative – with overly strong ideas and approaches to decision making. My overall impression was that Shaky was a rather strange, naïve "mother's boy" who had just arrived from some small Welsh village. How wrong I was.

During the Christmas break, John had been in touch with Chris Stamp and Track Records. As we had hoped, Chris now agreed to sign Shaky's album to Track Records. This album would now resolve Track's debt to Polydor.

So far, we had all worked for nothing except for a few expenses, but it was agreed that the production team would be paid royalties instead of a fee – John Fenton would receive a 1 percent royalty for producing the album, Alan Holmes would receive a 1 percent royalty as musical director, Mike Shaw (who had put up the £4,000 to make it all possible) would receive a 2 percent royalty and I would receive a royalty of 1 percent as engineer, all of which added up to a 5 percent cut.

By the mid-1980s, it became quite common for record producers to take as much as 4 percent in production royalty – on top of any fee. At the time of Shaky's album, however, 5 percent would have seemed a large number of points to give away. Nevertheless, this arrangement was more than justified by a number of factors. Not only were there no production, engineering and musical director fees at all, but Shaky himself did not have to lay out any money for the album. If the album did not sell, neither Shaky nor the record company would lose anything. But if it did well, everyone would make a little money. Shakin' Stevens agreed to this deal and we had contracts drawn up and signed with Track Records.

John and I were pleased with the results as we went into February 1978. John's idea and plans had worked. We had recorded and mixed the album for a budget of £4,000, contracts were signed giving us a percentage of the album, and we had a dozen or so tracks left in the can (technically owned by Mike Shaw) for a possible future project with Shaky. So far so good.

A few weeks later, Track Records went into liquidation. It seemed hard to imagine that Chris Stamp hadn't known what was coming. Chris left for the States. Our contracts were with Track Records, and although the album was released through Polydor, the company would not pay our royalties or honour the contracts. When we telephoned Polydor to discuss the matter, we were dealt with by lawyers and accountants, who as John said, "Are more interested in what the royalties would be on 10 percent of 90 percent of the retail selling price in British Bechuanaland than they are in our dilemma." Obviously, all was not well.

After 18 months or so with no royalties forthcoming, we contacted Chris Stamp, who was not interested. Neither Polydor Records nor the liquidator of Track Records was interested. If we thought that Shakin' Stevens himself might be sympathetic after our efforts to promote his music, we were again disappointed. Shaky was by now moving away from his old-style rock 'n' roll to being musically middle of the road and did not want to pursue the album. I telephoned John to see what he thought was happening and if he had any ideas on how to resolve the matter.

"Something's gone down," he said. "I'm not sure what it is, but basically no one is really interested in resolving it. It's out of our hands. I'm pissed-off because we could have released it with someone else. Shaky and his manager, Freya Miller, are getting into a new image. It's MOR – and I don't think they want him to be an old rocker anymore."

The four of us – John, Mike, Alan and myself – finally involved lawyers, and from March 1980 until October 1983 they exchanged hundreds of letters and phone calls, running up a considerable bill for us to pay. The lawyers threatened and blamed each other in these expensive letters and continually went round in circles. John telephoned me in May 1983 and said, "We're getting nowhere. I'm sure we'll never resolve the legal details. There are too many people trying to hide too many things. Everyone's pushing the blame around."

At one point, we were offered £100 each as a final, one-off payment, but feeling this was an insult we all refused. No royalties were ever paid, even though we had received a letter from Polydor in September 1981 agreeing to their responsibility. I settled my bills with the lawyers (£3,000) and pulled out of the litigation. I believe the tracks have since been released in other territories.

"I feel rather bitter about the whole thing," said John one day to me on the phone. "I think Mike might have been helped out in other ways, perhaps by The Who, who have always taken care of him since the road crash." (Mike had originally been a roadie for The Who and was involved in a bad crash in the late 1960s.) "He didn't get any of his investment back, and remember, he was company secretary of Track Records at the time. What I'd really like to do though," he went on, "is take out a full-page ad in the music press and have a photo of Mike in his wheelchair holding a cheque for the amount of money he had put in – and just have a caption saying, 'Polydor and Shakin' Stevens, where are you now?'"

In retrospect, it was not an earth-shattering album, but it was good and solid 1950's rock 'n' roll and had been fun to record. There was absolutely no good reason not to pay the percentages as agreed. Track, Polydor and Shaky all made some money from the album. It was one of those projects that, had we been paid, we would probably have forgotten about. Unfortunately, all four of us have bad memories of Shaky's attitude, the thousands of pounds paid to lawyers, and the contracts that proved to be worthless.

By the early 1980s, Shaky had become very successful with many Top 10 novelty hit songs. For me, Shaky will always live up to his name.

Chapter 21. Roxy Music
26 September 1978

It was now more or less 10 years since I had started work in the recording industry, and in many ways, I felt I had reached my first watershed. The previous decade of hard graft, adrenaline rushes, stress, bad diet and drugs had begun to take their toll on me, both physically and mentally. I had frequently worked as many as 120 hours a week, subsisting on fast food, copious cups of tea and various narcotics. The most popular drug had become cocaine. During the previous five years, there had been very few sessions where it was not in abundance.

The years from 1971 to 1978 had been, on the whole, a wonderful time for me, especially the sessions with Tim Rose, Kenny Young, Jeff Beck, Murray Head, Dana Gillespie, Bob Marley & The Wailers, Robert Palmer, Alex Harvey, Steve Winwood and John Martyn. On these sessions, I had been entirely serious about getting good results and trying to concentrate on the job I was there to do, even during times of extreme chaos. Work always came first, and my aim was to allow those around me to relax and enjoy the experience of recording without being dazzled either by technology or by the studio environment.

By the late 1970s, the music business was going through some major changes, most of which I neither welcomed nor felt were necessary. I was becoming disillusioned with the whole music business circus. The principal elements in my disillusionment were the impact of the punk phenomenon and the increasing importance given to the roles of a burgeoning army of accountants, lawyers and A&R men. Perhaps these two factors were not unconnected, at least in part. Many of the exponents of punk had an attitude to business as anarchic as their approach to music, and because of this, some record companies had lost substantial sums of money. Ironically the "revolution" backfired, and the result was that – by the late 1970s and early 1980s – the record companies had total control and the trend was for "manufactured" pop records turned out by heavyweight name producers.

Back in 1978, I was beginning, belatedly, to come to terms with punk, but although I was involved with one or two projects, I soon realized that this type of music was not for me. True, it had swept away some of the pretentious dross that had pervaded the rock and pop music scene at the time, but for me the better-quality music was thrown aside along with the rubbish. The style of bands and musicians I had spent the past 10 years recording and dearly enjoying were now the dinosaurs in this post-punk age, and many of the musicians that I rated highly had simply disappeared from the scene.

Although, ideally, I would have liked a break at this point to rest my brain and body, I still needed to work in order to earn a living, so I continued to look for new projects. In February, after working with Maggie Bell on the theme tune for the television show *Hazell*, I teamed up once again with Andy Mackay (ex-Roxy Music) to co-produce his second solo album, *Resolving Contradictions*. Andy was a thin, 5-feet-10-inch-tall ex-schoolteacher who was friendly, laid back and amusing. Projects with him were always fun. By March, we had put together various plans and budgets for the album, and on the 14th went into Basing Street's Studio One to record a few drum tracks and ideas with Peter van Hooke. Peter was a seasoned and inventive drummer who went on to have success producing Tanita Tikaram's first album, *Ancient Heart*.

A week later, on the 21st of March, I loaded up my Triumph TR4A sports car (bought on the day my son James was born) with the multitrack tapes while Andy filled his Bristol with his equipment, his wife Jane and their two whippets. We drove southwest to Golant and Sawmills Studio on the river Fowey, in Cornwall. Two of the musicians from the disbanded Roxy Music were involved: Phil Manzanera on guitar and Paul Thompson on drums and percussion. In addition, there was Mo Foster on bass and Ray Russell (who had been the *Rock Follies* musical director) on guitar.

Sawmills Studio was in a unique location only accessible by the river Fowey or a two-mile walk along a railway line. I had worked there for the first time with Paul Kossoff and Back Street Crawler three years earlier, in April 1975. We had recorded two tracks for the single *All the Girls are Crazy*. I had positioned Paul's guitar amplifiers outside the studio wall and blasted the surrounding valleys with 400 watts of Marshall, recording the natural echo returns. The studio was run by Tony Cox and Jerry Boys, whom I had known since the Olympic days. Sawmills, as the name implies, had previously been a wood mill and was located in a cove. A writer had lived here in the 1960s when it had acquired the nickname "Cannabis Creek".

We loaded our equipment into a small, outboard-powered boat, and towing a barge laden with the larger items, headed downstream from the small harbour at Golant. We passed many small dinghies, larger cruisers and fishing boats, before meeting some of the large ships that, loaded with china clay, regularly headed down to Plymouth Sound and the English Channel. At 3 mph, we chugged into the creek, which was also only accessible at high tide. We moored the boat and barge at the quayside.

It was incredibly quiet, with just the sound of a few birds and rustling trees. We unloaded our bags and equipment and walked the 50 yards to the large, three-storey building. It all looked very rough-and-ready and supplied only basic living conditions. Many of the upstairs rooms were furnished only with assorted single beds and cushions on the floor. The kitchen had a scruffy, lived-in look, with piles of wood drying by a large AGA stove. There was a small team looking after us and running the studio, including the owner Tony Cox, the engineer and maintenance man Jerry Boys and an assistant named Simon. After a cup of tea, we were shown around.

There was a separate building that housed a small live studio with an even smaller control room. There were additional living quarters in a wooden chalet hidden up the creek amongst trees. This could sleep four people, but the main accommodation was up in the large mill house. On one side, it was enclosed by trees and on the other the creek and the river Fowey. It was a beautiful location and an excellent place to live, regardless of the studio. Tony had been here for the past six years and had become used to bringing all supplies in via the river. This had included the desk, a 24-track tape machine and Hammond organ.

Andy and I achieved a great deal of work in the two weeks we were at Sawmills and returned to London pleased with the way the album was going. We now had drums, bass, guitars, keyboards and saxophones recorded on most of the songs. I went off to work on demos with Murray Head, who having left Island Records, was looking for a new recording deal and wanted my help. Meanwhile, Andy and his wife Jane went to China for a holiday.

On his return from China, Andy and I resumed work on his solo project, recording at Basing Street and Roundhouse Studios. Andy had brought back a vast collection of gongs, cymbals, flutes and unusual percussion instruments from his month in China, and these now became a big part of the overall sound and dynamics of the album.

There was also another short trip to Sawmills for a few more overdubs and a batch of new ideas from Andy, sparked off by his recent trip to China. Again, the sessions were smooth and enjoyable, with many ideas and experiments recorded to tape. We would start recording about midday and then work long into the night. During the days, however, we took many breaks and would walk in the woods, make trips to the local village of Golant or just sit in the Cornish sun.

Having finished recording at Sawmills, we moved back to London and Roundhouse Studios in Chalk Farm. Here, we recorded the final overdubs, little touches, vocals and "top lines". Ray Russell came in and played guitar and worked on brass and string arrangements. There was always plenty of spliff around on Andy's sessions in those days, and we worked in a very pleasant environment.

I had been having many problems with my sinuses over the past year and took this opportunity to go to hospital and have some tests. The diagnosis was a blocked sinus cavity and a polyp, and they would let me know when the necessary operation would be. I went to Paris for a weekend with John Fenton to record his latest project – the band Overdose – in a plastics factory that John had managed to "borrow". It was the usual Fenton mayhem, always feeling close to the edge. For me, Paris is always beautiful and worth visiting, but although we successfully recorded six tracks, I was still in need of regular wages and a proper job.

During the time of making *Resolving Contradictions*, Andy Mackay, Bryan Ferry and the rest of Roxy Music had patched up their differences and decided to reform and record a new LP – *Manifesto*. I was brought in as engineer by the band, who asked me to meet them at Ridge Farm Studio in Surrey. Ridge Farm would eventually become a beautiful residential studio with a swimming pool, state-of-the-art control room and isolated studio booths. However, at this time, it was just a large, empty barn with a collection of basic sound recording equipment at one end. This included an MCI desk (not my favourite), JBL monitors (not my favourite) and a few microphones. I was thankful that these included Neumann U87s, AKG D 12s and Shure SM57s.

The original idea had been that everyone should work in the same room – musicians, equipment and myself. Although this way of working eventually became very appealing to me in the 1990s, with .O.rang, SPA, The Dear Janes and The Throwing Muses, at that time I found the concept of not having a separate control room completely alien. After a half-hearted attempt at getting a sound, I moved the desk, 24-track machine and monitors into a small 6-by-8-foot cupboard at one end of the barn. Now at least I could hear some separation when trying to get a drum sound.

The band was Paul Thompson on drums and humour, Phil Manzanera on guitar and broken leg, Andy Mackay on saxes and whippets, Alan Spenner on bass and mayhem, Bryan Ferry on keyboards, vocals and ego, and newcomer Paul Carrack on piano and caution. Apart from Paul, these were all musicians I had known and worked with before. The band had a large collection of songs, riffs and ideas, so we decided just to set up and play, treating the occasion almost as demo sessions.

I arranged the musicians in a large circle to aid visual communication. Seen left-to-right from my position in the cupboard were Thompson, Spenner, Carrack, Ferry, Manzanera and Mackay. From the 10th to the 21st of August, we recorded a vast array of backing tracks, most of which were done in the form of jams that were further developed later. Some of these ideas were just left as jams, outtakes or "possible", but out of all these recordings we collected at least 10 pieces that we could call master backing tracks. On the 22nd, we went straight into overdubs, editing and repairs to our 10 main songs.

All the band members and I lived and slept in the house – all that is except Bryan, who stayed in a cottage on the grounds and would disappear there for hours at a time – very rock 'n' roll. Bryan was at the peak of his success as a solo artist, having released three albums in the previous few years. During my time working with him, I found that Bryan could be charming and likeable one minute and then difficult and remote the next. There was often friction between Bryan and the other band members, all of whom appeared to get on well with each other. However, Bryan was a star who had dated Jerry Hall, sold millions of pounds worth of albums, and appeared in fashion magazines. Alan Spenner would often start conversations with Bryan by saying, "Male model though you may be..."

Above the "control cupboard" was a large seating area where everyone gathered for playbacks, food and drugs. As usual for the time, there was much use of cocaine on the sessions. This had been the favourite drug on numerous sessions of the preceding years. A friend of Roxy Music's called "The Doctor", a smartly dressed 35-year-old, would turn up two or three times a week at Ridge Farm to deliver supplies, often with several beautiful women in tow. Some of these women would stay for a day or two, watching the proceedings and partying, but others left with "The Doctor". We had afternoon tea brought to the barn at 4 p.m., and all ate at a large, oak table in the main house each evening. Living conditions were very good, and we were well looked after by the team of Frank, Richard and Zoe. We could go horse riding during the day if we desired, and at night there was an old, wood stove sauna in which to relax.

Wonderfully romantic as this may sound, such pleasures were somewhat outweighed by the long recording days, the constant requests for sound and equipment changes and the conditions created by working in a hot and sweaty cupboard. Most irksome of all was having to deal with Bryan, his ego and the E.G. Records management office. Working on Andy's album as co-producer had been an entirely pleasant experience, and I was treated well and respected, but engineering for Roxy Music was very different. Bryan and his management appeared to treat me as they would have treated any lackey engineer.

The date came through for my operation (26th of September) and it fitted in perfectly with Roxy's plans, which were to take two months off and then overdub and mix at Basing Street Studios in November. However, at the beginning of September, the management suddenly changed their plans and suggested we all go to New York without a break and finish it there. I explained that I had an appointment with a scalpel. I was reluctant to change these plans, as I would then have to join the queue all over again. Justifiably, the manager was interested neither in my plight nor in my schedule and offered to pay for the operation privately if I stayed with the project and went to New York to finish the album.

"Oh, just cancel it, Phill. We'll pay for the operation privately when the album is finally finished."

I objected to this feeling of being bought and refused, suggesting they use Rhett Davies if they wanted to continue before November. I wanted to keep to my schedule and have a break after finishing the overdubs at Ridge Farm during the first week of September.

They decided to continue without a break. Rhett accepted the offer to take over and later that month went to New York with Roxy Music, building a relationship with them that would last 20 years. I was pleased with this arrangement and very willing to hand the project on to someone else, having become tired of working on big-name sessions with all the accompanying ego and bullshit.

Robert Palmer now turned up from America to play two dates at the Hammersmith Odeon. He wanted me to record them for a possible live album. I went to Oxford on the 10th of September to see one of Robert's concerts before doing the recordings in London. I wanted to check out the band and see what equipment I would need. We recorded the two concerts at the Hammersmith Odeon on the 12th and 13th of September with my former colleague Ray Doyle and the Island Mobile truck. We mixed on the 19th at Basing Street's Studio Two. Only Robert and I were involved, and I had no communication from any of the staff at Island, with whom I had little to do since the break-up with Chris Blackwell.

On the 25th, there was a reception for Robert at the West Kensington Hilton Hotel. All the usual characters were there, including record company personnel, tour promoters, assorted musicians, wives and girlfriends. The reception, staffed by an army of waitresses, was held in the main function room, which was laid out with tables of food and drink. I spoke to the few people I knew, picked at various food dishes and drank a little red wine. Within a couple of hours, I was ready to leave. I found Robert in order to say goodbye, but instead of leaving I was invited up to his room, where we spent the next hour partying on our own.

The room could have been in any city in the world, with a large, 6-foot square bed, overstocked mini bar, beige carpets and framed prints of the countryside on two walls. Robert played me some of his new demos, told me of life in Nassau and opened a bottle of brandy. We had a great time, talking about the hassles in New York while making the album *Double Fun*, our past glories, his surprise at some of Chris Blackwell's actions towards me earlier in the year and our plans for the future. Robert appeared to be in good form – he was positive and happy and enjoying the current tour. We had a good few brandies, some nice grass and lines of excellent cocaine. As I was no longer involved with Island Records or Chris Blackwell, and now did not work with their artists, this was the last time I saw Robert in a business environment. From then on, it was purely social. Around 2 a.m., I checked into the Communard Hotel in Hammersmith for what was left of the night, and in the morning made my way to the Middlesex Hospital.

Information, blood and various specimens were taken, and I adjusted to the routine of hospital life in a ward of predominantly old men. The next morning, I was prepared for the operation. Having been given a pre-med, I quietly drifted away. The next recollection I have is of finding myself in the operating theatre and hearing disjointed voices.

"Okay, let's stop... the bleeding... get... him upright. Okay... that's good... got to stop... this bleeding."

They pulled me into an upright position and inserted a small balloon into my nose. When it was in the required location, it was gently inflated to help stop the bleeding. It seems that during the previous four years (and probably the previous night in particular), the use of cocaine had worn thin the membrane at the bridge of my nose. This had helped me to haemorrhage. It certainly appeared stupid to me now to have snorted so much cocaine 36 hours before a nose operation where "drilling" would be involved.

I came around on the ward looking, as my visitors John Fenton and Anne Wightman said later that day, "a total mess". There was a collection of bruises across my chest caused by the vigorous treatment I had undergone while on the operating table, and blood still covered my face and hair. After a clean-up, I was visited by a physiotherapist, who explained why I had pains in my chest. "Don't worry, sir," she said, "it's just been caused by them lifting you about during the operation. It should all calm down in a day or two." She banished my fears that I was having a heart attack and I was then given the "all clear". I stayed in hospital on various medications for a week.

Finally, one morning after the doctor's daily round, I was declared fit to go home. The Ward Sister (late 20s, black curly hair, green eyes and the most wonderful smile) gave me the good news, along with a list of dos and don'ts once I was home. When it was finally time to leave, Sister said, "Goodbye Mr. Brown. Now remember, don't do any work or anything really for the next six weeks. Just lie on your back, taking it easy. Oh, and Mr. Brown, I should think about giving your nose a rest." As she said this, she looked straight into my eyes and gave a huge knowing smile, adding, "You really should think about it. Your nose was pretty poorly, from what the surgeon told me."

I was embarrassed and looked away but felt impressed at how she had dealt with the somewhat delicate subject of drug abuse. "Well, thanks again for everything," I said, and left.

I returned to Sussex to rest and generally think about what I really wanted to do, what alternatives there were, ways of moving on and ways of getting out. It would take time to adjust to the idea of having lost various Island relationships and not working again with Robert Palmer, Chris Blackwell, Steve Winwood or directly with any Island Records artists. I had been on a roll for the past five years with wonderful sessions, great musicians, varied studios and the occasional good party. I had come to the end of an era in more ways than one. Gone was the approach, attitude and feel of the '60s and '70s. Gone was the freedom of "we can do anything". Gone was the illusion that my health could survive anything. Also gone were a great many of my favourite musicians, to be replaced by a gathering army of managers, lawyers, accountants, consultants and A&R opinions. I had found the Roxy Music sessions to be a disappointment – not in the case of the musicians themselves, but in the time wasted on egos and bullshit from outside. I wanted that "freshness" again and the feeling of "event".

I decided to take things slowly, look around for bands and musicians with whom I might like to work and to leave the big sessions alone for a while. I was still depending on offers of work to make a living and for long-term survival, but now had enough money to take six months out if necessary.

I started by deciding to go on a clean-up diet, and on Alan Callan's advice, had a consultation with his wife Claire Callan – a reflexologist. I went to her for treatment in November 1978 with a desire to break a mild cocaine addiction and concern for having taken Valium for 10 years. I was put onto a diet of raw salad. I was not allowed alcohol, cocaine, Valium, meat, coffee, tea, eggs, fish, cheese, milk or dope. I managed to give up everything bar the dope. After six months, I felt brilliant and never did go back to meat, Valium or cocaine. Thank you, Claire.

Dave and Phill – The Pictures, 1978

Chapter 22. Paul Carrack
19 March 1980

I tried to do what the Ward Sister at the Middlesex Hospital had said, and spent four weeks taking it easy, resting on the sofa, reading *Initiation* (an autobiographical novel by Elisabeth Haich) and listening to all kinds of music. Initially, having a break from London and the recording process was fine, but by the end of October 1978 I was feeling bored and restless. Although part of me wanted to escape from the music business and the feeling of endless sessions, there was an equally strong side that needed the buzz, excitement and the adrenaline rush of being in the thick of it. As I had not received many telephone calls offering work, I decided to spend some time in London just hanging out. Having not worked since September with Roxy Music, I was anxious to find something for the winter months if possible.

I called in on the crew at Basing Street Studios – I still did the occasional session there and treated the offices as a London base. I found Robert Ash recording basic tracks with The Only Ones in Studio One, while Phil Ault was downstairs in Studio Two mixing some television backing tracks. I spent some time in each studio, catching up on the latest news and gossip, watching and listening to the proceedings and drinking some of the ever-present supply of tea. Not wishing to be in the way, I left after a couple of hours and went around the corner to Alan Spenner's house in St Luke's Road – partly to continue my quest for work, but mainly to see Alan and find out what he was up to.

Alan's residence at 14A St Luke's Road was a detached house, the only one of its kind on the street, with a tall, brick wall surrounding it and a pair of large wooden gates to allow entry. It was a large house with flaking white paint and a battered, scratched front door. I made my way along the path, stepping over a couple of boxes of various empty wine, beer and spirit bottles. The curtains at the bay window (the only room visible downstairs) were, as usual, drawn closed. I could hear the muffled sound of music as I began to bang on the door. After a long while, someone heard, and the front door was opened.

I entered the hallway, where there were stairs off to the left and a circular window set high on the wall. Straight ahead of me was the kitchen, and to the right a door led into a large room about 15 by 24 feet, being two rooms knocked into one. With the combination of the low lighting, stacks of equipment and clouds of blue cigarette smoke, it was difficult to see anything at first. Dimly visible were Alan and what appeared to be most of the members of Kokomo, along with Paul Carrack, who were set up and rehearsing under the name of The Retainers.

I had known Alan Spenner since the days of Olympic Studios in Barnes 13 years earlier, during sessions for Joe Cocker and The Grease Band. He was now about 30 years old with long, dark brown hair and heavy eyebrows. Alan exhibited three-day-old stubble, was chunky (not fat) and had the stance of someone who exercised too little and drank too much. As usual, he was wearing black boots, faded jeans, a T-shirt and thick woollen cardigan, and was standing by his amplifier – bass guitar in one hand and the remains of a roll-your-own cigarette in the other. Alan was a hero of mine, both as a player and as a person. At 20, he had played at the Woodstock Festival with Joe Cocker, later joined Spooky Tooth, and in 1973 had formed Kokomo with another Grease Band member, Neil Hubbard. Over the previous 10 years, Alan and I had worked together with a wide and varied assortment of artists in addition to Joe Cocker – Kenny Young, Murray Head, Robert Palmer, Dana Gillespie, Steve Winwood, Jim Capaldi, Jess Roden, Roxy Music and (of course) Kokomo. Above all, we trusted each other and were good friends.

I sat down on the floor in a corner near to the drums, but out of the way. As the band continued to play through songs and discuss arrangements, I checked out the room. There was little visible floor space, as most of it was covered with equipment, cables, boxes and people. Around the walls, piled almost to the ceiling were flight cases, speaker cabinets, amplifiers, PA systems and cardboard boxes. Pushed into the bay window, there was a Hammond organ and Leslie cabinet littered with coats, bits of clothing and tea mugs. Apart from the equipment and boxes around the walls, there was a Marshall 100-watt amplifier, two Fender Twin Reverb amps, an Ampeg Portaflex amplifier, a Yamaha CP-70 electric piano, an old Moog synth and what looked like bits of broken gear piled up in one corner. A half-buried upright acoustic piano protruded from a vast heap of tied-up newspapers, and there were mic stands, an array of foot pedals and effects boxes, leads, ashtrays and clutter. It was chaos.

The little bit of carpet I could see had several generations of tea and coffee stains on it and two large burns. The room had originally been painted white, but the little of it that was now visible was covered in black scuffs and there were large chips missing from the paintwork around the doors. The only daylight entered through a partly obscured window, four feet above my head. There was a strange, indeterminate smell that was a combination of damp, tobacco, joss sticks, sweat, electrical equipment and curry. I feared there might also be the hint of some dead rodent or half-eaten sandwich trapped behind a speaker cabinet.

As I sat there taking all this in and thinking it was more untidy than usual, I became aware of the band playing and how good it all sounded. Besides Alan on bass, they had Jeff Seopardie on drums, Neil Hubbard on guitar, Mel Collins on sax and Dyan Birch on vocals. I knew all these people well and had worked with them many times during the previous 10 years, with one exception – Paul Carrack, who was playing piano. I had met Paul only recently, during the Roxy Music sessions for *Manifesto* at Ridge Farm – on that occasion he had appeared calm and professional and had spoken very little. Paul was short and stocky with thinning hair, a dark beard and a pair of eyes that looked straight through you. In appearance, he was an ordinary looking bloke who might enjoy an evening down the pub playing darts with a beer and a fag. With hindsight, he looked like a demo for Phil Collins. Besides the band Ace, Paul had played keyboards for Squeeze and Nick Lowe, securing a solid reputation among other musicians. His manner was quiet and detached with little verbal communication, and he appeared just to let things slide along. Sally later said, "On a charm level, he rates zero," but he played well, wrote great songs and had a wonderful voice.

In the environment of Spenner's house with whatever drugs they were on, they were all quiet, calm and reserved. Neil Hubbard, a sweetie and very laid back; Jeff Seopardie, Mr. Cool, an extrovert like all drummers; Mel Collins, "Mellow Mel" – a gentleman, charming, talented and polite; and Paul, withdrawn. And then there was Spenner – a twinkle in his eye and a broad grin on his face, swaying as he played, cigarette in mouth. I loved his playing and his attitude. I was having a great time sitting on the floor and listening to them play, and I spent the remainder of the afternoon and evening there. Later that night, while the band were in the local pub, I helped Brendan Walsh to plug up microphones and assemble an 8-track system for him to record the rehearsals. We converted a small upstairs bedroom into a control room and ran mic cables and foldback leads down the stairs. I borrowed an AKG D12 and D224 from Basing Street and Brendan blagged a couple of mics and headphones from his friend "Mad Pete" in Powis Square.

Brendan Walsh was a typical shady music business survivor. Over the years, he had been a roadie, sound engineer, manager, publisher, promoter and dealer. He was now a 30-year-old wide boy, a cool and relaxed hustler who worked really hard getting projects together for artists and then took his cut. I liked him and found him to be one of the genuine "good guys". I liked his straightforwardness. He had a solid, hands-on attitude to wiring and cables, earths and amplifiers, desks and tape heads, and it all showed – the sound quality of the equipment was very good. The band had an excellent batch of songs, and once they had returned from the pub, they persuaded me to stay and record demos for them at the house. As in the old '40s musicals, it was a case of, "Let's do the show right here."

The musicians had access to varying quantities of hash, grass and cocaine, but due to their unnaturally laid-back manner, I felt there were probably some darker drugs around as well. Alan gave me the wink and invited me into his and Dyan's bedroom. Amongst the chaos of clothes and yet more musical equipment, there were two album covers strewn with bits of cardboard, a pack of Rizla papers and a number of small plastic bags. There was a round mirror lying on the bed on which had been placed two piles of powder, one white (large), one brownish (small), three razor blades and an empty biro. There was also a tube made from a £5 note that was beginning to unroll.

"It's great you could help us out with these recordings," said Alan. "We really appreciate it. By the way, Brown, how's your nose? Repaired? Shall we get rolling?"

There followed three wild days of work, beginning on the 31st of October. I was upstairs in the bedroom with the 8-track recording equipment while a full band stormed away downstairs. We ate little, but did take regular breaks to make tea (sometimes with toast), roll joints and make trips to the pub. By November 2nd, we had recorded, overdubbed and mixed six songs. It was agreed that Brendan would take these demos to various record companies and see what interest he could generate.

I returned home to Sussex, and over the next two weeks received a number of telephone calls offering paid work. During 1979, I spent time at the Marquee, Easy Hire Rehearsal, Basing Street, Wally Heider and the Roundhouse Studios, with a selection of artists including The Movies, Runner, Jim Capaldi, Dire Straits and Bos Tweed. In the meantime, Brendan went around all the record companies with The Retainers' demo tapes.

One of Brendan's meetings was with Dave Bates, the A&R man at Phonogram Records. (By the mid-1990s, Phonogram was part of the Polygram empire, along with A&M, London, Philips, Island, Polydor, Vertigo and others.) During his 20-minute meeting with Dave Bates, Brendan played some of the house demos of The Retainers and discussed "various possibilities". I never found out exactly what he said, or how he achieved it, but Brendan only played two or three tracks to Bates and came away with an album deal. However, it was a solo deal for Paul Carrack. Perhaps Dave's decision was influenced by Paul's track record (writing the single *How Long* and his success with the band Ace) or maybe the situation with The Retainers was not fully explained, or possibly I had just misunderstood the arrangement. For whatever reason, Paul now had a deal. He asked me to co-produce the album and to use the rest of the band – The Retainers – to work with him on the recordings. Although this didn't seem to me to have been the original plan, the band accepted these arrangements and prepared to record the album.

Before this could happen, it was necessary for Paul and myself (as producers) to go to the A&R department of Phonogram Records and have a meeting with Dave Bates. This was duly set up, and we played him three other songs that had been recorded at Alan's house. We discussed budgets, possible studios and the musicians we planned to use. Dave was good-looking – 6 feet tall with dark hair and a boyish face. He was wearing jeans and a blue shirt and sat at a tidy desk with just a few papers piled up at one end and a ReVox B77 stereo tape machine at the other. This tape machine was connected to an impressive sound system.

Dave's attitude was cool and confident, and he had all the record company techno jargon down to a tee. Most of the time, he appeared to be more interested in his own project, The Blitz Brothers, (a band of which he was a member, along with producer Chris Hughes) and played us their new single – twice. I was unused to this kind of meeting and felt ill at ease. Although I was better known as an engineer, I had coproduced various artists (albeit without marked success), including Amazing Blondel, Dana Gillespie, Robert Palmer, Jim Capaldi and Andy Mackay. However, up until now, the majority of these artists had come through Island Records or friends and associates, and although I had assembled budgets, booked musicians and organised studio time, I had been to very few A&R meetings. There was a lot to learn, and the first lesson was, "Dave is in control". I thought him arrogant, egotistical and quite possibly "public school", with a few hang-ups. After 40 minutes, the meeting ended, and as Paul and I were getting ready to leave, "Master" Bates turned to me and said, "So Phill, how do you hear the album? What's it going to sound like?"

This has since become the most common, and (for me) the worst question that can be asked by any A&R person. I've never really worked to a fixed, tried and tested formula, so every album I work on may sound different, even with the same artists. If I had any formula at all in 1979, it had developed naturally over the previous 10 years and would have been made up of a combination of things, including training under Glyn Johns and Keith Grant, knowing studios like Basing Street and Olympic very well, using similar mics on a daily basis and knowing what sounds and performances I might be looking for and how to get them. Most significantly, I had embraced the whole idea of the Island way of working, whereby you captured the band's performance and attitude, and only helped steer the project back on course from time to time if required. My only personal production preferences were for open, warm sounds, with plenty of "air".

All this is very different from knowing beforehand what the finished album would sound like. Dave knew my track record and the musicians involved, (the plan to use the members of Kokomo, plus Tim Renwick on guitar, Andy Newmark on drums, and possibly Richard Bailey, Noel McCalla, Kuma Harada and Martin Drover). The question "How do you hear the album?" seemed even more irrelevant than usual. I felt trapped, but I had to say something. I had been inhibited by the afternoon's antics and was now thrown by this particular question. I was feeling slightly panicked and out of my depth. "Well... it's going to be cool... you know, like laid back, smooth, funk... er... (TING! Inspiration floods into a scrambled brain) Doobie Brothers-ish," I said.

"Oh great," said Dave. "Okay, I'll leave it to you."

I left the office with Brendan and Paul. Turning to Brendan I said, "Well, at least I didn't say 'Man.'"

During 1979, there were many delays and sidetracks, due mainly to the availability of the musicians. We finally started work on Paul's album at RG Jones Studio in Wimbledon on the 5th of November. A year had passed since the initial recording of the demos in Spenner's house. I brought in Alan Callan to help with arrangements and production. The theory was that with Paul in the studio with the band and me in the control room engineering, we could do with another pair of ears on the project. I had recently worked with Alan on an album for the guitarist Bob Weston (ex-Fleetwood Mac). I liked Alan's production ideas and thought his relaxed attitude would be perfect for this project. I also wanted his help in focusing on song arrangements. If anything, this was my one worry and criticism of Paul and the band. They were laid back, great musicians and just grooved, but I sometimes felt they misplaced their priorities and wandered from the plot. I wanted to make the songs as tight and immediate as possible (i.e., commercial) while still capturing the spirit.

Things did not get off to a great start in the studio. Paul didn't appear to get on well with Alan, and the vibe was tense. The second day, on hearing Alan discussing some BBC Radio 4 programme, Paul said, "You're either a cunt or a genius." That threw Alan. It was probably just Paul's dry humour, but on top of everything else this remark helped to worsen an already uncomfortable atmosphere. Apart from this relationship problem, I wasn't happy with the control room's JBL monitors, and it was a hell of a hike for everyone out to Wimbledon each day. After four days and many late-night discussions with Brendan and Paul after sessions, I delivered the news to Alan that he was out. Alan was obviously disappointed with this decision, but he had many years' experience in the business and took it in his stride.

This left just Paul and myself responsible for production. The first decision we made was to move from the studio in Wimbledon to good old Basing Street's Studio Two. Unfortunately, this was not available until January, so we took a break until the New Year. Not all was doom and gloom, however. We had managed to record three master backing tracks from this first week's recording.

At the end of 1979, I was still feeling disillusioned with the music business and now generally fed up. I had worked during the year with Jim Capaldi (in the South of France), Bob Weston, The Pictures, Reg Laws and Dire Straits (all in London). I had also made a trip to Los Angeles, Long Beach and Las Vegas with Steve Smith to record Bos Tweed. However, there had not been any truly special albums or projects to work on.

The sessions were no longer the be-all and end-all of my life (as some earlier ones had been), but they gave me money to live and allowed me to postpone any real decision. Along with the feeling of there being a shortage of talented artists, I was becoming aware of much more interference from the A&R departments. They now appeared to have more say in the overall sound of an album or how they wanted it mixed than ever before. This, fortunately (for them), coincided with the advent of computer-automated mixing and the ability to retain endless alternatives during mixing. Before 1979, I was not really used to this form of input or the speed at which a total winner could become a turkey in the eyes of the record company. Albums I had recorded with The Pictures and Reg Laws were not released (both with Arista Records), and Jim Capaldi's album *Sweet Smell of Success* only just saw the light of day.

Bos Tweed's project was abandoned. Perhaps I was losing my touch. I certainly didn't find work easy anymore.

Worst of all was a personal sadness. Lowell George had died of an accidental overdose while touring his solo album on the East Coast of America back in June. It was another name to add to the list of people I had worked with who were now dead, joining Brian Jones, Jimi Hendrix, Keith Relf, Paul Kossoff, Lou Reisner, Mark Bolan, John Bonham and Sandy Denny. With Lowell George no longer there to inspire, the end of the year also confirmed my feelings: it was finally the end of an era.

With a break for Christmas behind us, Paul and the musicians all gathered at Basing Street's Studio Two on the 17th of January 1980. We worked approximately 15 hours a day, every day, until the end of February. Everything went well, and it was a pleasure working with musicians of this calibre. The studio, however, was in a sad state of repair, having had little done to it for many years, but I knew it well and could usually coax along the old equipment. As usual, I recorded as much as possible live, with everyone heavily screened off and using every available space, including cupboards and passageways. We worked on the songs with two main bands. Richard Bailey on drums, Kuma Harada on bass and Winston Delandro on guitar made up band number one. Andy Newmark on drums, Alan Spenner on bass and Tim Renwick on guitar were band number two. Neil Hubbard and Mel Collins were playing with both groups of musicians. There was nothing special on the technical front – AKG, Beyer, Neumann and Shure microphones and recording to a 24-track analogue tape machine at 30 ips with no noise reduction.

The majority of the songs on the album were love songs. These we arranged with sparse musical instrumentation and were played clean and tight, with a fat, solid bass and crisp, even drums. It was easy adult rock. Hubbard played mainly rhythm guitar with plenty of stabs and "chukkas" and the occasional "lick", while Renwick and Delandro delighted in covering all the lead and solo guitar parts. Mel came up with some great brass arrangements. At times, I thought they were close to being an English version of Little Feat.

We moved to Studio Two at the Roundhouse on the 3rd of March and prepared to mix. The Roundhouse had become my new favourite mixing room, with a Harrison desk, old EMT echo plates, valve compressors and excellent monitoring. Paul's was the sixth project I had mixed there in the past two years.

We finished on the 16th of March, cut the 1/4-inch tape of the album mixes into the running order, accurately timed the songs and made copies. Paul, Brendan and I had spent the greater part of 18 months discussing, planning, recording and mixing this album – now it was finally finished.

The three of us sat down in Dave Bates' office at Phonogram. I was already uneasy and waiting for more bullshit. I handed the 1/4-inch tape copy of the mixes to Dave, who was sitting behind his desk. He laced up his ReVox machine and sat back. On came the first track, *Beauty's Only Skin Deep* – a track we thought was a possible single. Dave listened, eyes closed, sitting back in his chair with his legs resting on the desk and said nothing. Then track two played – *There's a Good Chance*. Halfway through the song, Dave stood up, stopped the ReVox tape machine and looking vaguely in my direction said, "Phill, this doesn't sound anything like the Doobie Brothers."

I was floored and unable to say a thing. It took me awhile to even place the previous conversation about the Doobie Brothers and to realise why Dave had brought them up. I did not work again for Dave Bates for 14 years (two weeks with Robert Plant in 1994).

Paul's album *Nightbird* was released, but with almost no publicity and little radio play for either the LP or the single. I was particularly disappointed with the album's cover artwork. Not surprisingly, it sold few copies and failed. I felt 1980 might be a repeat of 1979.

Paul went on to have moderate success with a Nick Lowe-produced record (*Suburban Voodoo*), and later sang for and had hits with Mike + The Mechanics. Dave Bates was consistently promoted throughout the 1980s, and by the end of the decade he was head of A&R at Phonogram.

Chapter 23. Murray Head – On the Road
10 October 1981

By the spring of 1980, I was beginning to come to terms with the changes that had been going on during the past few years within the music business. I came to the conclusion that – for me – the late 1960s had been a fantastically exciting time as I trained to be an engineer, while the '70s had been a time to realise my ambitions with hard work and wonderful fun – with some of the best sessions and characters. After Dave Bates' negative reaction to Paul Carrack's solo album in March 1980, I was beginning to think that I should take a break from sessions and have a re-think as to whom I wanted to work with, where I wanted to work, and the amount of control I wanted the record company to have. I decided to take time out and follow up some alternative projects of my own. These included Dana Gillespie, David Malin and The Volunteers.

In April 1980, I helped Brendan Walsh move the sound equipment owned by him and Paul Carrack from Alan Spenner's house in St Luke's Road. We set it up in the basement of Screaming Lord Sutch's house, just around the corner in Powis Terrace. Here, we put together a basic 8-track recording studio, with a recording room in the basement and a control room upstairs at the back of the house. Starting in May, we became the "demo kings", recording, overdubbing and mixing songs for artists and bands like Dire Straits (a great version of *Romeo and Juliet*), The Movies, Larry Wallis, Mel Collins, The Volunteers, Steve Swindells, Jonathan Perkins and many, many more. For me, at first, it was fun – a constant challenge with very little real pressure. However, after four months or so, I began to feel as though it was becoming a permanent way of life. It looked as though 1980 was going to be the year of the demo.

By September, I needed a change from making 8-track tapes in a terraced house for 10 hours a day and £5 an hour. Relief came in the form of a phone call from old friend and work colleague,

Murray Head. He asked me to help him organise and rehearse a new touring band, first going to Canada and then moving on to France. He now had a new manager (Michael Deeny), a new record label (Phonogram), and another chance at stardom following recent successes in France and Canada. Although we had had our differences of opinion in the past – the failed *Nigel Lived* album and the unsuccessful attempt at salvaging the Joe South studio time – I still believed in Murray, and unwilling to give up on him, said yes.

The band I assembled with Murray consisted of Trevor Morais on drums (The Peddlers, Björk, Howard Jones), Alan Spenner on bass (Joe Cocker's Grease Band, Kokomo), Alun Davies on guitars (session player, Cat Stevens), Pete Veitch on keyboards (Penguin Cafe Orchestra), Geoffrey Richardson on guitar and viola (Caravan), and Dyan Birch on backing vocals (session singer/Kokomo). I spent a good deal of time back at Murray's flat – Toad Hall – with members of the band, choosing songs and discussing stage ideas. During the weeks of arrangements and rehearsals, I began to feel quite close to the project, and accepted Murray's offer to go on the road and do the front-of-house, live sound mixing.

We rehearsed at SUMA Rehearsal Rooms in Chelsea at the end of September and flew to Canada on the 3rd of October. We planned to use this month of concerts to work the band in and get things tight. We played in the east of Canada, taking in Rimouski, Three Rivers, Montreal and Quebec City. On one occasion, I was able to drive up to Le Studio at Morin Heights, north of Montreal, for an evening with my brother Terry. He was recording yet another Rush album – over a 10-year period, he produced six platinum albums with this band.

During this warm-up month, everything went surprisingly well, and I enjoyed the freedom of mixing for two hours a night in a different venue. If it was a good night for us all, there was much celebration. If it was bad, it was forgotten, and we looked to the next night to get it right. Overall, the tour was a success.

Murray was unsure about a couple of the band members. By the end of the first two weeks, he had felt that Alun Davies did not really have the desired playing style and vibe. Also, while we were on the road, Murray found Dyan Birch difficult to deal with. Then, just before flying back to London in early November, Michael made an announcement, "I'm afraid the French tour is, uh... uh... o... uh... delayed," he stammered. "We'll probably go in January now and take the next two m... m... months off." This was a disappointment, but it did give Murray an opportunity to make changes to the personnel of the band.

During January 1981, we rehearsed for five days at Nomis Studios, West London, and then had a full dress rehearsal on the M Stage at Shepperton Film Studios. Phil Palmer (a session player, later to join Dire Straits) had replaced Alun Davies on guitars and Ginny Clee had replaced Dyan Birch on backing vocals. Ginny became a popular addition in more ways than one, having close encounters with a member of the crew, then one of the band, and allegedly with the manager. Alan Spenner and I referred to her as "Ginny Clee with the silent t," and were not on her list of conquests.

On the 28th of January, we moved to France for a month's tour. We were now using 34 channels of inputs on the desk, including ones for viola, mandolin, accordion and two radio mics for vocals. All the musicians and I travelled in a 35-foot-long Travel Cruiser that belonged to Trevor Morais. This was a left-hand drive American motor caravan, built of fibreglass on a truck chassis with a seven-litre engine. There was a sleeping area for five at the back of the truck and an area with a television and a sound system. There were storage spaces, a toilet and a shower, and towards the front of the cruiser there was a well-equipped kitchen and a seating area that could convert to three more bunks. Next to the driving seat there were two luxurious armchairs. Alan, Trevor and I were licensed and insured to drive the cruiser and took it in turns driving throughout the day and night. Murray's manager, Michael Deeny, was also on board organising the tour and acting as our tour manager, assisted by Tony Wiggins. Murray had his French girlfriend, Diane, with him and Trevor brought Denise, a woman he had met in Montreal in October. In all, there were about 12 of us.

The road crew was made up of Ernis Costasczuk, the backline roadie; Doug Beveridge, the PA engineer; Craig Sherwood, the stage monitor engineer; and Mick Bullock and Lyn Scoffin as lighting engineers. The 12 tons of equipment and five crewmembers travelled in two 6-ton trucks.

Besides the concerts, we recorded a live album over three nights in Clermont-Ferrand, Aix-les-Bains and Lyon, and made a promotional video in Paris. On these occasions, I ran the mobiles and Doug took over the front-of-house PA mix. We crisscrossed France many times during the two months of the tour, often staying in Lyon at the Hotel Frantel. This was on Rue Servient, above the Banque de Lyon. As was usual on the tour, I shared a hotel room with Alan Spenner. This was mainly because I was a friend, knew him well, and was one of the few people who would deal with him when he was drunk or out of it.

Life on the road in France was a new world to me, and reality blurred very quickly. There was alcohol and drug abuse by everyone involved after each show. Alan had arranged for "packets" to be posted out to him twice a week, and because I shared a room with him, I was often offered a small line either 45 minutes before the start of the show or afterwards while we changed our clothes and waited for instructions from Michael as to where we would eat that night. Coming back from one of these restaurants one night with Alan the worse for drink, I was left alone to get him back to the hotel. Everyone else had moved ahead. Alan was very depressed. As we were walking across the Rue de la Caverne bridge high above the town, he suddenly climbed onto the brick parapet and swayed over the streets below, looking as though if he did not jump he would probably fall. For 10 minutes (which seemed like an hour), I talked to him, trying to be normal and calm. Finally, I talked him down to ground level. He gave me a huge hug and we returned to our room and drank the mini bar dry. The episode on the bridge was never mentioned again.

Personal relationships were tested more and more as the tour progressed. Murray began to play distracting mind games on everyone, triggered by stress and cocaine abuse. He would do this nearly every day – before, during and after the concerts, in restaurants and also while traveling, making some of the drives intolerable. Alan was the only one who dealt with it well, and in fact gave the impression of enjoying it, setting up a whole series of games of his own. It became difficult to judge what was truth and what was scam, but because of that there were wonderfully guarded conversations, and we developed a good, if uneasy, humour. Ginny and Geoff became a little scared of Alan, who continually wound them up and then played on the fact that he disturbed them. When not mind-fucking each other up, we watched films on video at the back of the cruiser – Mel Brooks' *The Producers* being the favourite. Trevor, when away from the sound check, concerts and traveling, spent any time left with his girlfriend Denise, finding the chaos not to his liking.

Some nights, we were booked into hotel rooms in the local town; other nights we slept in the cruiser as someone drove us to the next venue. The crew were the real workers in France. They would pack up 12 tons of equipment, load the trucks and drive to the next town, take a few hours' sleep, then unload, set up and be ready for a soundcheck at 4:30 p.m. After the concert, this cycle was repeated. Occasionally, I drove the 6-ton lighting truck to give Lyn Scoffin (the lighting technician) a break and some extra sleep and to give myself some space. I found driving the truck through the night quite an adventure, and enjoyed the few drives that were offered to me.

Murray was plagued by small injuries and colds during the tour and was now having cortisone injections before every show due to a throat infection. Girlfriends and wives turned up at various venues around France, usually with little warning, and added to the game of surprise. We all survived, even if some marriages didn't. Only three couples out of the six were still married three years after the tour. We returned to England on February the 23rd. A week later, on the 2nd of March, we finished and mixed the live album, *Find the Crowd*, at FarmYard Studios.

The touring had been very successful for Murray, with considerable demand for videos, records, television interviews and more live performances. It was decided by Michael Deeny that the band and I would now take a four-month break and then re-group for a longer, three-month tour of France in August. Murray, meanwhile, would follow up with radio interviews and appearances on television.

I had been offered a studio album with Alvin Lee of Ten Years After, and feeling refreshed from the road work, said yes. I then spent three months from April 21st to July 17th with Alvin, working at his home studio in High Wycombe. He had a perfect 24-track studio built in a barn connected to his house. It had a beautiful 1974 Helios desk, Tannoy monitors and basic outboard equipment. I found it a cosy and warm environment, and the sessions started encouragingly well. There was Steve Gould on guitar (also the songwriter), Mickey Feat on bass (I had worked with them both in the band Runner in December 1978), Tom Compton on drums, and Alvin, of course, on guitars.

We worked five-day weeks with weekends off. During the week, I slept in a room in Alvin's house and returned home to Sussex late each Friday night. Alvin and his wife were great hosts and tried to make me feel relaxed and at home. However, in the studio things were very different. There were two opposing views about how best to arrange and record the tracks, with Steve and Mick in one corner and Tom and Alvin, who were old friends, in the other. As the weeks passed, this became distracting, confusing and energy draining. I found myself being drawn in favour of Steve and Mick's ideas, while Alvin appeared to be chasing some long-lost attitude and approach. I slowly lost interest in him and the songs, and finally the whole album. (I have not listened to it since the day of the final mixes.)

Having finished Alvin Lee's *RX5* album, it was refreshing to get back with Murray and some anarchy. We met and rehearsed during the last week in August, before two days at Shepperton Studios with full stage setup on the 4th and 5th of September. Tim Renwick (Aretha Franklin, David Bowie) had replaced Phil Palmer on guitars, and Stan Coles was the new tour manager. Apart from these changes, it was the same band and crew. This was to be round three – a tour of Europe, mainly in France, but with some dates in Italy, Germany and the Netherlands. With the Travel Cruiser serviced and restocked, our wives and children waved us off from Toad Hall and we headed south to Dover. On board was a large box containing T-shirts to sell at the concerts, and 1 pound of sticky black hash (only Trevor knew the location of this item). The journey over on the ferry was pleasant and calm, everyone having had four months of sane living to quieten down and return to some form of normality.

On arrival at Calais, France, we climbed back on board the Cruiser and drove out towards customs. Before we had driven 50 feet, we were flagged down by a customs officer, "Okay, pull up at the entrance on the left," he said to Trevor, through an open window. We pulled into a large hangar. An officer came on board and checked our passports and the vehicle papers, before looking through a few cupboards. When he saw the large cardboard box, he inquired about the contents and did not seem too happy. We had no papers for importing T-shirts and they were immediately confiscated.

Two more officers now came on board and began systematically going through all the boxes, cases and bags. We were all asked to leave the Cruiser and to wait in the customs hall. Tim Renwick was petrified and convinced that we would all be busted. Geoff was also worried and became very quiet. I was pretty numb to it all, feeling somehow protected by being on the road. It was yet another problem for Michael Deeny to resolve.

We were held up for more than two hours before finally being allowed back on board to continue our journey. As we boarded the Travel Cruiser, a customs guard gave each of us a T-shirt. "One each for personal use," he said. Once out of the area and on the open road, Trevor asked me to take over driving while he went back and retrieved the pound of dope. It was hidden in the chemical toilet tanks. So, with a large spliff, we set off for our first town, a few hours behind schedule, but with much celebration. With all the drama and subsequent escape, the four-month break was soon forgotten. We were back on the road.

Again, we crisscrossed France, each time passing through Lyon and staying at the Hotel Frantel. I think the novelty of having a rock band staying at the hotel had worn off long ago for the staff, and we had difficulty getting phone messages, late breakfasts or late-night drinks. Alan and I complained to Michael after one breakfast fiasco, but he would not take us seriously and rejected our views. However, later that day, when an important message from the USA went astray and failed to get through to him in time, he changed his mind and agreed something should be done. It was decided to raid the hotel, and Michael (as the "Big Man") would come up with a master plan. Pete would act as the "Big Man's" assistant.

Michael as the "Big Man" had been the obvious choice for all of us. We had spent many nights listening to Michael recall events and stories from his Irish past. One favourite story was Michael's alleged involvement in a tear gas attack in the House of Commons in the early 1970s. It appears the army was using tear gas in Northern Ireland, and often fired it into domestic houses. This was causing great distress to those people who came into contact with it. After various Westminster politicians had said it was safe and harmless, a decision was taken to show them what it felt like. It was planned to explode a tear gas canister in the confines of the Parliamentary Chamber itself. Michael recruited a terminally ill man to deliver the tear gas, but unfortunately the man died before carrying out the task. A second man was now hired for the attack, and this time all went to plan, with the Irish "delivery man" concealing the canisters in his hollow artificial legs.

As we travelled around France we bought or stole several fire extinguishers (of the powder or foam variety), and during the more boring trips honed our plan to the minute. We made straps to carry the fire extinguishers, discussed what clothes to wear (very important), picked up a street map of Lyon and planned our escape route. Finally, after a triumphant gig at de L'Olympia in Paris on the 15th of September, we made a detour to Lyon so that Pete could time the lifts at the Hotel Frantel. We were ready.

After just a few hours' sleep in the Travel Cruiser, parked outside of town, we got up, had breakfast and collected together the fire extinguishers and masks from various cupboards and storage areas. For extra effect, Murray brought with him the stage gun that fired blanks – at the time none of us considered the dire danger this prop might cause, but later we thought better of it. Making our way to Lyon, we headed the Travel Cruiser towards the hotel. To our surprise, there were police everywhere, and we joked that they had been tipped off and were waiting for us. By the time we reached the hotel, we all realised that the attack would have to be postponed until another day. On each side of the street there was a neat row of guards armed with rifles or machine guns. We drove on past the hotel, out of Lyon and onto the autoroute towards the next venue. Later that day, at soundcheck, we saw a newspaper that carried the story that Prime Minister, Raymond Barre, would be visiting Lyon on the 16th. It appeared he too had chosen to stay at the Hotel Frantel. Undeterred by these events, we made a new date for the raid and a few adjustments to our plan of attack – the first being to lose the gun. The second was to keep up with the local news.

We were scheduled to pass through Lyon in three weeks' time. First, we travelled north and played Amsterdam. Sue (Murray's wife) and Sally joined us here for two nights and for a further three days of the tour. Both the band and the concerts were now very tight and well-polished with a sophisticated stage show. There was a combination of electronic drums, full drum kit and percussion, and an assortment of instruments that included piano, organ, accordion, acoustic guitars, viola and electric guitars. The musicians often had to change instruments very quickly during the two-hour show. One song might require thumb piano, accordion, mandolin and percussion, while another might need electric viola, electric guitars and a full rock setup. These transitions were possible because Geoff and Pete were able to play many different instruments. Murray performed two songs while walking around the concert hall with a radio mic, much to the delight of the audience. All the old favourite songs were there including *Last Days of an Empire*, *Say it Ain't So, Joe* and encores from *Nigel Lived*.

On the 10th of October, we arrived back in Lyon at about 3 p.m. and parked the Travel Cruiser at the Hertz car rental depot near the main railway station. Trevor, Denise, Geoff, Tim and Ginny did not want to be involved, and were left there awaiting our return. I had been nominated to be the getaway driver. Alan, Pete and Murray would be the main attack force, and Michael was still the "Big M-m-m-man". We changed our clothes and left all our identification in the Cruiser before hiring a large black Peugeot saloon. Into this we loaded our bags of extinguishers, clothes and masks and climbed in.

We drove out of the Cours de Verdun and along Quai du Dr Gailleton and Quai Jules Courmont before turning right onto Pont Wilson. None of us noticed, as we passed it, a massive building on the left – the police headquarters. We then entered Rue Servient. I parked the car outside the hotel building and everyone bundled out and collected their bags from the boot. The hotel lobby was on the 10th floor, while the other nine were owned by the Banque de Lyon. Pete, unfortunately still carrying the gun, called the first lift. When it arrived, he switched it off and called the second one. Murray was recognised at this point by one of the bank employees and came back to join me in the car.

Alan, Pete and Michael carried on with the plan and took the lift to the hotel lobby. As they entered the lift with their bags, they looked like any other group of visitors who were about to check in. This was with the possible exception of Alan, who was dressed in a black jumpsuit and looked like a member of the Special Air Service. As the lift ascended, they took the fire extinguishers and masks out of their bags and strapped them on. The doors opened, Pete switched off the lift and all three raiders burst out, spraying the lobby, the counter, and the hotel clerks with white foam and powder. The security guards left, women and children screamed, and the male desk clerk fainted. Two minutes later, as chaos reigned in the reception area, the attack force was back in the lift and coming down the 10 floors. Murray got out of the car and went 'round to the back, opening the doors and the boot and sticking black gaffer tape over the number plates. With everyone in, we moved off rapidly and joined the dual carriageway, heading back towards the railway station.

There were two things I had not really noticed before, or at least not thought through. First, the hotel lobby was on the 10th floor, while the other nine were owned by the Banque de Lyon. At the first opportunity, the hotel had rung the bank, where they immediately hit the panic button. The second point was that the police headquarters was only a mile down the road. As we rattled down the carriageway, the police were going past in the opposite direction, sirens blaring. A third factor then re-entered my head – the French police carry guns.

By mistake we turned off one exit too early. I stopped, Michael leapt out and pulled off the gaffer tape and then he was back in, and we were going again. I was trying to read the map and get directions back to the railway station, while Alan, sitting between

Pete and Murray on the back seat, was reciting one-liners from the film The Producers at the top of his voice:

"Flaunt it baby, flaunt it!" "Let's play the countess and the chauffeur! Watch the road Brown, watch the road!" "I can't take my eyes off you!" "Pull over!" "Next week we could play the Abduction and the Cruel Rape of Lucretia – you can be Lucretia and I'll be Rape." "Don't forget the chequies Michael. Can't produce concerts without chequies!" "Just say oops and get out!" "No way out... No way out... No way out..."

All I knew amongst all this noise and chaos was that we were on the wrong side of the river Saône and having difficulty finding our way back to the station. Michael came to the rescue and stuttered commands at me. Somehow, we managed to compose ourselves, and drove sedately into the Hertz depot, parked the car and removed our bags. Trevor had seen us coming and started the engine of the Travel Cruiser. We climbed on board to much cheering, and within five minutes were cruising down the N6 at 110 kph. It was one hell of a rush – perhaps a bank job next?

By 8 p.m., we were in Auxerre, where Michael treated us to a wonderful meal of seafood and champagne. The chef had a stutter, and at first refused to serve Michael, who he thought was making fun of him. Once he realised Michael had a similar problem, there were drinks on the house and a relaxed atmosphere. Murray's girlfriend Diane joined us there later, bringing with her a video of the raid.

She had checked into the hotel earlier in the day and had recorded the whole thing from the balcony above reception.

The next day we read about it in the papers: "Mystere: Hotel pris d'assaut par Trois inconnus", or "Mystery: Hotel Attacked by Three Unknown".

Chapter 24. Red Box
4 September 1984

Although during the previous two years I had recorded tracks with Dire Straits, Marianne Faithfull and Alvin Lee, most of my time had been spent recording demos at Brendan Walsh's 8-track studio, touring with Murray Head and working with David Malin, and The Volunteers. I had found my niche during the 1970s, but the music scene had changed a lot since then, and I now felt somewhat adrift. I continued to look for creative and as-yet-unsigned artists – enter Harlequins.

We met at the North London Polytechnic (they were all students) in late 1981. I had been asked by a friend of a friend to help them with information as to how to get a recording contract. At the time, the band consisted of Simon Toulson-Clarke on guitar and vocals, Julian Close on sax and vocals, Paddy Talbot on keyboards, Rob Legge on bass and Martin Nickson on drums. I liked all the members of the band immediately, but it was Simon and his songs that I thought had something special. His vocal lines and melodies were strong, commercial and most importantly, memorable.

Over an 18-month period, we worked on demos of several different songs at my house in Sussex, Jacobs Studios in Surrey and The Old Smithy Recording Studios in Worcester. During this period, I had got to know Simon well. He had been Harrow-educated, loved playing football and rugby, read a great deal, enjoyed computer games and had a passion for ocean sailing. He was of solid build and usually wore jeans, T-shirts and pullovers. With his fair hair, blue eyes, fresh look and softly spoken voice, he seemed charming and easy-going.

By the summer of 1983, we finally had five demo tracks that I thought we would have no trouble in getting signed, and I took them to Max Hole (A&R at Warner Brothers Records). I had known Max for 10 years, right back to the start of his own record label, Criminal Records. I had always respected his opinion in the past, and unlike many record company bosses, he listened to music with a keen interest – Little Feat being one of his favourite bands of the '70s. He said he liked the recordings but did not think they were "right for Warner's".

Sometimes, it's hard to know what conclusions to draw from a comment like this. An A&R person who dislikes your tape but wants to avoid hurting your feelings will usually say, "It's good, but it's not for us." It may be hypocrisy, but at least you can walk away retaining some confidence.

Ian Carlile, the manager of the band, was not put off by Max's lack of enthusiasm. He raised £5,000 from a friend in the city, and in September 1983 we went into Regents Park Studios, St John's Wood, to master two songs. We planned to release a single. The two tracks we recorded were *Chenko* and *Valley*. For these recordings, we used additional musicians: Tim Cross on keyboards (Mike Oldfield) and Tim Renwick on guitar (Paul Carrack, Al Stewart, Elton John). With these finished tracks, we were now in a position of some strength and no longer needed to borrow money from a record company to pay for recordings. However, we now required a record company who would be excited enough by our two master tracks to release and distribute them – a one-off singles deal.

Instead of again attempting to deal with a major record company, we approached several small, independent labels, and had our most positive reaction from John Hollingsworth at Cherry Red Records. He loved the songs and the overall sound, and within a week of hearing them agreed to release the tracks. I was extremely pleased that after two years of planning, demos and gigs we would finally be releasing our first Harlequins record. A name change was suggested by John at the last minute – after a discussion this was welcomed by everyone involved and they finally signed as Red Box.

The single *Chenko* received great interest and airplay from BBC Radio 1 DJ Janis Long, and we had a minor chart hit. Over the next few months, Max Hole became interested again, and got back in touch with their manager, Ian. When John Hollingsworth moved from Cherry Red to the A&R department at Warner Brothers, Ian took this as a positive sign and the band signed an album deal with WEA (Warner Brother's parent company) in March 1984.

The night before signing, three of the band – Paddy, Rob and Martin – left, not feeling able to commit themselves for the required five years, and only Simon and Julian signed as Red Box. Such an occurrence is not unusual. Bands frequently disintegrate either just before or soon after signing contracts with a record company. Some musicians become aware for the first time that 100 percent commitment is required of them, some realise that they have other interests that take priority or cannot be set aside, and others cannot face the reality of the rock circus. However, in the case of Red Box, I had had no inkling of any such problems. The band had seemed to be an extremely tight unit, each of them appearing to be fully committed to their music, and I was surprised when three of them decided to pull out at the last moment.

Although the project survived this difficulty, another more serious crisis was to follow, and in retrospect, I wondered if the outcome might have been different if the original, highly motivated five-piece band had stayed together.

We now needed a new band of musicians. I brought in Ginny Clee on vocals and Chris Wyles on drums. Julian introduced us all to Simon Edwards on bass. The follow-up single was to be *Living in Domes*, with the B-side a cover version of the Buffy Saint-Marie song *Saskatchewan*.

We went into Konk Studios on the 2nd of July to record. We laid down a basic drum part on a LinnDrum and put down guide acoustic guitar and vocal tracks. Then, one by one, we overdubbed drums, bass, percussion, guitars, sax, keyboards and more drums. Many friends helped out – Anthony Head and David Malin (singers), Kevin Jarvis (keyboard player and arranger) and Tim Renwick. Like *Chenko*, the A-side, *Living in Domes* was inspired by the plight of the Native Americans, and the lyrics drew heavily from the novels *Touch the Earth* (by T.C. McLuhan) and *Bury My Heart at Wounded Knee* (by Dee Brown).

The backing track was tough and hard with lots of drums, percussion, rhythmic cellos, vocal chants and Indian war cries. When it came time to record the main army of backing vocals, we cleared the studio area of the mound of drums and percussion instruments, positioned a playback monitor under the control room window and plugged in two Neumann U87s back-to-back.

The lyrics were written in large letters on enormous sheets of paper that were attached to the studio walls. This made it easier for our 20 singers to read the words while we recorded. Ginny sang beautifully and suggested a number of great vocal ideas. The day was excellent, with everyone involved having a good time and performing well. "This is better," I thought, as I drove home after the session. "It's what recording is all about – fun, adrenaline and great results."

Tim Cross, the keyboard player on *Chenko*, came in for a day and overdubbed marimbas and strings to *Living in Domes* and a collection of vibes and pipes on *Saskatchewan*.

With the tracks completed, we moved to Trident 2 in Strutton Ground, Westminster, on the 13th to 15th of July to mix. For *Living in Domes* we mixed two 7" versions and a dark-humoured 12". During mixing, some sections were pared down to unaccompanied vocals, which produced a very beautiful effect. Our favourite 7" mix was an edited version of the 12", and this became our master. The B-side, *Saskatchewan* was a gentle 12/8 with big vocals, a hypnotic drum loop and drifting sax. The sessions had been more of an event than work, and everyone involved was excited with the results. We delivered the final mix to Max, who much to my surprise declared the mix of *Living in Domes* to be "too aggressive".

On the 9th and 10th of August, we went back to Trident 2 to remix. We achieved a better mix of *Saskatchewan* – it was more to the point, stripped down and gentle. The vocals were made smaller, and we favoured the pipes and had less sax. We did three different mixes including a 12" version. However, *Living in Domes* was more difficult, as the power (what Max had called aggression) was in the playing and singing. I tried to tone it down by using reverbs, echo and EQ. The chant vocals were placed back in the mix, but I thought this just made it feel weak. Trying to stop the mix taking its natural course was frustrating, and Simon and I fought for hours to try and get what we thought Max wanted – even getting side-tracked into a dance version. After 15 hours, we called it a day and left with four alternative 7" mixes.

The results were again not acceptable to Max.

"I don't think it's a 'world-class' mix," he said to me on the phone a week later. "Let's get Simon, Ian and Julian and have a crisis meeting."

The night before the meeting, Ian, Simon, Julian and I got together to discuss our plan. We all preferred the first mix of *Living in Domes* and the direction in which the band seemed to be going – it was something that had been worked on consistently for the previous three years.

"You know," said Simon, "'...Domes' isn't supposed to be sweet. I mean it has tough lyrical content. It's supposed to be hard. Aggressive, even."

"It's important that we are all solid on this," I said. "If you are going to win long-term, we must stick together. Once the record company gets a foot in the door on discussions about overall sound and mixes, it's all over."

They nodded. "As usual, Phill, we'll listen to you," said Ian with a smile.

The 4th of September 1984 found me sitting in an office at WEA with Simon, Julian and Ian. We were there to have our crisis meeting with Max Hole. At the meeting with Max, I laid out our preferences strongly and clearly – for the mixes, the band's direction and our reluctance to "tone it down". When I had finished, Max turned to the others and said, "So, guys. What do you think?"

Silence.

Max looked at Simon, "So, Simon. What do you think?" I waited for Simon to say something like, "Yes, what Phill said. That just about sums up what we think."

Then, to my disbelief I heard him say, "I don't know Max. What do you think?"

I was stunned, thinking, "What about all the discussions we've had?"

"Would you mind leaving the room, Phill?" said Max.

I left the room, and I was soon to discover, the entire project.

Having been sacked from this project, at first I was hurt, and then very angry. Although it was only really all about a "pop song", at the time it seemed as though we were creating something significant – the climax of three years' work – and I found it difficult to let go. It probably took a couple of years to really accept it. I was annoyed that Simon had not supported me, but with hindsight he always appeared to be slightly in awe of the record companies. With Red Box, it seems he was easily diverted from the original vision, particularly after the departure of Paddy, Rob and Martin. For their part, other interests had taken priority. Martin went to work full-time at Sotheby's and Paddy eventually became the owner of an airline company. Meanwhile, Julian stuck with the project, but if he had an opinion, he kept it to himself.

The two years following my split with Red Box were made harder by my continued friendship with Simon Edwards, Chris Wyles and Ginny Clee, who were still members of the band. They kept me informed of current events – video shoots, newly recorded tracks and new producers. The next Red Box single released, *Lean on Me (Ah-Li-Ayo)* (produced by Chris Hughes, who was managed by Max Hole), was a number two hit. This made Max's decisions look even more right and mine wrong. However, success was short-lived, and both of the albums that were released basically failed.

My relationship with Max Hole was soured from that point on. I did no further work for EastWest or Warner Brothers for nine years. (In 1993, I was brought in by Dave Stewart and Max Hole to remix and finish Nan Vernon's LP, *Manta Ray*, and the Jonathan Perkins *Miss World* album, both for Anxious Records.)

By the early 1990s, Max was promoted to managing director at EastWest Records, Julian Close was successful as an A&R man at EMI Records, and Simon (just one year after leaving WEA as an artist) was "re-hired" as an A&R consultant by Max Hole, for EastWest Records.

In 1993, Simon and I got back together, and along with Alastair Gavin, wrote and recorded an amazing album as SPA.

Chapter 25. Go West
13 March 1986

I survived sessions for the second Go West album, *Dancing on the Couch* for just one day.

Having set up in Studio One at Wessex Studios with Gary Stevenson producing, we were recording drum samples. Gary was large – 6 feet 1 inches tall with a solid build. He was friendly and was fun to work with. During the early 1980s, after running his own demo studio, he had become very successful as a producer. He usually worked with "machines" as opposed to musicians, and owned a Fairlight CMI (Computer Musical Instrument), as well as an E-mu Emulator (two early digital sampling keyboards).

We recorded multiples of six samples of each instrument – snare, tom toms and bass drum – with different tunings, locations, "live" and "dead". Shaun, the assistant engineer, logged each sample. Tony Beard, Go West's road drummer (and ex-Kokomo) was doing the honours. He made this boring task as pleasant as possible.

The process entailed moving the appropriate drum, stool and mics (Sony C-48, Shure SM57 and Neumann U87) to three main locations around the room. Tony would then give a vocal identification by calling out the name of each drum and its tuning and location. He then struck the drum six times at five-second intervals. Then followed a new tuning, vocal identification and more hits of the drum, with Tony trying to keep the strikes as even as possible. This was a far cry from the spontaneous days of Kokomo, or even Go West's first album – recorded in only three weeks at Chipping Norton Studio at a cost of under £35,000.

That first album had been massively successful and had given the band two Top 10 singles with *We Close Our Eyes* and *Call Me*. The live band had consisted of Tony on drums, Graham Edwards on bass, Alan Murphy on guitar, Peter John Vettese on keyboards and Carol Kenyon and Sylvia Mason-James on backing vocals. The band was fronted by two singers – Richard Drummie and Peter Cox. Go West were managed by John Glover, whom I had known since the early 1970s at Island Records, when he had managed the groups Free and Amazing Blondel. I had worked for him many times over the previous 15 years and enjoyed his humorous company. It was John who had recommended and introduced me to Gary Stevenson some months earlier, with recording the second Go West album in mind. As they had not decided where the album would finally be recorded, they willingly accepted my suggestion of Wessex, with its large recording space and excellent facilities.

Wessex Studios had originally been built as a church and was bought and converted into a recording studio by Les Reed and the Thompson brothers in 1965. Les Reed co-wrote many successful songs for '60s artists, including *Delilah* and *It's Not Unusual* for Tom Jones. The studio was later acquired by Chrysalis Records in 1975. Over the years, many influential musicians had recorded at Wessex, including Melanie, The Moody Blues, Frankie Vaughn, Alan Price, Leo Sayer, The Four Tops, Queen, Connie Francis, The Pretenders, Stevie Wonder, King Crimson, The Sex Pistols, The Clash, and Pete Townshend.

Bill Price was the studio manager and chief engineer at Wessex, Stuart Stawman and Dietmar Schillinger were engineers, Kevin and Shaun were assistants (tape ops), Richard Hill was on maintenance and Joyce Moore was the studio booker. In reality, Joyce ran the place (she would become my manager upon leaving Wessex in 1988).

Betty Edwards made tea and cleaned. Betty had started working at Wessex in 1967 after she had seen a note pinned to a tree in Highbury New Park that read, "Tea lady and cleaner required. Could be same person. Phone 359 0051." She would work at Wessex until the sale of the studio in September 1993 – a total of 28 years.

There was a great deal of recording equipment at Wessex that had been collected through the '60s, '70s and '80s. This included a 48-channel SSL computerised desk, a Mitsubishi 32-track digital tape machine, two Studer A800 24-track analogue machines, Eventide and AMS outboard equipment, an assortment of old valve microphones, EMT echo plates, spring reverbs, UREI and Neve compressors, and monitors including Tannoy, UREI Time-Align and Yamaha. I felt very comfortable working at Wessex, and it became a good replacement for my previous "home" at Island's Basing Street Studios. During 1985 and '86, I had worked here with Virginia Astley, King, T.V. Smith and now Go West.

After 12 hours, we had well over 1,000 possible samples and at least three very bored people in Shaun, Tony and myself. "Okay," said Gary. "Time to fire up the Fairlight." Gary then entered a basic rhythm pattern from the keyboard, along with the "best" 60 drum samples. Gary turned to me and said, "Okay Phill, now let's choose the snare we'll use on the album."

I left the project at that point. Gary's approach to the recording was anathema to me. I was used to hearing a whole kit of drums and making them work as a unit, and I always found it very difficult to separate a kit into bass drum, snare, toms, hi-hat and such. Getting a great snare or bass drum sound individually was not enough – I wanted to know if they would all work together. From my experience, if one had a big bass drum sound and a great snare sound with wonderful tom toms, it did not automatically mean one would end up with a great drum sound – in fact, often the exact opposite would happen. Over the previous 18 years, I had often worked with drum machines, tape loops, sound effects and samples, but always in addition to a live musician's feel, performance and vibe. This planned approach really wasn't my preferred way of working. I knew I wasn't the right man for the job and did not relish the thought of spending the next few months "painting by numbers".

The album was recorded and mixed by John Gallen at Puk Recording Studios (in Denmark) and finished six months later. At the beginning of August, I was working with Robert Hart – another John Glover-managed artist – at Gary Stevenson's home studio in Stoke Poges, Buckinghamshire. We were recording eight tracks for an American television show. Gary arrived one night on a brief break from Puk with a DAT copy of rough mixes of the new Go West album. The first song was played, and it sounded amazing – beautifully clean, with an excellent top end and a truly massive sound. I was very impressed and listened carefully, all the time trying to remember that this was just a rough mix. I tried to analyse what made up this great sound and wondered how I might achieve such a result myself. The second track was equally impressive in its sound structure, but by the time I was halfway through listening to song number three, I began to have doubts about this incredible sound. Although John Gallen had done a wonderful job, to me it did not sound "real", despite the inclusion of "live" keyboards, bass, sax, percussion and guitar.

Coincidentally, in the previous year of 1985, Talk Talk released the highly successful *Colour of Spring*, which became one of my all-time favourite albums. This also made some use of the Fairlight CMI and machine-controlled percussion, but Talk Talk made considerable efforts to make the drums sound "real" by using a selection of samples for each drum sound, and introducing minor "mistakes" in the sounds, e.g., rim-shots and missed hits.

Perhaps the sound of the second Go West album was just too good. Although it cost three or four times as much as their debut album, *Dancing on the Couch* was far less successful. Meanwhile, for the next six months, I continued to have difficulty finding the right projects to work on. The 1980s were difficult.

That is, until I met Tim Friese-Greene.

Chapter 26. Talk Talk
5 September 1986

On the afternoon of the 5th of September 1986, I walked into Wessex Sound Studios in Highbury to collect tape copies of the single *Hand of Fate* by Paul Roberts (ex-Sniff 'n' the Tears). I had spent the previous two days in Studio One mixing a 7" and a 12" version, but due to a line up problem with one of the stereo machines, I had been unable to take a finished copy home with me at the end of the session.

As Stuart Stawman, the studio engineer, went off to find my now completed copies, I wandered into Studio One and found engineer Dietmar Schillinger setting up microphones for a session. Tim Friese-Greene was also there, sitting in the corner playing the Bösendorfer piano and smoking a Silk Cut cigarette. He was wearing dark grey trousers and a faded green sweatshirt. With his large, gangly, 6-foot-3-inch frame, black hair and huge bushy eyebrows, he reminded me of some 1930s movie gangster. I had not seen him since April 1982 at Battery Studios when we had briefly worked together on an album for Tight Fit – a "manufactured" pop band of the time that enjoyed brief success with their single of *The Lion Sleeps Tonight*.

Tim would take whatever he was working on very seriously and this applied to the Tight Fit sessions. He would spend a great deal of time working on sounds, arrangements and getting everything "just right". In contrast, I could not take the sessions seriously at all and had wondered what I was doing working with this band and their leader, a non-singing male model. I was also uncomfortable at Battery Studios, where there were constant interruptions from the office staff and management. After four days, Tim and I agreed that it was not really working and that I should leave the project, after which he would continue with one of the house engineers. There were no hard feelings between us, and we parted on good terms – I thought of him as a gentleman and a genuine guy. Now, four and a half years later, we had met by chance at Wessex Studios. Tim and I chatted for a while and I congratulated him on the Talk Talk album, *Colour of Spring*. "That's the kind of band I'd love to work with," I said. "The vocals, melodies, rhythms – they've got the lot. Great album." Stuart brought in my tape copies, and I left Tim to his session.

Two months later, at the beginning of November, Tim rang me at home. He asked me if I was serious about wanting to work with Talk Talk and whether I would come and meet Mark Hollis.

On the 6th of November, I drove to Tim's house in Stanmore just north of London, and over a pint and a ploughman's in the local pub, I spent two hours with him and Mark Hollis. Mark was about 5 feet 9 inches tall – thin with an angular face and shoulder-length, light brown hair. He was dressed in jeans and a white shirt. He looked like a very regular guy, polite and softly spoken, with a sardonic humour that I warmed to immediately. We sat in the pub and covered many topics, including football, hair loss, my days at Island and Olympic and the current music business scene. Through all our chatter, there was no mention at all of Talk Talk or their plans. As I got up to leave, Mark said, "Are you going back into London? Could you give me a lift?"

As we headed back into town, I was now just a driver. It was 4:30 p.m. and the evening rush hour was beginning to get under way. I was no longer at a job interview, my defences were down, and I was relaxed and off guard. We chattered away, discussing kids, cars and various hideous politicians. As I dropped Mark off at a convenient tube station, he asked me, "What's your strongest overall memory of the Olympic days?"

I answered immediately, "Oh... it has to be 1 a.m., November 1967."

"Who was that with?" he asked.

"Traffic."

Without further comment, Mark smiled and shut the car door.

I drove off thinking about Mark and recalling memories of the 17th of November 1967. It was my second week at Olympic Studios and my first all-night rock session, recording overdubs on the song *Heaven Is in Your Mind* for Traffic's debut album, *Mr. Fantasy*. The drugged atmosphere, the large collection of people and the dim lighting had stuck in my mind. Whenever I thought of Olympic, Jimmy Miller and 1967, I always remembered this

Traffic session. By 5:30 p.m. I was back in town to set up for rehearsals and pre-production for the Paul Roberts album, *Kettle Drum Blues*. This was due to start at the end of November.

About a month after my visit to Stanmore, I received a telephone call from Tim Friese-Greene.

"The new Talk Talk album is due to start sometime in May next year," he said, "and the guys would love to have you on board. I'll ring you in the new year with an update."

I was really pleased with this news, as 1986 had been a tough year for me with little work and emotional chaos. I had been working at various markets, selling Indian gear – trying to make some money.

On the 11th of May 1987, we all met at Wessex's Studio One – Tim Friese-Greene on keyboards and production; Mark Hollis on guitar, keyboards and vocal; Lee Harris on drums and Paul Webb on bass. The band liked to make recording an event, not just another session, and succeeded in creating a unique environment. They brought in their own lighting, which consisted of a 1960s oil projector, a strobe and four sound-activated, flashing disco lights.

We placed the strobe in the studio and housed it in a clear plastic dustbin to try and eliminate the clicking noise as it switched on and off. Particular care was taken when setting up the oil projector, which was positioned in the control room so that it shone over the desk, the monitors, and onto the ceiling. Joss sticks were lit and left burning in the studio, hallways and control room. Once the atmosphere had been organised, we set up the equipment and microphones.

The drums were placed in a booth near the microphone cupboard and screened off to avoid as much leakage as possible. Lee arranged the disco lights around the drums to give him his own personal light show. Mark's guitar amplifier – an original Vox AC30 – was positioned along the far wall of the studio and placed at the beginning of a long "corridor" made of screens. The microphones were positioned at the other end. I constructed a roof out of screens and a large double mattress to reduce the sound leakage in the corridor to a minimum. (I had seen Pete Townshend use this setup with The Who on *Quadrophenia*.) The keyboards were arranged in a cluster in the middle of the room, and with this basic setup we were ready to begin recording. Apart from the lighting, this was a fairly usual setup and gave away nothing of the extraordinary events to come.

Perhaps due to the comment I had made during my conversation with Mark back in November, we approached the album as if it was night-time in 1967. I used no Dolby noise reduction, and we confined ourselves to equipment and microphones that were around prior to 1967 – Neumann U67, Neumann U48, Shure SM57 and AKG C12a. The musical equipment included a Hammond organ, a piano, two harmoniums and the Vox AC30 amplifier. The few exceptions to our 1967 "time frame" included a Neumann KU 100 "dummy head" binaural stereo microphone, a set of contact mics for Lee's drums, and a Mitsubishi 32-track digital tape machine.

Otherwise, we used relatively old-fashioned equipment where possible. The lighting created an atmosphere that could only be described as psychedelic. This was fun at first, being quite relaxing, and I was blissfully unaware that we would spend most of the following year in this almost total darkness. We all disliked the sound of the Solid State Logic (SSL) console and tried bypassing it whenever possible. We hired Neve and Focusrite mic preamps and EQ units and plugged our mics directly into these instead of the SSL. We only used the SSL as a monitor desk for our returns from the Studer A800 and the Mitsubishi and to feed headphones, monitors, etc.

In our dark cocoon, we settled in to work. Lee started proceedings by playing a selected rhythm hypnotically for many hours, only stopping occasionally to hand-roll a cigarette or to adjust his lighting. As we recorded the drums, sometimes Mark and Tim would play along on guitar and keyboards. These performances from Mark and Tim were treated as guides and were replaced later once the drums were mastered. We worked five-day weeks (Monday to Friday) from 11 a.m. to midnight during May, June and July. I drove back and forth to Sussex every day. Work was carried out in almost total darkness, except for the oil projector in the control room, the strobe and three Anglepoise lamps in the studio. This had a very strange affect upon our sense of time. As we arrived at 11 a.m., the lighting would be adjusted, and the day would begin. Within an hour or two, it was difficult to tell whether we had been working for two or 12 hours. "Was it 2 p.m. or 10 p.m.?" Our studio environment felt so completely isolated that we rarely even thought about what might be going on in the world outside. Slowly, I began to find the extreme concentration coupled with the strange lighting and atmosphere emotionally and physically draining. It reminded me of the Stomu Yamashta sessions for the *Go* album 10 years earlier in 1976.

Over a three-month period, we worked patiently, slowly layering instruments and refining arrangements. Paradoxically, I found the music, the intense atmosphere and the extreme lighting conditions created both a tranquil and an agitated state of mind, sometimes almost simultaneously. I loved what we were doing – the raw sounds and textured layers of instruments – but I felt somehow removed from proceedings, while at the same time right inside the sound. It was all-encompassing and dreamlike. I had never before been so absorbed by a sound or a way of working as with these sessions.

Once we had the backing tracks recorded for the six songs (working titles: *Modell*, *Camel*, *Maureen*, *Norm*, *Inheritance*, *Snow in Berlin* and *Eric*), we made safety copies and transferred our 24-track analogue masters to the Mitsubishi digital 32-track machine. We recorded them in the desired running order of the album and left approximately two minutes of clean tape between each song on side one. These gaps would be used later to record an intro and two "link" sections. We began to build up our songs, adding electric guitars, Dobro, acoustic 12-string guitar, piano, harmoniums, Hammond and percussion. Great care was taken over sounds and approach, and many hours simply disappeared. After many weeks had passed, we finally took a break.

Almost three months later, on the 19th of October, just after the hurricane of the 16th, we resumed at Wessex's Studio One for overdubs. I moved into a rented flat in Stamford Hill to avoid traveling three hours a day through difficult road conditions.

On the first day of recording, Mark arrived and after tea and toast said, "I'm happy with all our backing tracks except one – *Maureen*. I think the feel of the track is great and just what I was looking for, but ideally it should be down a semitone in pitch. Is it possible to take it down? I don't want the tempo to change." Tim and I sat there quietly, thinking through the options available to us. With the technology available at the time, these options were sadly limited, and we both reached the same conclusion.

"Digital detuning with a harmoniser is the only real choice if we are to keep the speed unchanged," said Tim.

"Well, can I leave it with you?" said Mark. "See what you can do." He put on his coat. "I'm just going up to see a game." Mark spent the afternoon at Highbury football ground watching Arsenal play, taking Shaun the assistant with him.

The task Mark left us with was far from simple. The studio was equipped with an AMS dmx15-80 digital delay/harmoniser, which enabled the pitch to be changed without affecting the tempo. Unfortunately, when we tried using this machine, it constantly generated digital errors, so Tim rented a more sophisticated version. Track by track, we detuned and re-recorded the main instruments to clean tape on the Mitsubishi digital machine. This was asking a great deal from the harmoniser, and it did not handle certain instruments well. The machine also generated digital errors, so we ended up having to stop, rewind and drop-in every five or six seconds on all our relevant tracks.

Tim and I took it in turns with the record button, as neither of us could continue for more than 20 minutes at a time. By 11 p.m., we had had more than enough and called it a day, resuming our task on the following morning. From time-to-time, Mark would call into the studio to see how we were getting on, but most of the time he was wise enough to stay away. At last, after three days of intense concentration, we finished detuning the instruments. I made safety copies and slaves, and once again we were ready to overdub.

First to be worked on were our link sections with a woodwind quartet. These were arranged by Tim and Mark using a Variophon – an early-1980s German-designed instrument that was played by blowing down a mouthpiece while holding down the relevant note on a mini keyboard. It can be heard on a number of Talk Talk recordings, notably on *The Colour of Spring*. There were five different sounds that could be selected, including flute and sax.

We preferred working with one of the sax sounds – nicknamed "Chris Wood" by Tim (Chris Wood had been the sax player with Traffic). The quartet recordings went very smoothly, and within three days we were finished with the link sections.

We now moved into overdubs on a grand scale, slowly building up parts and textures. Over the next three months, an army of musicians came and played. Most of these overdubs we later erased, through no fault of the players, who included David Rhodes and Bernie Holland on guitars and Larry Klein on electric bass. Among the few who survived on tape were Nigel Kennedy on violin, Danny Thompson on acoustic bass, Simon Edwards on guitarrón (Mexican bass), Mark Feltham on harmonica, Robbie McIntosh on guitar, Martin Ditcham on percussion, Henry Lowther on trumpet and Hugh Davies, who brought in his homemade instruments called Shozygs (these consisted of springs, egg slicers and metal rods connected to batteries that would give off sounds when moved towards each other, at times generating sounds similar to the Ondes Martenot or Theremin). We would record eight tracks of our guest musician and then mix down the best bits to a master track on the Mitsubishi.

Sometimes, out of all eight tracks over a nine-minute song – a possible maximum of 72 minutes – all we ended up with were a few seconds of music. These individual notes or clusters were duly bounced to our master track, and then the next musician was brought in to record another eight tracks. Some musicians were treated to the full length of side one, some 22 minutes. Recording the eight tracks would take about three and a half hours. We would then spend two days sorting out the performances and mixing down.

It was a slow process.

On one occasion, Tim had just finished playing a guitar part. Before we stopped recording, he put the guitar on its stand to come into the control room for a playback. As he took his first step, he caught the lead with his foot and the guitar, which was still plugged in and crashed to the floor, giving off a grand explosive sound. After the playback, we erased the guitar part but kept the accidental explosion at the end, moving it to a more desired location in the song.

The name of each instrument was not always written clearly on the track sheets – some took on nicknames or names that gave an impression of the overall effect. On *Eden* (working title *Maureen*) there were "Sea Life", "Smykes", "Beach Boys" and "Martin's Grannie". On *Desire* (working title *Eric*) we had "El Gringo" and "Chris Wood". On *I Believe in You* (working title *Snow in Berlin*) there were "Stilts", "Gringo", "Blobs" and "Brief Encounter".

At the beginning of December, we recorded a 25-member adult choir for *I Believe in You*. I thought it sounded absolutely beautiful, but the next day Mark, after listening to a playback, said, "It sounds too good – like The Cliff Adams Singers. Can you erase it?" It took me a few minutes to grasp the joke about Cliff Adams and then to realise he was serious about losing the choir. I copied it to a slave reel we had for "ideas" (just in case he changed his mind) and then erased the original. Because it was nearly Christmas, we could not get another choir until the middle of January. Later, we re-recorded the parts with six 12-year-old boys (the Choir of Chelmsford Cathedral).

On Friday the 18th of December, we packed up, went to our prospective homes and prepared for Christmas. For me, this two-week break went by in a blur, and by January 4th we were back at Wessex working on the final overdubs before mixing. One evening I had suggested that bowed guitar would sound good on the instrumental section of *Snow in Berlin*. "Okay then," said Mark, "here's a bow and a guitar. Go do it."

"But I don't know how to play," I said.

"It's easy," said Mark, "and you've had 20 years of watching musicians. Just move your hands around like everyone else. It's all chance."

I was set up in the studio with headphones, a cello bow, Mark's Rickenbacker Country Gent guitar and the strobe light. "Okay," said Tim, "here it comes." The tape rolled. I played. After three takes, Tim said he had enough, and I should take a break while he mixed down the "surviving" notes. Half an hour later, I was listening to my cluster of bowed guitar notes and feeling great warmth towards Mark for allowing me the opportunity to be included on his album. It was the last overdub – we were ready to mix.

I used few effects during mixing – just an ancient spring reverb (found in an old rack at Wessex), an EMT echo plate and a digital delay. The majority of the sounds were kept as we had recorded them. By the middle of February, it was complete.

Tim and I mastered *Spirit of Eden* at Abbey Road on the 11th of March 1988. We had finished seven months' work, spread over an 11-month period. The album was delivered to the A&R man at EMI Records, Nick Gatfield, who it is rumoured broke down in tears. One thing is certain – he was disappointed with *Spirit of Eden*. I think he was expecting *Colour of Spring* – Part Two, and not an album sounding as if it had been recorded in the late 1960s. There was no track that was an obvious single, and the dark, non-commercial nature of the album was not going to help airplay or sales. The album was put on hold.

Sometime later, I heard a rumour that EMI had sued Talk Talk on the grounds of "Technical Incompetence" in the production of *Spirit of Eden*. I was stunned. A wave of paranoia briefly overtook me – "Technical Incompetence" sounded as though some blame might be attached to me as the engineer of the album. However, it soon became clear that EMI were referring to a get-out clause in the recording contract ("technically acceptable") to support their claim. They resented spending such a lot of money on what they thought was a non-commercial album – it was not radio-friendly and had no three-minute track to release as a single.

Initially EMI won, but the court judgment was overturned on appeal. Tim, with his usual discretion, did not tell me about the case until the appeal stage, and I appreciated that very much. After winning the case, Talk Talk left EMI and moved to Polydor Records. The important "get-out clause" was now changed by most record companies to "commercially satisfactory".

Spirit of Eden was finally released on EMI Records and went on to sell over 500,000 copies. It was cited as influential by many new indie bands and appeared in many magazines as one of the "all-time top 100 albums." Over the past 30 years, I have received more offers of work from this album than any other I have worked on – including Bob Marley or Dido's *No Angel*, which has sold 16 million copies.

Shaun, the assistant, resigned his job the day after we finished mixing – left the business and moved to the West Country.

And finally, I arrived home... Sally said, "If you ever work with that band again, you move out."

Postscript:

It took me over 20 years to find out that we were not sued by EMI for 'technical incompetence'. It was just Tim and Mark's perverse humour – again. Talk Talk sued EMI because they missed their renewal date for further albums. Keith took this opportunity to sue EMI and get out of any future deals.

After *Spirit of Eden,* 1988

Chapter 27. Talk Talk
11 February 1991

My second project for Talk Talk – the album *Laughing Stock* – began at noon on Saturday the 22nd of September 1990, back at Wessex's Studio One. During the previous three and a half years since the completion of *Spirit of Eden*, I had worked with Tim Friese-Greene on an album for Brian Kennedy (*The Great War of Words*) and we had generally kept in touch. However, this was not the case with the other members. I had not spoken to Mark, Paul or Lee since the day we packed up our belongings and left Wessex in February 1988. It therefore came as a surprise to find that Paul was no longer with the band.

As Tim, Mark and I sat in Control Room One and discussed our immediate plans, Lee, Darren (the studio assistant) and a roadie unpacked flight cases and set up equipment. Lee again assembled the oil projector in Control Room One and lit incense in and around the studio (he said this time it was to eliminate the smell of cat's piss). Within an hour of arriving, it felt like old times, and there was an easy atmosphere. After the last album, I felt a little apprehensive, but I thought I knew what was in store.

"I'd like to move the sound on from Spirit of Eden and perhaps not use the Neumann head or contact mics on the drums this time," said Tim. "Instead, maybe we could try out some valve mics – what do you think? There are no demos so I can't play you anything. But at least we won't be chasing the past. I'll just set up this keyboard and Variophon by the desk, and then we should probably make a list of any hire gear, mics, etcetera, that we might need. Okay with you?"

"Yes to everything," I answered. "How long do you think the album will take?"

"Oh, about five months," said Tim. "We can't possibly take as long as we did with ... *Eden*."

This turned out to be a bit of an underestimation.

I joined Lee and Darren in the studio and helped to arrange the ever-increasing mound of equipment that was now beginning to cover the studio floor. I retrieved the entire Wessex collection of valve microphones from the mic cupboard – two Neumann U48s and three AKG C12As – and plugged them in to allow them to warm up. We rolled the Bösendorfer piano out of the way against the far wall, as we planned to use Mark's baby grand instead. I couldn't make final placements for the instruments until we had decided on a location for the drums. Lee was still unpacking snare drums, cymbals and hi-hats, but was making some progress. Having finally set up the drum kit, we moved it to every possible location in the large studio (with a capacity of 80 musicians) to check out what affect this would have on the sound. We hired a collection of valve mics from Dreamhire, including Telefunken U47, Neumann U48, M49 and an AKG "The Tube". These, along with the old Wessex collection, were carefully listened to before we decided on the rented Telefunken U47. We worked on the positioning of the drums for four days and eventually settled on the sound of the kit when placed near the far wall opposite the control room window.

The usual rock arrangement when mic'ing up drums consists of about 10 microphones, all close to the kit – bass drum, snare, hi-hat, tom-toms, overheads, ambient, etc. On *Spirit of Eden*, we had used about six – the Neumann head, contact microphones, bass drum and snare mics. This time, however, we placed our single U47 mic 28 feet away from the kit near the control room window. This microphone broke on day three, but was miraculously repaired by the Wessex maintenance man, Richard Hill, using parts from a Neumann U48. Our solitary drum mic became a hybrid of the Telefunken U47 and the Neumann U48.

Having decided on a position for Lee's drums, we could now find a place for Tim and Mark. Tim was set up with DI boxes on his Korg synthesiser and Yamaha CP-70 piano about 10 feet away from Lee. Mark's guitar amplifiers were this time put in the old vocal booth (which was now a mic store) to eliminate any leakage of the guitar parts onto other microphones. Mic'ing up the drum kit at such a great distance created a delay of between 26 and 33 milliseconds depending on the temperature and humidity of the studio, so I set up close mics to feed the headphones. The close microphones on the bass drum and snare, along with the keyboards and guitar, all had to be delayed between 26 and 33 milliseconds to bring them in sync with the main drum mic (this delay had to be checked daily). Lee, Tim and Mark were all on different headphone sends with wildly differing mixes. Mark's mix was dry and upfront, Tim's was spacey with a large amount of reverb and Lee's was mainly drums with just a little dry guitar and keyboards. They were all fed the close drum mics, most of which I was not recording. I only recorded the distant U47/U48 and snare (Shure SM57) and bass drum (AKG D 12). We had already created a relatively involved setup just to be able to record the drum kit – mainly from the single microphone. However, this was just the beginning, and more complications were to follow.

The studio was now more or less free from unwanted flight cases and equipment, allowing us to make full use of the large, open space at Wessex. The keyboards – comprising piano, two harmoniums, Hammond, Korg and CP-70 – were all arranged down the middle of the studio. This still left plenty of room for guitar setups, bass, percussion and any last-minute guest musician. I started to make detailed recalls, having learnt how useful they had been during the recording of *Spirit of Eden*. Darren made a note of the serial number of each mic and measured every instrument setup minutely – from three locations. Often when we were happy with a sound, we would leave it all set and go back to another instrument that had already been prepared. This was to help us keep as fresh an attitude to the performance as possible. We were again working on SSL and tried very hard not to use EQ, preferring to change mics and positioning rather than to boost some missing frequency. The sound in the room was all-important. As there was a "hump" in the room's sound at Wessex, we usually took out frequencies around 190 or 200 Hz.

After a few weeks, we developed a routine. This was to choose a drum pattern and then for Lee to play it continuously for 12 hours, day after day, until we "found" a master that would satisfy both Tim and Mark (Lee appeared to have very little say in the process). We worked with a Studer A800 24-track machine with Dolby SR at 30 ips to make editing easier. Each reel lasted for 16 minutes, but because the songs were unusually long, one reel contained only one or two takes, and soon we had 48 reels of 2-inch tape stacked up. We were constantly listening to takes and would erase any that we felt had no chance. At this stage, only Mark appeared to know exactly what the desired result was. As with *Spirit of Eden*, we worked in almost complete darkness, with an oil projector in the control room and the odd red light in the studio. Later, during overdubbing, when we had a guest musician or were looking for "that special vibe", we brought out the strobe. Most musicians said nothing about this eccentric lighting technique, except for Martin Ditcham when recording a shaker. He eventually asked for the strobe to be turned off, as it was flashing at a completely different tempo to that of the track and making life very difficult for him.

Tim's and Mark's interest in playing along to Lee's drumming waned within a week or two and both preferred to be in the control room because, as Mark had said, "The control room is the only place I can really hear what's happening without my ears going numb. Those cans are fucked." Sometimes, Mark played along on a guitar plugged into a DI box in the control room, and Tim would place weights on individual keys on the organ to give Lee some form of musical atmosphere, but most of the time it was just Lee drumming away. We occasionally used Martin Ditcham to play along as a human metronome, and he would spend many days sitting in the dark, in the mic cupboard, playing a shaker at 60 bpm.

We started with *Ascension Day*. After approximately six days, we "captured" it – our first master. The kit was now set up for *After the Flood* with a different snare and a different cymbal. Because we were using just one microphone, it was important that the kit worked within itself for each song, so changes had to be made. The next day, we recorded both the album and the 7" versions of this song. We were rolling!

Then, just as we seemed to be making some real progress, we got bogged down with two tracks – *Swabi* and *New Grass*. Everything suddenly ground to a halt. During the following three weeks, we tried every possible combination of musicians, instruments and recording methods – Lee with Tim and Mark, Lee with Mark, Lee on his own, Lee with Martin, Lee with click track, and half Lee/half drum machine. At one point, we had an unbelievable 21 reels of "possible" or "hold" (as a reference) takes of *Swabi*. A couple of times, we started to overdub on a version of *Swabi* only to abort the track some days later and go back to Lee and more drum takes. We listened to them countless times before throwing them all out. It was tough on everyone, especially Lee, who developed a stress-related illness similar to flu and was often away sick in bed for whole weeks at a time. For a period of some 17 days, we would arrive at 11 a.m., get a cup of tea from Betty, turn on the oil projector, turn out the lights and play back the previous night's takes of *Swabi*. By 4 p.m., we had usually decided which takes to keep and which to erase and Lee would be back at the drums, head bent low, nodding, as we recorded more versions.

With Tim and Mark being such perfectionists – each in his own way – it sometimes took hours, even days, to get a sound they were happy with. Once, we took five days to get a guitar sound, with Mark simply playing the same two chords over and over again at very high volume on the AC 30 amplifier. He was trying to recreate a sound he had captured one night at his home. After a day or two, the guitarist with a band that was mixing in Studio Two (Calum MacColl of The Bible) telephoned on the studio intercom to say he had learnt the part now and was willing to help out if we were "having problems". Mark smiled wryly and went back to his two chords and the job in hand, much to the dismay of the Wessex staff, who said they were finding the "noise" difficult to take.

The setup was permanent, with leads and mic stands taped down. We had a lock out at Wessex until further notice. As recording progressed, I built up pages of recalls, with information concerning each instrument on each take of each song. My theory was that if I logged the type of mic, its exact location and any amplifier or equipment settings, the same setup could be recreated when and if required. I made full use of the 48 channels available to me on the SSL desk with its highly efficient patchbay. Once we had a master, I would make safety and slave copies (five slaves per song) on another 24-track Studer. Each tape was striped with SMPTE time code on track 24. This was to enable us to synchronise and lock other machines to our master reels.

Whenever Lee took a break from drums, Tim and Mark would record ideas with guitar and piano to the backing tracks. Sometimes, they would try out ideas or arrangements by playing along to click tracks. Sorting out these click tracks and making a note of the length of each section took up a good deal of time. Most of the songs were 9 to 12 minutes long, but the length of each verse, bridge, chorus, etc. was not decided at this point. The songs were being constructed in the studio, and often our approach was an immediate reaction to the previous overdub, or the instrument being recorded.

Lee came back from one of his weeks off and cut some more drum tracks, but at the end of November Mark called a halt and decided to work on the tracks we had already succeeded in recording. These were *Myrrhman*, *Ascension Day*, *After the Flood*, *Taphead*, *New Grass* and *Runeii*. These became the six songs for the album, and we also had a 7" version of *After the Flood*. *Swabi* was left unconquered.

Tim and Mark now required a calm, uninterrupted atmosphere conducive to intense concentration, so Lee and Darren (the assistant) were requested to stay away from the control room as much as possible. This upset both of them. They spent many hours in the pool room upstairs above Control Room One, killing time until they were needed for recording, setting up or for recall purposes. With the backing tracks now recorded, Tim, Mark and I settled down to five months of overdubs, editing, offsetting and fly-ins.

Until this point, I had been renting various flats around Highbury, in North London. Not only was this costing anything from £65 to £200 a week, but it was also very unsatisfactory not having the privacy of my own place to come home to. I decided that I would probably get more out of my time off and in the long run save money if I bought my own flat. Within a few weeks, I moved into 13 Balfour Road, right opposite Wessex Sound Studios. This was a great improvement. I now had a few home comforts, privacy and space, although I was concerned about taking on a mortgage at 13.5 percent.

Life settled into a daily routine, working from 11 a.m. until midnight or 1 a.m., Friday to Tuesday. Wednesday and Thursday became our weekend. On working days, we had our supper on our laps in the control room – either curry or pizza. We rarely took breaks, although there was a daily ritual at 6 p.m. when Mark would have a pint of Guinness, usually at the studio, although sometimes he would walk up the road to The White House pub, nicknamed by Mark "The Shite House". I would often take this opportunity to slip up to see Richard in maintenance and roll a small joint. It helped to make the job of sitting still and listening to the same track for hours on end a little easier.

We hated interruptions or outside noise. Due to our mics being wide open, we picked up every noise around the building – children in the school playground opposite, Bill Price mixing in Studio Two, Betty making tea or people playing pool upstairs. We got very little help from Bill and the staff at Wessex on this matter, who were beginning to think we were all very weird. I feel this was mainly due to our withdrawn state and lack of conversation or small talk. At one point, Bill even offered me "therapy".

Simon Edwards came in and recorded most of the bass parts, using a wide collection of instruments including five-string, fretless and guitarrón – the Mexican acoustic bass used on *Spirit of Eden*. By Christmas, Mark had recorded 70 percent of the main guitars, and Tim was almost finished with the keyboards. All was going well. However, although the daily work was not difficult to handle, the combination of sitting in the dark in front of a desk full of red LEDs with the oil projector turning round at half a revolution per minute began to affect my state of mind. Added to this, there were many days when we took a section of a song that lasted for just a few seconds and played it repeatedly for many hours.

I find it very difficult to describe the "space" that we all travelled to during the making of this album. The combination of continuous darkness, the oil projector (which made everything I looked at appear to move) and the process of listening to the same six songs over and over again, put me in a very dark emotional state. I think Tim and Mark were there too, but each to a different degree. The result was less and less communication, and the three of us often went for hours without talking or looking each other in the eye. After *Spirit of Eden*, I had thought I was fully prepared for their approach and had even told Sally in June 1990, "Oh, don't worry. I know what I'm in for this time. It won't be another ...*Eden*." But I had moved out anyway.

Each night, I would go back to the flat and sit up until 3 or 4 a.m. watching crap television, drinking brandy, smoking dope and occasionally writing to old friends. It was an isolated existence, and I felt very cut off from the outside world. I began to find dealing with anyone from outside the team of Mark, Tim, Lee and Darren very difficult. This applied to my own family and home life. I found their noise and their orderly, planned lives very difficult to adjust to during my few visits home.

We stopped work for two weeks at Christmas. This was the first break for three months. I tried to go shopping in Wood Green on two occasions but had to pass and go home – I could not deal with the crowds, the light or the noise. Sally, who had not wanted me to work on another Talk Talk album, just got on with her life, putting up with the situation as best she could.

On getting back to work in January, we found that Mark had changed the arrangements of two of the songs. The first alteration would involve an edit to cut out a section of a chorus on the track *Ascension Day*. This was relatively easy. I took all the additional information, now digitally recorded on Mitsubishi 32-track, and copied it back to our master and slave analogue tapes (editing a digital tape with a razor blade is not to be recommended). I then cut down our chorus on the analogue copies, re-striped the tapes with SMPTE time code and made new safety and slave copies and a new Mitsubishi digital master.

The other change was more difficult, as it required the adding of 35 seconds to lengthen a verse in *After the Flood*. I copied the analogue master up to the required verse onto a new Mitsubishi digital tape. Then, by offsetting the 24-track analogue master machine, and using different information from our slave tapes, we dropped into the new Mitsubishi digital master – drums, bass, guitar and piano – and lengthened our verse. The next step was to remove the offset from the 24-track analogue master and slave tapes and drop-in the remainder of the song. Once this was all completed and checked, I made new slave and safety copies. It took a couple of days to do all this and get set up again, ready to overdub. The first Gulf War started, but no one talked about it. Life carried on as before.

Unlike *Spirit of Eden*, Mark and Tim wanted to record as much of the instrumentation as possible themselves and not rely on a stream of visiting session musicians. Also, as nothing was planned and we were playing by the rules of chance, accident and coincidence, we needed to try out almost every idea and combination of sounds before we knew we had the right part or texture. We started working with the five slave copies per song – one slave each for vocals, strings and woodwind, percussion, storage and a current one for new ideas. These were in addition to our 48-track analogue and Mitsubishi master reels. Things could get crazy, with a possible 175 tracks per song to make use of.

Our list of recalls was now 2 inches thick and each song had its own file – this would hold track sheets, microphones used (location and angle), compressors, amplifier settings, Hammond drawbar positions, room temperature and all other relevant information. We continued to overdub more and more instruments and textures, including harmoniums, pianos, guitars, cellos, violas, double bass, percussion, harmonica, melodica, drums, water heater, boiling kettle, Hammond organ and Variophon. There was also sampling, looping, offsetting, and the odd backwards effects. When working this way, it is very difficult to know when a song was actually finished. We still worked by recording eight tracks of our desired overdub and then mixing the best bits down to a master track on the Mitsubishi.

On *Spirit of Eden*, I had played bowed guitar on the instrumental section of *I Believe in You*. Now, Mark asked me to guest on *After the Flood*, my favourite track on this album. This time, I was given a cello to play. After rolling a joint and turning on the strobe, I held the cello like a guitar and played through the song, plucking the strings. As the track finished, Tim's voice entered the cans from some distant land and said, "Try keeping only to the high notes. I'll send it again." Two more takes and 20 minutes later, I was told to take a break while Tim and Mark selected their favourite bits. I sat in the studio listening to the track on headphones and tried to savour the feeling of what it felt like to be on that side of the glass. When I entered the control room an hour and a half later, Mark said, in his usual sarcastic humour, "Listen to this, you bastard. You've got the best lick on the album."

By the end of February 1991, we started on the vocals and final overdubs, and although exactly what these were going to consist of was unknown at this point, we all felt we were "getting there" – at last.

During March, the projector was moved next door to Studio Two and we started mixing. Initially, the projector was set to revolve in the opposite direction but was put back to "normal" (clockwise) after four hours, because we all found it too disturbing. The way we worked was still inconsistent, in that while one song might take only six hours to mix, another would take three days. *New Grass* took 11 days to mix. The process of mixing and concentrating acutely to minute details for 12 or 15 hours is very draining. To try and achieve this level of efficiency, day after day, for that amount of time felt like pure insanity to me. I felt drained mentally and my energy level was extremely low. I have never listened to *New Grass* since the mastering session at Abbey Road.

In spite of all this, by April 10th, we had a CD and a vinyl version of the album (in typically perverse Talk Talk fashion, the vinyl version was longer) and sent it over to our A&R man and managing director at Polydor, David Munns, while we finished off the 7" version of *After the Flood*. We had used 50 reels of 2-inch tape, nine reels of Mitsubishi digital tape (20 miles of tape), 10 DAT cassettes and 18 computer discs. We had spent 1,700 hours over eight months recording, editing, re-recording, overdubbing, offsetting and mixing six songs. The result was Talk Talk's fifth album, *Laughing Stock*. It was finished! It was stunning! It was not commercial, but instead had a dark, Pink Floyd/Beach Boys feel done '90s-style.

Curiously, despite all the time spent with every last musical and technical detail, the album sounded to me as fresh and spontaneous as five guys playing live in a room. Over the next three years, I would meet many musicians and fans and would receive letters from a wide assortment of people, all of whom had been inspired by this album. I felt it was one of the best pieces of work I had ever been involved with and I am still very proud of this album.

During the mix of the 7" version of *After the Flood*, we had a phone call from David Munns at Polydor. Mark took the call and repeated David's thoughts to us: "I can't stay in the same room as that album."

On the afternoon of Tuesday the 30th of April, after we had mixed a 7" version of *After the Flood*, and a couple of album remixes, the Talk Talk sessions finally came to an end, and we all departed to our respective homes. Tim and Mark loaded their vehicles with their harmoniums, guitars and amplifiers and drove to Suffolk. Lee headed back to his house in Stamford Hill with his vast collection of drums and cymbals, and I packed up my mics, speakers and safety copies and drove to Sussex. After eight months of almost constant work, we just stopped. At the end of most albums, especially one that had taken so long to record, there would usually be a studio playback for the record company. At the very least, there would be a quiet drink for those involved. Instead, we just packed everything up and left.

That evening, I settled Sally, Becca and James in front of my 12" Tannoy speakers and turned out all the lights. "I just want 40 minutes of your time to play you what I have been up to for the past year," I said. "Please listen. Questions will be asked later." I then played them the whole of *Laughing Stock* at a moderately loud volume. Nobody said a word. When it was finished, Sally turned on the lights, and life continued as before. She made no comment on the album and never listened to it again.

Over the next few months, more rumours and comments filtered through from the record company. For some unknown reason Polydor believed that the title *Laughing Stock* was directly aimed at them, i.e., that Polydor was a laughing stock for signing Talk Talk and releasing an un-commercial LP. Paranoia? Not understanding Mark's new direction, Polydor later stated that they believed the previous album, *Spirit of Eden*, had been made to enable Talk Talk to be released from their previous contract with EMI. Much later, in 1997, we discovered that the album *Laughing Stock* had been deleted in the UK a few months after its initial release.

In the aftermath of *Laughing Stock*, there were divorces, breakdowns and retirement.

Lee put all his energy into Hypersanity, later to become .O.rang. (see chapter 29).

Tim withdrew from the music business for a number of years, returning only to release his own "home" albums (as Heligoland) and the occasional string arrangement.

Darren left Wessex Sound Studios (just as Shaun had before), abandoned his desire to become an engineer, and went to work for FX Rentals, the hire company.

Mark took a four-year sabbatical, re-emerging in 1995/6 with a solo project and more grief from Polydor. See chapter 32.

Chapter 28. Alan Spenner
28 July 1991

I found adjusting to family life in Sussex very hard as I tried to come to terms with not working with Talk Talk anymore. Although the days with Talk Talk had ended up being difficult, it was now very strange not to be getting up and going to Wessex Sound Studios, turning on the oil projector, turning out the lights and listening to one of the six songs. After finishing *Spirit of Eden*, I had spiralled down into a bout of depression that had lasted for many weeks. Now, on finishing *Laughing Stock*, a similar situation arose.

I felt emotionally numb, drained of energy, shell-shocked and unable to relax. Conversations with Sally were difficult, and I could not deal with the hectic lifestyles of Becca and James, who were then 17 and 14-years-old, respectively. I returned to the flat in Balfour Road and spent the following three months in a somewhat hermit-like existence. I spent many days just sitting on the floor drinking, smoking, listening to music and watching television. I was now "rolling" to obliterate, not to inspire. I did not want to feel a thing.

Around 11 a.m. on Thursday the 1st of August, the telephone rang at the flat. A quiet and gentle voice said, "Yeah... Hi, Phill... It's Neil Hubbard... I... I've got some bad news to tell you... Alan has died. Dy [Alan Spenner's wife, Dyan Birch] wanted me to phone you." Alan Spenner had died sitting in a chair at his house on the morning of Sunday the 28th of July. I couldn't answer. "I'll ring you later with more details, funeral, etc.," added Neil. "I'm sorry to be the one..."

I hung up the phone and sat down on the floor. "No Spenner. Not now, you bastard. All the times you were close to death in France, with Richie Hayward and the brushes with smack, you got through all that – what happened? SPENNER!"

I drew the curtains, lit a couple of candles and rolled a joint. Then I put on Steve Winwood's track *Vacant Chair*, with the chorus "Only the dead weep for the dead" – LOUD. Spenner had played bass on this track at Chipping Norton Studios in late 1976. I was feeling lost even before this particular piece of news arrived. I spent the day sitting on the floor, talking to and thinking of Alan. What a waste. He had been one of my favourite bass players and during periods over the past 20 years, a very good friend. The last few years had been hard for Alan, and having lost all confidence he had stopped playing bass and left the music business. I was angry, mainly with myself for not having been in touch just three weeks earlier when I had been making a copy of old Kokomo tapes for my neighbour, Liz. I had thought of ringing Alan then and driving out to Essex, but as usual I put it off. Now I regretted it. I had wanted to see him for a good chat and to discuss *Laughing Stock* with him – Alan would have understood the experience I had gone through.

Alan was cremated on the 7th of August. A large assortment of friends and work colleagues turned up – Steve O'Rourke from Pink Floyd's office, David Enthoven from E.G., Brendan Walsh, Paul Carrack, Tony O'Malley, Mel Collins, and Neil Hubbard and Chris Stainton from the old Grease Band. As we all waited outside the chapel for the hearse to arrive, there was an uncomfortable silence. A great many people were wearing dark glasses, and everyone just stood around, staring into space, and looking numb. Some, red-eyed from hours of crying or drinking – or both – looked at their watches nervously. Alan was 10 minutes late. This was nothing new, as anyone who had worked with him had found out almost immediately.

Alan was always late. Late by minutes was normal, late by hours not unusual. On one occasion in the mid-1970s, after being consistently late for 11 a.m. starts, he burst into a session at Basing Street at 10:59 a.m., bass in hand, uttering the words, "See, you bastards. I can be early." He was, in fact, a complete day early – 24 hours too early. He went home and arrived the next day at 1:30 p.m.

Now, from the silence, Dy's voice echoed round the gathering. "COME ON SPENNER!" For a few seconds, a ripple of laughter rang through the awaiting crowd before the gloom and numbness returned. I had heard Dy yell that a thousand times – backstage at Kokomo gigs, touring in Canada with Murray Head, trying to get him out of a studio control room to do another take, or trying to get him out of a toilet before he did another line.

Finally, the hearse arrived and the service commenced. I remember little Henry (Alan's 8-year-old son) laid a note on the coffin, and several people stood up and spoke about Alan. Most were in tears. Mel Collins, next to me, was in terrible shape – I was just about keeping it together. As the curtains closed, we filed back out to the courtyard past the display of flowers. Murray Head was standing by the door as I came out. We hugged and wandered off to a quiet corner.

"God, Alan would have hated this," started Murray. "All standing around morbidly. He'd want a fucking party."

"Yeah, I know," I said, "but this has been the vibe since I arrived. It's hit everyone hard. I mean we all expected him to die years ago, but not now. It's really come as a shock to me."

"No, look at them," continued Murray. "They're all bloody ridden with guilt. No one wanted to know about him or take on the liability and now it's all too late."

"I feel guilty about it too," I said.

"Of course you do. So do I. We all do. We let the fucker down."

"God, this really is grim," I added. "I wonder what Alan would make of it?"

As Murray and I stood there in the warm sunshine, a huge wave of blue-white smoke billowing from the chimney above us was hit by a down draft and enveloped us all. With a wry smile on his face, Murray said, "Yeah, that's typical Spenner – covering us all in his shit. I feel as if he's all around me now."

"God, this is horrific," I said as I inhaled the smoke. "This fiasco can't be the best way to say goodbye to such an amazing person. What an awful situation."

"Don't worry," said Murray, "It's probably what Spenner thinks too."

From June to November, I did very little. I now felt after six months that it was time I made some serious work plans, preferably without record company involvement. Then a number of things happened around the same time. Simon Toulson–Clarke from Red Box got in touch. Having left Warner Bros. Records – after almost nine years – he wanted to work with me again. Ginny Clee telephoned and asked me to have a meeting with her group, The Dear Janes, and I bumped into Lee Harris (drummer from Talk Talk) in Stoke Newington Church Street. All three partnerships led to albums being recorded over the next two years. They were all relatively cheap projects (between £4,000 and £16,000) and were recorded without record company backing. Most importantly, there was no attempt to fit into some commercial/dance/indie/record company preconception. All three albums were approached in a refreshing atmosphere of experimentation, freedom, honesty and energy. The projects became debut albums for SPA, .O.rang, and The Dear Janes.

Chapter 29. .O.rang
14 November 1991

On the 14th of November, I was strolling back from the health food shop on Stoke Newington Church Street when I walked right into Lee Harris. He was shuffling along in his moccasins, his head bent low. I had neither seen nor spoken to Lee (nor Tim and Mark) since leaving Wessex on the 30th of April, and it was great to see him. I invited him back to the flat and we picked up some beers on the way.

It was about 4 p.m. when we settled into Balfour Road, curtains drawn, candles alight and joss sticks burning. We opened a couple of beers and talked. Lee told me of his feelings, his state of mind and general lack of well-being over the previous seven months – his sense of failure and of being inadequate and the spiralling darkness and void that took him over on finishing the album *Laughing Stock*. He described his numbness and anger. As I recalled my attitude to the album and my activities (or lack thereof) since finishing it, we both began to rebuild our confidence. We realised that we had both been through a very similar experience and were not going mad after all, as we both had thought might be the case. I had come out of it slightly better. From what Lee said, it sounded like he had suffered a mild breakdown four months earlier.

We talked into the night, reassuring each other over the past events and getting stronger by the hour. One topic we kept coming back to was our dream of making an album that was fun, adventurous and cheap, with no record company involvement. We both felt embarrassed by the huge cost of both *Spirit of Eden* and *Laughing Stock* – together adding up to a total bill of £700,000. "We can do it Lee," I said in typical *Young Ones*-style. "All we need is a desk, my Tannoy speakers, some microphones and a multitrack machine. Could be 2-inch, could be a Fostex – it doesn't really matter. Technology isn't the problem – a good location is."

"You should come and talk to Paul," answered Lee, referring to Paul Webb. "He has a desk, Fostex and an Apple Mac. We've already been writing some songs and we have about eight finished on DAT. I'll bring you a copy. We recorded them at Paul's house just 'round the corner. I'll give him a bell tomorrow. We could always rent somewhere for a month or two. We've been working under the name of Hypersanity."

That night, it all seemed so easy. Lee and I appeared to be on a similar wavelength and got on well. There was great enthusiasm between us, and I had faith in his abilities as a creative musician.

Over the next few weeks Lee, Paul and myself met and discussed what we would need to build a home studio that was well enough equipped to record finished master tapes. Paul was a small, light-framed guy, and like Lee, laid back and easy-going. He appeared to spend most weekends taking Ecstasy and clubbing. Slowly, between the three of us, a plan was formed. We needed a large room, as we wished to record drums, Hammond, percussion, electric guitars, choirs and such live. We planned to work mainly with musicians and live instruments and to create our own samples and layered sounds. Lee and I talked about working fast, capturing the moment, being spontaneous and making it fun. We both wanted to prove it was possible to make a great album this way and for it to be cheap – say under £20,000. Lee asked a business rental firm to start looking for suitable premises around the Stamford Hill area, and we fine-tuned our growing list of requirements.

I had finally regained some confidence on the work front and asked Joyce (ex-Wessex booker and now my manager) to look out for interesting projects. I informed her that I was up for any necessary A&R meetings if it might lead to something positive – preferably projects with live bands. In December, two meetings of this kind were arranged – one with the band All Other Animals at MCA and the other with Nan Vernon at Anxious Records. Although, initially, I worked with neither of these artists, the meeting at Anxious did lead me to finishing off and mixing an album with Jonathan Perkins and his band Miss World. This project had been started by producer Chris Thomas at Dave Stewart's (Eurythmics) house in the South of France the previous summer. By the beginning of January 1992, I was quite busy again – mixing the Miss World album at Wessex's Studio Two, catching the occasional gig with The Dear Janes and keeping in touch with Lee and Paul to discuss our plans for a studio.

After inspecting various premises, Hypersanity settled on an industrial unit at the Millmead Business Centre in Tottenham Hale. The unit had previously been used as some form of studio and already had a large, soundproofed room built within it, perfect for our main live recording room. There was a large lounge area and two small rooms, about 8 by 10 feet, one of which we intended to use as our control room. Lee was owed Talk Talk royalties by EMI Records amounting to several thousand pounds, and convinced that these would eventually come through, he re-mortgaged his house and put up £16,000.

Paul donated all his equipment, and I agreed to donate any equipment I had plus three or four months of my time in order to build the studio and record an EP. We then hoped to sell the finished EP to an indie record company – we particularly fancied the label One Little Indian.

Lee, Paul and myself all agreed to divide the income (advances, royalties, etc.) three ways after expenses and Lee being repaid. After the initial three-month period, I was to be given two weeks free studio time to work on my own projects. As for equipment, we had settled on leasing a Yamaha DMR 8 – this comprised a digital desk and 24-track machine. This, along with Paul's Fostex 16-track analogue machine and two tracks of Pro Tools on the Apple Macintosh computer, would give us a great deal of scope in handling data and constructing songs. As a bonus, when mixing down, the DMR 8 desk became a full 24-track digital mixing desk with computerised control of faders, EQ, echo effects, panning, cuts, etc. – with the facility to store mixes and recalls.

Work began on the studio in May. Graeme Jones, the maintenance man at Wessex Studios, came and laid mic cables in the studio, control room and the lounge area and monitored our mains electricity supply for any spikes or surges. I filled the roof spaces and some of the wall cavities with foam, and in the control room I hung heavy carpets on the walls and floor. This room turned out to be very tricky to set up for sound – it always felt too live and bass-heavy. I borrowed a 1950's BBC acoustics book from Bill Price at Wessex, and we constructed bass traps for different frequencies. Once they had been built from the prescribed materials in the correct thickness and size, I screwed them to the wall, mostly behind the desk area. One afternoon, I drilled straight through a hidden mains cable in the wall and fused the whole unit. We had to hack the plaster and cement away by torchlight and join the wires with a plastic adapter. It was three hours before we had any electricity.

By the beginning of June, the studio was completed and all the equipment was set up in our control room. Paul's analogue desk and machine plus a large patchbay were laid out down one wall, and the DMR, mic preamps, digital decoders and DAT machines were positioned across the centre of the room, forming an L shape. The studio now had a pool of instruments and equipment, including a Hammond organ with Leslie cabinet, a large drum kit, various unusual percussion instruments and a Marshall 100-watt, plus Peavey amplifiers, guitars (acoustic, bass and electric), a small PA system and microphones, plus all the old Talk Talk lighting, including the strobe, oil projector and disco lights. The lounge area had two chairs, a sofa, a television and video, a sound system, a fridge and single cooking element. We felt completely self-contained.

We decided not to record any of the songs that Lee and Paul had already demoed, but to start afresh, while we learnt and got used to the new equipment. "We'll just see what happens," said Lee. "Let's roll a spliff, get a rhythm happening and fire it through the PA system, plug up some mics, roll the tape and party."

During June and July, we recorded musicians, friends and ourselves "wild" onto 28-minute digital tapes and slowly built up a library of instruments, performances and sounds comprising over eight hours of continuous music. The atmosphere in the studio (now named by Lee, "The Slug") was relaxed but concentrated. This brought out many excellent performances and ideas from a large assortment of musicians including Emily Burridge, Mark Feltham, Simon Edwards, Anthony Thistlewaite, Matt Johnston, Martin Ditcham and Graham Sutton. We recorded in the control room and the lounge as well as in the studio itself. At night, when the building was almost deserted, we used the corridors and stairwells.

Lee had a plan forming in his head and would spend hours and then days sifting through the tapes and loading sections into the Pro Tools computer programme. He would edit, tune, stretch and treat the relevant stereo sounds, before re-locking up with my master DMR tapes and "placing" the performance where required on a particular song. It was very similar in approach to Talk Talk and also very time consuming and slow. Paul would take off on days like these and go to the floatation centre in St Johns Wood, leaving Lee and me to it. (The floatation centre had tanks of a strong saline solution where one would float in total darkness, and when wearing earplugs, total silence.)

It dawned on me during July that this rather slow way of working was not what I had had in mind when we set the studio up. Our original plan, I thought, was to record tracks fast and spontaneously. The process of writing and making computer overdubs became more protracted as we began to put the music together. I would sometimes sit at the desk for seven hours at a stretch, waiting for Lee to be satisfied with his work at the computer. By the middle of August, my donated time had run out, and we had only completed three songs. However, at least they were finished, mixed, edited and ready for a deal.

Keith Aspden was the manager for Talk Talk and for Lee, Paul and Mark Hollis individually. He had shown little interest in what he called our "hippie ideas of making music for little money" and had only been down to the studio on two previous occasions. Now that the tracks were finished, Keith was brought in and we played back our three songs. "Great stuff," he said. "It'll be a great LP."

We explained how we wanted to arrange things with the contract between the three of us and the importance of keeping control of the project – now named .O.rang. (Lee's new name, after briefly calling it Moratorium). Keith nodded and left with a DAT copy of our first three songs – *Little Brother*, *Mind on Pleasure* and an untitled eight-minute dance track. I talked to Lee about the EP now becoming an LP and my lack of any more time. He replied with, "I think we should play the tracks to some record companies and see what they offer. An EP would be great, but within two more months we could probably finish the album." A couple of days later, I dropped off a cassette copy to A&R man Steve Ferrara while at a meeting with Echo Records about the trio Zoo.

I was having severe doubts about my involvement with .O.rang long before the contracts finally appeared. For me, the pace was too slow and far too close to that of the previous Talk Talk sessions. Lee and I had had talks about it and decided that I didn't have to be present all the time during the painfully slow computer editing process, but for me it went much deeper than that. Although we had talked about an equal partnership in the approach to the album, it was very much Lee's show. He had something personal to prove to Mark and was determined to get everything just right and sounding just as he heard it in his head.

When the contracts came through, Lee and Paul were referred to as "The Artist" and I was referred to as "The Producer". This was certainly not what Lee, Paul and I had agreed on between us. I was offered a standard production contract with a 2 percent royalty. So much for a three-way split. I got Joyce involved, and with the help of lawyers and a heart-to-heart with Lee, I managed to add a 15 percent share of any advances to the contract. Steve Ferrara signed .O.rang to Echo Records, and the album *Herd of Instinct* was released in 1994. When .O.rang signed to Echo, I received £1,500. This was my only payment and worked out at less than £125 a week. But on the whole it had been fun.

The album received a collection of good write-ups from the critics, but unfortunately sold few copies. I thought on the whole that the album was very good, and the working approach of Lee had given results, though it was not as focused as Talk Talk.

Chapter 30. Throwing Muses
7 November 1993

In August 1993, I was working with the Throwing Muses in New Orleans, recording their album *University*. One afternoon, I was in the kitchen of the studio, standing by the sink and making a cup of tea, when the band's manager came in.

"How's it going?" asked the manager.

"Oh, okay."

It was hot – in the 90s with 80 percent humidity. The ceiling fan did little, but it was therapeutic. I didn't really mind the heat because I was having fun – up to now that was.

"So, what's happening?" continued the manager.

"Oh, we're just having a break," I said, as I fished into the cup with my fingers to remove the tea bag.

"Why?" said the manager.

"Oh, we had a couple of interruptions."

"Such as?"

"Oh, just Ryder." Ryder was band member Kristin Hersh's two-year-old son.

"Stay there," said the manager, and left.

I'd been in New Orleans a couple of weeks recording at Kingsway Studio, which was built in a large, beautiful colonial house in the French Quarter, and I was feeling quite at ease. The house was owned by Daniel Lanois and was full of classic equipment he had collected over the years, much of it purchased from various studios that had either closed or had been re-fitted. The desk was the API from the 1970's Electric Lady Studio set up by Jimi Hendrix, and the outboard equipment included valve compressors from Media Sound in New York. There were three pianos, two Hammond organs, about 35 guitars (from the '50s and '60s) and a room full of amps, including Vox and Marshalls.

The studio was not laid out conventionally with a separate studio and control room but was a large open space (the entrance hall) with four non-soundproofed rooms around it. There was a marble floor in the hall and a wide, wooden staircase that led to two more floors above. The equipment was all housed in this hallway area, and with the combination of a large, open space, marble floor and plaster walls, it was extremely live. I found this interesting rather than difficult, although there was the occasional problem with extraneous noises from other parts of the house. I had the drums set up in the hall just a few feet away from where I was sitting at the desk, with close microphones and distant ambient mics on the first landing in case they should prove to be useful for the sound. Kristin's guitar and vocals were set up at the far end of the room with screens to help stop any live guide vocals leaking onto other instruments. The bass was placed between the two of them, close to the drums.

The incident with Ryder had happened 15 minutes earlier. We were coming to the end of a great take on the song *Surf Cowboy*. It was a mid-tempo hypnotic track, and the musicians were locked in and grooving. It had been perfect right from the start, and we were now just a few bars away from the finish of this track. Suddenly, a scream echoed around the building, bursting through our concentration. Drummer Dave Narcizo looked at me over his shoulder and smiled but continued playing until the end. The cry was Ryder, playing with his nanny in an upstairs room.

"Unlucky," I said annoyed, but not wishing to make a big deal. "Don't worry, let's take five minutes and then do another take." I made my way to the kitchen to make a cup of tea.

Their manager returned to the kitchen within a few minutes, bringing the band with him. This consisted of Kristin on guitar (and the band's singer and songwriter), Dave on drums and Bernard Georges on bass.

"Tell them what you just told me," said their manager.

I sat down at the kitchen table. Dave, Bernard and Kristin joined me. Their manager stood at the back. Inside, I began to panic. I had walked into the sort of situation I had been trying to avoid ever since I had met their manager four months earlier, during the recording of Kristin's solo album, *Hips and Makers*. This project had Lenny Kaye producing and was recorded in a converted stable (Stable Sound) in Rhode Island. The 16-track machine had originally belonged to Pete Townshend and was close to 23 years old. It was now owned and operated by engineer Steve Rizzo, who had worked on demos with both Kristin and the Throwing Muses many times in the past. Steve had been very helpful in settling me in and making sure I was happy with the monitors and equipment. We had spent many late evenings together, repairing the relays on the 16-track (with slivers of matchsticks) and getting it ready for the next day's workload. On these occasions, we had talked on a variety of subjects including Glyn Johns, Jimi Hendrix, drugs and Talk Talk.

At that time, I had only just met everyone and had been quite positive in my feelings for the manager.

Now, at the kitchen table in New Orleans, I thought for a moment and said, "It's nothing really. I was just saying how we had been disturbed by Ryder, and in fact I came out here to make a cup of tea and to avoid a post mortem – exactly what we are now going through. But, as we are here, let's face up to the fact – we have just lost a possible master."

Silence, with the exception of Karen Brady, the studio manager, and Trina Shoemaker, the assistant engineer, who could both be heard making phone calls in the office just off to the left at the end of the kitchen. "Look," I added, "I'm not trying to make an issue out of this. I just want to get on with the album. I don't like distractions." Dave stared at the box of Fruit 'n Fiber on the table. Bernard appeared to nod in agreement. Kristin, sitting quietly beside me, looked straight ahead and said nothing. It was the manager who spoke:

"This is the way we want to do things."

"Fine," I said. "But we are paying $1,200 a day, and over these past few days have not really made full use of the time. With Ivo [Watts-Russell] from the record company [4AD] being here for the weekend and the breaks to deal with Ryder, we have sometimes only achieved five or six hours of real work a day."

The manager made a comment telling me I couldn't run his life. No one else spoke.

"I'm not. But I have been flown out here to make an album, not to be part of your lifestyle."

Kristin spoke for the first time, "I want to have some quality time with my kid."

My head buzzed with conflicting emotions, but mostly I was angry with the manager. I had become wary of him and had been dealing with him in what I thought was a very diplomatic way. I recalled the previous recording sessions in Rhode Island and the difficulties Lenny Kaye had been through. I also disliked watching other people play happy families, whomever they were. If I was in the studio I just wanted to work – if not I preferred to be on the roof in the sun, in a bar on Bourbon Street or at home with my own children. I did not find it very easy or productive to be constantly on call for 14 hours a day, only to work for five.

The way I usually worked was now quite different from the chaotic conditions in studios during the 1970s. Over the past 10 years, I had got used to working only with the members of the band who were being recorded and with those closely involved, and I hated distractions. There was also the fact that Dave, Bernard, Kristin and I had spent the first week on our own. For me, this had been the best five days' recording in years. We cut two or three masters a day and the atmosphere between us all had been great. Then, the manager turned up with Kristin's brother, her son Ryder, a 5-week-old Weimaraner puppy and an "attitude".

"Well, I would like some 'quality time' to make this album," I replied, getting annoyed at yet another time-wasting exercise.

Kristin spoke calmly, "I like having Ryder here. I want my family around me."

"But what if we all decided to do that?" I said. "It would be chaos."

"Well, perhaps just mothers then," said Kristin, also beginning to get annoyed.

This situation could get out of hand. I needed to backtrack and divert the discussion from the obvious route it was taking. "Look, I'm English. I have a different view on things. It's the Victorian upbringing. When I'm in the studio, that comes first – family second. But it's different here – the 'Great American Family' vibe. Fine. I'll adapt." I lit one of Trina's Marlboro cigarettes that were lying on the draining board. Silence.

In my head, memories of other people I had pissed off darted through. The big bust-up with Ginny Clee from The Dear Janes just a month before, my frustrations with Nan Vernon, who had changed her mind daily during mixing, manager Keith Aspden at the end of the .O.rang album, and even the difficulties with Richard Perry on Harry Nilsson's album all those years ago. These episodes briefly came to mind – perhaps I'm just a difficult bastard. Now I appeared to have done it again – while trying to make a cup of tea. "Look, it's fine," I said. "We'll work 'round it."

I picked up the remains of my tea and went back to the studio. Bernard followed. "I think you're right," he said quietly. We played Kristin's solo single *Your Ghost* LOUD. Dave and Kristin wandered in after 10 minutes and we got back to work. The manager sat at the back, saying nothing. The rest of the afternoon and evening were subdued, but we ploughed on, achieving little. Kristin, Ryder and the manager went for dinner at a Vietnamese restaurant on the other side of town. This was a two-hour round trip, which was a further source of annoyance for me.

Dave, Bernard and I went to the local pizza place, two blocks away. The manager had been the band's A&R man, had married Kristin and was now their manager. It seemed tough on Dave, who had been performing with Kristin since high school and was a founding member of the band. Dave and Kristin appeared to have a great relationship, and they were like brother and sister. I sensed that they had a special friendship. I wished that Dave and Bernard were more involved in the day-to-day decision-making, but they both appeared to accept that "what the manager says, goes".

On leaving the pizza restaurant, I noticed a large sign on the other side of the street. It read, "Homicides – New Orleans 173, Boston 64." When I left town two weeks later, it read, "Homicides – New Orleans 254, Boston 89."

I met Kristin on the stairs, close to midnight. "Sorry, Kristin, if I upset you, but the album is my main concern," I said.

"No problem," said Kristin. "I like the distractions. Remember Rhode Island?"

I did. Her concentration span had been so short that she had read a book at the microphone between vocal takes to avoid getting bored. We made our peace and she went to bed. I stayed up with Dave and Bernard playing pool and listening to *Dark Side of The Moon*. Ironically, a few days later, we used Ryder to yell over the intro to the song *Snake*. It's a pity we had not been working on this track instead of *Surf Cowboy* a few days earlier. The subject was not mentioned again by anyone until Sunday the 7th of November, when I was back in England.

That Sunday was just three weeks before I was due to return to New Orleans and finish the album. Joyce, my manager, had been trying to resolve my production contract for almost four months. In the end, their manager had refused to deal with her – it was a stalemate.

I rang Kristin to see how she was, and to get a plot on what we had left to do. She spoke for just a couple of minutes, sounding a little detached, before handing me over to the manager. Obviously, she did not feel like talking. The manager sidestepped the important topics, saying, "Don't worry Phill. We'll get the contract sorted as soon as the budget is agreed." This was not as easy as it might sound. I had no part in, or control of, the budget – this had been put together by the management without consulting me, despite the fact that I was co-producing with the band and was ultimately partly responsible. However, I had now been sent a copy and had talked it over with Joyce.

There were a few items on the list I was unhappy with – "child care", "transport", "office expenses" and "cello overdub" adding up to around $17,000. In my production contract, I was responsible for any overrun and it would come out of my money, so since the projected budget for the whole album was already up to $190,983, (out of a possible $200,000) this sum of $17,000 could be decisive. Instinctively, I knew I should avoid discussing this with the manager.

After a long and heated telephone conversation with the manager, I left the project.

The album was overdubbed and finished by Trina Shoemaker, the assistant engineer at Kingsway, and was then taken to Larrabee North Studios in Hollywood for mixing with David Bianco.

Obviously, I was disappointed not to have followed the album through to the end. There was only one of the final mixes I really disliked, and that was *Like a Dog* – originally a wonderful live performance of band and vocal. For some reason, the track was treated with effects and the vocal mic was gated, creating an unsettling effect on the drum sound – very tatty. I had to give Warner Bros. my permission for them to use the recordings that I had produced, and at this point I finally received the signed contracts. I was paid any monies due and the matter was resolved.

Kristin sent me a note a few months later, while on tour in England to promote the album:

"Sorry it got weird. I hope none of us have stomach-aches anymore. Hips and Makers sounds beautiful. Love, Kristin"

I noticed that she didn't mention *University*.

Chapter 31. Fusanosuke Kondo 23 May 1994

By May of 1994, I had the distinct feeling that I was going around in circles. Although I had worked on some interesting projects from 1991 to '93 with Miss World, Bark Psychosis, Nan Vernon, Roger Beaujolais and Kristin Hersh, the combination of .O.rang, The Dear Janes, Throwing Muses and a god-awful band called Billy Rain had resulted in a rather negative feeling towards music, musicians, managers and business affairs in general. The changing deals and unrewarding hassles with .O.rang and The Dear Janes had all but confirmed my worst impressions of the music business of the 1990s, neatly summed up by the word "greed".

Sessions in the late '60s and early '70s had – on the whole – been fun, with a relaxed and friendly attitude shown by those involved. At that time, there had been fewer A&R men and managers to deal with, and we had been left to get on with the job in hand. Now, there were armies of managers, consultants, A&R men and various other record company departments – all with an opinion on how to record, mix or approach a particular song or artist. It appeared to me that everyone and their mother had an opinion, and in addition to this they were slow to pay the bills after the work had been completed. Into this gloom came Fusanosuke Kondo, a Japanese blues artist. To my pleasant surprise, I found Fusa to be completely honest and forthright; he had no apparent ego problems and his business approach appeared impeccable – he was a breath of fresh air.

One morning in April, I received a telephone call from Alastair Gavin, Fusa's musical director. I had known Alastair since 1991, when he and I had begun to work with Simon Toulson-Clarke on a project that became the SPA album. "Look, Phill," said Alastair, "I'm about to record an album with this Japanese blues player. I wondered if you would like to engineer the album? I've already mentioned you to Fusa, and he would love to have you involved. He'll pay you £300 per day and all expenses. I've already toured with him in Japan and the band are a good crowd. It could be fun."

I was delighted with the idea of working on a project simply as the engineer. I wouldn't have to worry about dealing with budgets, record deals, studios, managers or contracts – no pressure. I said yes.

We started at Protocol Studios on Benwell Road, Highbury, on Monday the 23rd of May 1994. Although the studio was relatively cheap, at £400 per day, it had good facilities – a great-sounding DDA desk, a wide selection of microphones and a large studio and control room. The band (named "The Grub Street Band") consisted of an excellent bunch of players – Yoshinobu Kojima on keyboards, Kenji Omura on guitar, Fusa on guitar and vocals, Peter Lewinson on drums, his brother Steve Lewinson on bass, Alastair on keyboards and Ray Gaskins on sax.

I set Fusa up in the control room with guitar and guide vocal, along with DIs for Steve's bass and Alastair's keyboards and computer. The rest of the band were scattered around the studio room, with Koji in the live area, Pete in front of the control room window and Kenji's guitar amps out in the passageway. Ray Gaskins and his sax moved between a purpose-built booth in the studio and an area at the back of the control room.

I immediately hit it off with Fusa – he was 43 (a similar age to me), 5 feet 10 inches tall, thin, with long, straight black hair, an infectious laugh, and a wonderful glint in his eyes. He appeared extremely friendly. In Japan, he was a big star, having had many pop hits in the 1980s and several appearances in television soap operas. All the proceedings were to be videotaped on Hi8, with the idea of making a promotional documentary – *Fusa in London*. They filmed everywhere – in the studio, in the control room, out on the streets and in restaurants.

We arranged and recorded one song per day with all seven musicians playing live. The days were not long and we often finished work around 7 p.m. and went for a meal. All the musicians were easy-going and fun to work with, except Ray who never stopped talking and re-telling jokes. Ray was a large, black New Yorker with an ego and voice to match his size. He was, however, very good at maintaining energy within the band and was useful when it came to writing lyrics. Within two weeks, we had all the tracks covered. Most of the band members now went home, and Alastair and I got down to overdubs – percussion with Martin Ditcham and lead vocals from Fusa.

By the end of June, we were at the Roundhouse Studios on Chalk Farm Road and mixing two to three songs a day. During this mixing period, Fusa asked me if I would go to Japan later in the year and tour with him and the band. I had always wanted to see Japan and liked the idea of being back on the road, so I answered in the affirmative and became the eighth member of The Grub Street Band. We finished mixing on the 3rd of July, and mastered the CD, entitled *23A Benwell Road*, at Abbey Road on the 4th. The project had been smooth and easy and a great deal of fun.

I now returned to Sussex and took a break for a couple of weeks. My daughter Becca was due home from six months of teaching in Nepal on the 10th, and I had planned to pick her up from the airport and spend some time with her. On the 6th, I gave blood (for the first time) at a mobile unit in the village. I felt pretty rough after this bloodletting and had a dull ache in my side, finally going to the doctor's on the 8th. He thought I probably had a colon infection and told me not to eat for a day or two.

On Sunday the 10th, I awoke covered in a rash and in pain. On returning to the doctor, I was immediately sent to the Accident and Emergency department of the Kent and Sussex Hospital in Tunbridge Wells. Here I was put on a drip of fluids and painkillers, and due to a lack of bed space was moved into the cancer ward. Although somewhat anxious, I still thought I would be out later that day or the next, with everything sorted and an end to the problem. However, at the end of three days, I was still there, connected to drips and not having seen a doctor. On complaining to a nurse on night duty about the situation, she replied, "If you have a complaint, Mr. Brown, I suggest you speak to Virginia Bottomley [then Secretary of State for Health]."

I could not think of a polite reply to her remarks and said nothing. Finally, I managed to win over a male nurse who, later the next day, disconnected me from my drips and took me up to the outpatients department. Here, I sat in my pyjamas and wheelchair and joined the queue. On examining me, the doctor moved me from the cancer ward to the surgery ward. This did not make me feel any easier.

I now spent the next two weeks in hospital having X-rays, ultrasound scans and other tests – probes, tissue samples and a barium enema. I ate nothing during this period and lost almost two stone (28 pounds). A French-Canadian guy in his late 60s had also been admitted on the same day with similar symptoms. We would exchange notes on our various tests and sit outside in the sunshine talking of Canada, the Second World War, our desire to get out of hospital and food. We planned to go for a meal together to celebrate when we were both eventually released. One morning, towards the end of week two, he died of a stroke. I was floored – what next?

The hospital finally discharged me on the 24th of July. The diagnosis was diverticulitis. "Many older people suffer from this complaint and I'm sure you'll learn to live with it. Just drink plenty of water," was the parting comment from the consultant's assistant. Feeling feeble, I spent the next three weeks resting, taking gentle walks and eating small meals, slowly building up my strength.

In late August, feeling somewhat recovered, I took my son James for a week's boating trip in Norfolk. This stress-free lifestyle suited me and I felt great. By September, I was well again and making the occasional trip to London to see friends and hang out – but these trips were rare and I had no great desire to be back in the studio. Most of my time was spent gardening, walking, reading, and listening to demos sent to me by my manager Joyce. Few of these excited me enough to play them more than once, and I slowly drifted back to listening to albums by Neil Young, The Vulgar Boatmen, Van Dyke Parks and Sibelius. Plans were finalised for the Grub Street Band tour – it would be a comprehensive tour for the month of October.

On the 6th of October, I met Alastair and Pete at Heathrow Airport and we boarded our plane to Japan. "I've got a woody already," said Alastair, "just thinking about those beautiful women. Phill, you won't believe it, the women in Japan are amazing." I took a couple of sleeping pills and drank a large brandy, hoping to sleep most of the way to Tokyo. I would have welcomed any way to relieve the boredom of the 12-hour flight. I floated in and out of sleep, waking long enough to eat the occasional meal or to take a swig from a two-litre bottle of mineral water that I had purchased at Heathrow. I was trying to follow the hospital's advice.

We arrived at Narita International Airport on Friday the 7th and were met by Fusa's manager, Mr. Nobuyuki Yamazawa. Nobu would turn out to be an excellent character – friendly, witty and charming – who delighted in doing Elvis impersonations. He seemed to work 20 hours a day. Nobu drove us the hour and a half into Tokyo and we were checked into the Hotel Ibis in downtown Roppongi. Here, we met Steve and Ray, who had flown in from America. The hotel rooms were very small (this is quite common in Japan) and the bathroom was an all-in-one plastic unit, containing a small sink, toilet and sit-in bath. There was just enough space in this claustrophobic room to stand and use the sink, although drying oneself after a bath had to be done back in the main bedroom. I felt for Ray, who must have had difficulties.

The band and I spent the next three days rehearsing at Tuzuki Studio, using all the sound equipment we would have on the road – plus lights and crew. The evenings were spent relaxing in the hotel, eating at wonderful restaurants, playing in the huge amusement arcades or exploring the city. I found being in Tokyo an amazing experience. The pavements were crammed with people, bicycles, drinks machines, telephone boxes and old guys cooking food, while the roads were overflowing with traffic. Overhead on giant pillars were four-lane motorways cutting right through the city. (Imagine the M4 going across Piccadilly Circus and you will have some idea of the effect.) There were bright neon lights and giant video screens everywhere, and speakers on poles spewed forth distorted music and information. It reminded me of a set from the film *Blade Runner*.

At midday on Thursday the 11th, we left Tokyo and travelled by train to our first concert in the city of Fujieda. I was very happy to be back on the road. It instantly brought back memories of touring with Murray Head some 14 years earlier – hotel, Travel Cruiser, concert hall, restaurant, hotel – no thinking necessary. This time, however, we travelled everywhere by rail – usually first class – on the Shinkansen "bullet train". This was a wonderful experience.

The train ride was smooth and quiet and gave little impression that we were scything through the countryside and cities at 190 mph. We ate take-away meals out of little wooden boxes purchased at the station and read or listened to CDs and cassettes.

The concert in Fujieda went surprisingly well for a first night. There were the occasional chaotic moments for me, the band and the crew, but it went down well with the audience, and the promoters were pleased with the results. After the show, we were all taken to a sushi restaurant. Although I am 90 percent vegetarian, I love sushi, and this was some of the best I had ever eaten. "A little better than London, eh?" said Fusa. We sat drinking sake from square wooden bowls, eating a selection of tuna, eel, shrimp and rice, and being interviewed by the local press.

The Western members of the party knew little or no Japanese, but Fusa's knowledge of English was excellent. Most of the journalists also spoke English well, although there were the occasional reversal or additions of the letters "l" and "r". This inevitably caused much amusement. Happily, the joke was shared by all, as it was hard not to laugh at such words as "Rondon" (the capital city), "Blob" Marley, and Jeff "Bleck". The combination of inconsistent English and bad Japanese resulted in a lot of good-natured humour, and soon we were all firm friends.

For the next three weeks, we fell into a routine, leaving our hotel midday and catching the train to the next city, doing a soundcheck at 4 p.m., followed by a light snack backstage before the concert. These usually started early, about 7 or 7:30 p.m. After the show, I would make my way backstage, signing autographs on the way. Sometimes, I would be given album covers of records I had made and asked to sign them. These young Japanese, usually men, often produced albums I had worked on during the 1970s (before they were born) including Jeff Beck, Led Zeppelin, Bob Marley, Rolling Stones, Sly Stone and Steve Winwood. It was a wonderful boost to the ego. Once everyone was ready backstage, we would be taken out to eat with another round of noisy interviews.

We travelled to Sapporo in the north and to Hiroshima in the south, taking in most cities in between, including Nagoya, Osaka and Fukuoka. During the three weeks we were on the road, I was completely won over by Japan – the countryside, its cities, the food and the people. It had the combination of centuries of tradition and ultra-modern technology. I had never been anywhere in the world that was so efficient. Trains arrived to the minute, crews set up the stage and sound systems identically every night, and managers and record company executives worked very hard to make the tour a success, often staying in their offices until 10 p.m. I was impressed.

In Fukuoka, we stayed at a truly wonderful hotel – The Hotel Il Palazzo. It was built to look like an Egyptian temple, with giant marble pillars, barrel-vaulted hallways and (compared to what we were used to) huge bedrooms. Most remarkable of all were the bathrooms. These were rooms about 8 by 10 feet, with a full-sized bath and a shower unit in the centre of the room. The floor was made of stone and was sloped to allow the water to drain away. It was one of the sexiest bathrooms I had ever seen. During the long after-concert meal, it became the topic of conversation for all the Western members of the band. Not being able to make ourselves understood to the many Japanese fans we were introduced to on these occasions became boring and frustrating. That night, however, we all had the same catchphrase, "You like shower?"

Halfway through the tour we reached Kochi, on the southern island of Shikoku. Here we were treated to the most fantastic, though somewhat bizarre meal. Most of the Western band members preferred to eat cooked food – usually beef – but I was very happy with the raw fish. Fusa usually ordered rice, vegetables and sushi for me, but on this occasion, he asked me if I would like to try "dancing shrimp" and some other local delicacies. I was game to try something new and left it to Fusa to order.

The waitress brought out a small wicker basket covered with a tea towel. On removing the tea towel my dinner began to leave the table. The "dancing shrimp" were live and hopping across the table. Kenji grabbed one and showed me what to do. He poured a little sake onto its head to subdue it, and then just ripped its head and shell off, and ate it. I tried. It was much harder to do than it appeared, and because I hadn't used enough sake, the shrimp struggled wildly in my hands. As I put it into my mouth, the tail slapped against my cheek – very strange and disconcerting.

With the "dancing shrimp" all gone, Fusa suggested we all try a large black fish that could be seen swimming around in a tank. "This very special fish," he said. "Should be very expensive." He called the waiter and spoke rapidly in Japanese. The waiter wheeled the tank to the table. The next event happened so quickly that none of us gaijin (foreigners) could believe it. He grabbed the fish with his left hand, held it on a plate, and with a razor-sharp knife sliced the fish into small pieces. Within a minute or two, the fish was placed on the table, its flesh exposed and the mouth still gasping. An extraordinary experience, but a tasty fish. Alastair could not believe it. He immediately took out his camera, photographed the fish and went back to his beef.

As if this experience were not unsettling enough, there was more to come. At the end of the meal, two large fish heads were brought to the table. I was presented with one and Fusa the other. I looked at my plate. The fish head lay on its side, with one eye showing. "Ah, you are guest of honour," said Fusa, "We now eat fish eye." I watched Fusa deftly extract the eye with his chopsticks and pop it into his mouth. I followed, to much applause from the band and the Japanese sound crew. I could not swallow it whole and decided to chew it like any other form of food. It burst and fluid filled my mouth. "Well, I think Phill definitely gets the award for tonight," said Pete. "Unbelievable."

"Yeah, thanks. I'm not sure I could do that again," I replied.

The next day, Saturday the 22nd, we arrived in Hiroshima to play in an unusual location – an underground car park. As usual, the crew were set up and ready for us. "You'll have your work cut out tonight," said Nobu. "It's a difficult venue to sound good."

The soundcheck was a nightmare – the sound from the PA echoed wildly around the concrete walls, floor and ceiling. Once the audience had filled up the large empty space, the sound did improve, but I was struggling with levels for most of the concert. The band also had a difficult time on stage, as everything they played bounced back at them off the walls. That night, after another noisy and interrupted meal, Pete, Alastair and I sat in the roof bar of the Namiki Hotel, overlooking Hiroshima, drinking salty dogs and talking of the difficulties of long-term relationships, affairs, being on the road for several weeks, long studio hours and marriage. The bill for our six drinks came to £80.

The next day, I went to the Peace Memorial Park with Fusa, Alastair, Pete and Steve. We set off walking together, but very soon went our separate ways and each explored the park on our own. It was a beautiful area – a large, open parkland scattered with shrines, and in the centre, the ruin of a grand building, the image of which is known the world over. This building – originally the Prefectural Building for the Promotion of Industry, but now renamed the "A-Bomb Dome" – is all that remains of the old city that was destroyed by the nuclear bomb on the 6th of August in 1945. As I stood alone, staring at this ruin and thinking about the bomb that had been detonated directly above where I was standing, all manner of feelings swept through me. Exhilaration for simply being in Hiroshima, a place that had haunted me since my childhood; wonder at such a beautiful place with its paper streamers fluttering beside the shrines and the sound of the wind chimes; and deep sadness for the thousands of victims, whose names were written on large stone blocks listed below the words "Genbaku Shi" – killed by the atomic bomb.

Just inside the entrance to the park was the museum. I wandered around and took in the facts displayed on the walls: "Bomb dropped at 8:15 a.m. as children went to school and adults made their way to work" – "equivalent to 12.5 kilotons of TNT" – "92% of buildings destroyed by blast and fire" – "13 square kilometres of ruins" – "the thermic rays left an imprint of clothing on people's skin" – "immediately after the bombing there were large black flies, and maggots got into the wounds of many victims."

There were showcases of twisted bicycles, broken watches (that had all stopped at 8:15), before and after photographs of the city and the stone steps leading to the Sumitomo Bank. On these steps was the shadow of a man burnt into the concrete. It was more than I could take, and I broke down in tears. I had to leave. I sat outside in the late morning sunshine, shaking, and smoked a cigarette. Fusa came over. "Very difficult to look, isn't it?" he said. All I could do was nod. We went for a coffee at a nearby restaurant and I listened to two Japanese and one American discussing the casualties who had died within the first four months of the bomb being dropped. The American was quoting 160,000 casualties; the Japanese 360,000.

Later that day, as we were traveling to the airport to fly to Tokyo, Ray started to wind everybody up. "Have a nice morning at the park?" he asked. "I don't need none of them ghosts. I went for a steam. Why you guys need to put yourselves through that?"

"Oh fuck off, Ray," I said. "Typical that the only American amongst us doesn't bother going. Just leave it. We've all been through enough for one day."

It was fortunate that this Sunday was a traveling day and we had no concert to do that evening. Everyone apart from Ray was subdued, numbed from the day's events.

We stayed the night in Tokyo, back at the Ibis Hotel. Oddly, it turned out to be a fun night. The team of Pete, Steve, Alastair and I tried virtual reality Grand Prix driving at the amusement arcade and then had cheap noodles (£8) in a restaurant opposite the hotel. The next morning, I telephoned home before leaving for the remaining few concerts at Fukushima and Niigata. I needed to get word to Joyce that I was not keen to work with Bon Jovi in L.A. on their next album, as requested in a recent fax from her. The bill for the phone call was £115 – fuck, this country's expensive.

On the 26th, we headed back to Tokyo and our final concert in the Melpark Hall. To my amazement, waiting to greet me were posters declaring "Phill Brown Comes".

On entering the building, I left my bags backstage and went out to the sound desk where there was a further surprise – about 25 trainee sound engineers from the ESP Music Academy. During the soundcheck and the evening concert they sat behind me, watching me work – the whole event being video-taped for use later in the classroom. As was customary, photographs were taken and more interviews were given – this time before the show had even begun. The soundcheck went well and the concert was a great success – there's always an extra buzz playing in a capital city. After the gig, there was a small end-of-tour party backstage, after which we moved to a restaurant in Roppongi for one final band, management and artist meal.

I stayed in Tokyo for two more days to do television and newspaper interviews and some more studio work. Fusa's record company had asked me to mix three songs for a compilation blues album. The studio – Birdman West – was impressive, with vast amounts of equipment, including a 60-channel SSL desk, two Studer A800 24-track analogue machines, two Mitsubishi 32-track and two Sony 48-track digital machines, plus a wall of effects that had at least four of everything – echoes, reverbs, compressors, etc. I had never seen so much equipment in one studio. The price was £2,300 per day.

The mixing session went on until 6 a.m., and then, after picking up my belongings from the hotel, I was driven out to the airport by Nobu. All in all, it had been a brilliant trip, and I returned to London with renewed energy, a very positive state of mind and a desire to continue working, partly fulfilled by projects with Avril Jamieson and Roadside Picnic. There were also proposals to do another tour with Fusa in 1995 and to record a second album with The Grub Street Band.

Things did not go quite to plan. Within three months, I was back in hospital.

Chapter 32. Mark Hollis
21 June 1996

As I sat around at home recovering from my operation (see introduction), and during the time I had spent lying in hospital in a doped state, I had thought a great deal about my past and my own mortality – as one does in these situations. I came to the conclusion that for me, the late 1960s had been a fantastically exciting time as I trained to be an engineer; the 1970s had been a time to realize that ambition with hard work and wonderful fun – some of the best sessions and characters; the 1980s had been a time of disillusionment, re-think, new technology and accountants; and the 1990s seemed to be a time in the business world for the "corporate company rule" to really get a hold. The men in suits and ties (the ones I thought I had avoided by working in music) were now running the show – where was the rock 'n' roll? For me, the album *Laughing Stock*, broken relationships with The Dear Janes, SPA and .O.rang, and a loss of passion had so far summed up the 1990s.

Since finishing *Laughing Stock* at Abbey Road in 1991, I had had no contact with Talk Talk's Mark Hollis. He had returned to his house in Suffolk and an alternative lifestyle. In March 1995, he telephoned me to enquire how I was after surgery – he had heard rumours. We talked for a while, catching up on the past few years. Two months later, we met in Hampstead for a curry and an evening in the pub. Mark outlined his ideas for a second album for Polydor – a combination of classical, jazz and folk, using only acoustic instruments. He appeared in good form – relaxed, accessible and very amusing.

Mark's deal with Polydor had been for two albums. It had been rumoured at the time that he had received an advance of over a million pounds, although out of this he would have to pay the entire recording costs for both LPs.

In June, I drove out to see Mark in Suffolk. He played me his writing demos, produced with the aid of a computer and a sampler. He had used untreated samples of instruments and no reverb. I found the music stark, intriguing and at times very beautiful. He asked me to get involved. I was doubtful – I had planned that my return to work would be by easy stages, taking on lightweight things first. Also, following the gruelling experience of the two previous Talk Talk albums, I wasn't sure I was quite ready to spend another year of my life on a similar project. However, I was really pleased that Mark had asked me, and it did my battered ego a power of good.

A few weeks later, we had another meeting in London, this time with co-writer Warne Livesey, who was to produce the new album. Warne had worked on a wide assortment of projects including Midnight Oil, Paul Young, and Deacon Blue. I thought he was an unusual choice. Mark talked about his idea for an overall sound. "I want to capture a 1950's jazz approach, with the feeling of a complete band playing live around you – you know, everything on one mic and standing up for solos. How can we bring that approach up to date?"

Rather sarcastically I said, "We could make it stereo."

We decided on trying two valve microphones at the front of the studio room – a classic '40's or '50's approach – updated to stereo. We would record everything on these two mics, without changing the EQ or levels. We would move the musicians around the room to the required location in the final stereo image. The recording room would be all-important working this way, and a short list of possible studios was drawn up – AIR, Lansdowne, Master Rock and Westside.

In November 1995, the three of us went into AIR Studios at Lyndhurst Hall to have a trial day. This is a remarkable building – a huge church on a corner plot in Hampstead. The rumour here is that it had cost £16 million to convert into the assortment of studios, control rooms, programming suites, offices and canteen, and I could almost believe it. Beautiful, light-coloured wood drenched the walls, ceilings and floors. Machines and equipment lined the walls, and with a staff of 45 it was more like an offshoot of the BBC. We were in the smaller of the two main studios and started by setting up a selection of Neumann valve microphones – U47s, U67s and M49s. The walls in this room were adjustable, with floor to ceiling screens allowing one to split the size of the room into two-thirds or a third. Slowly, by changing microphones and adjusting the acoustics of the room, we arrived at the arrangement of a pair of M49s at head height (when sitting in a chair) at the front of the studio room, 3 feet from the control room window and using two-thirds of the available space. We were working on the beautiful sounding Neve desk from the original AIR Studios in Oxford Street – a classic desk from the 1970s. We checked our mic setup with a collection of instruments for sound and location – acoustic guitar, bass, piano, oboe, clarinet, bassoon, flute and drums were all positioned, checked, adjusted and measured. There was an easy atmosphere between everyone, although I was slightly thrown when Warne, who was drinking chamomile tea, asked John (the assistant) and me not to smoke in the control room. These would be "clean" sessions. This was okay by me for that day, but I wasn't sure I would be able to endure such austere conditions for a long-term project.

The day went well, and it appeared that the approach of using two microphones at the front of the room could work well. We then repeated the whole process at Master Rock Studios, and preferring the acoustics (which were more dead) we made plans to start recording there before Christmas. We had decided that Lansdowne Studios was too dead, and Westside Studios was too small.

Despite the fact that I wanted to be involved with Mark's new album, I now began to have serious doubts about my ability to work at this level so soon after coming out of hospital. Also to consider was the planned second album with Fusanosuke Kondo in February – something I was already committed to. After some thought I warned Joyce that I didn't yet feel fit enough to spend many months recording, leaving her to sort something out with Keith Aspden, who was still Mark's manager.

Joyce and Keith are both tough negotiators, and over the next week they faxed away at each other. It appeared Mark was willing to change the recording schedule and was offering good money – a potential £20,000. On Friday afternoon, I had just finished a telephone conversation with Joyce when Mark rang.

"Hi Phill. Just thought it would be best for me to ring you direct, because it feels like everyone's talking ultimatums."

"Yeah, I know," I said. "It doesn't take long. Well, thanks, it's um, like this – the Japanese project with Fusa that has been on hold has now been confirmed for February or March. But there is another thing; I'm not sure that after not working for nearly a year I should start back with something as intense as your album. I really wanted to do it, and I've been stalling slightly because I thought it might all work out. But between you and me, I'm still concerned about my health and don't think it's fair on you for me to start the album and then have to pass or whatever."

There was a short silence, and then Mark said, "I'm stunned, but totally understand. Studio life is never easy. Well, I don't know what to say. I really wanted you to do it."

"I enjoyed AIR. It was a good day, but since thinking about the time span of four months..."

"Well, I don't know what to say."

"Maybe I can be around for mixing?"

"But it's what you do when recording that I wanted. You have the right placing of instruments."

"Yeah. I'm sorry Mark, but I think it's best to pass."

"Okay. Well, let's meet up for a pint when you're in London."

"Yeah, that would be great. Best of luck with the project. Give us a ring and keep me informed. Maybe I can set up the room or something."

Mark took me up on my offer to set up the studio for these recordings, and in January 1996 I joined Mark and Warne at Master Rock Studios on Kilburn High Road and prepared the room. We deadened the room with additional acoustic panels, and I positioned our chosen M49s at the front of the room as a crossed cardioid pair. This is a technique developed in the early years of stereo, whereby two identical cardioid mics are rotated about 45 degrees to the left and right respectively.

"I think we should set up some close microphones, just for insurance," I said. "Later, if you want to bring something nearer to you, then you could use them."

It wasn't my fault, but this act of caution had unfortunate consequences.

We spent a couple of days fine tuning and then recorded our first song, *Om*, with Mark and Dominic Miller playing acoustic guitars side by side on a wooden riser and about 2 feet from the M49s. At the end of week one, I left them to it and Brent Clarke took over engineering. I spent March and April recording and mixing the second album (*Gravel Road*) with Fusanosuke Kondo and The Grub Street Band.

In May, Mark rang and asked me to meet him for a drink. By this time, he was living back in London. We went to two of the many pubs in Wimbledon and talked all evening about top end, energy, bass frequencies and the possibility of changing these things when mixing. This particular question made me feel that there was something on his mind, and as the evening progressed, I was sure he was going to ask me to work with him again. He didn't. However, three days later, he rang and said, "I've been thinking. It really makes sense for you to finish the album. There's just some woodwind, a few guitars and all the vocals to record and then mix. You could help me sort out some of those things we talked about. I've booked four weeks, with two more on hold from the end of August. What do you think?"

I was really pleased to be asked yet again by Mark, and now feeling more confident, having just finished my first album in 18 months, said yes.

"Great," said Mark. "We'll meet up in a few weeks and listen through together to the rough mixes."

On Friday the 21st of June, I arrived at Mark's house at about 5 p.m., and after a quick pint in his local we settled into his sparsely furnished music room to listen to the mixes. The floor was carpeted, and all along one 20-foot wall were shelves housing records, CDs and books. There was a Steinway grand piano at one end of the room and a hi-fi setup at the other – that was all. We sat on the floor directly central to the speakers and played the DAT of rough mixes.

The sound was not at all what I had expected. I tried to remember how it had all sounded back in January, and was surprised by the lack of air or room feel, the bright top end and the upfront energy of most of the sounds. This can't be the same as I set it up in January, with just two M49s at the front of the room, I thought. I now fully understood the implications of Mark's questions a month earlier. We listened to three of the backing tracks and then Mark stopped the DAT. "What do you think?"

"Well, slightly surprised. How are these mixed?" I asked. "Is this what's on multitrack or have the mixes been EQ'd, compressed or treated in any way? How much of our close mics were used?"

"I'll ring Warne and ask him," answered Mark.

Mark came back saying, "It appears there are close mics on everything. Warne said they're mixed in."

"Mixed into these rough mixes, or mixed together on multitrack?" I asked.

"Don't know," said Mark. "I'll ring Warne."

Mark was gone for at least 10 minutes and returned looking shaken and upset. "I can't believe this has happened," said Mark. "Warne says the close mics are on almost everything and they've been mixed to the multitrack tape that way."

We now spent some time going through the various options that were open to us. Neither of us could believe that there had been such a significant deviation from what we had originally planned. "Well, we've spent about a hundred grand, but if we have to," said Mark, "we'll re-record it."

I left Mark and drove over to Protocol Studios to set up for four days mixing with Theo Travis. We were finishing off his album *Secret Island*, started at Protocol back in early May. On Sunday the 23rd, and much to my surprise, I bumped into Warne Livesey making a cup of tea in the studio kitchen.

"I didn't think they had chamomile here," I said, coming up behind him and surprising him.

"Hey, Phill. What are you doing here? And yes, they do."

We talked briefly. I did not want to discuss Talk Talk, but Warne slid into the subject after a few minutes.

"Well, you know what artists are like," said Warne. "Mark knew exactly what I was doing – he listened and gave the okay. He can try it this other way just using the room mics, but you know it won't work."

I said nothing. After a year of working with him, how could Warne have failed to realize how important such details as microphone technique would be to a project like this, or more importantly to a perfectionist like Mark Hollis?

"The bass had no depth when 4 feet from the mics," continued Warne. "You know what I mean?"

Again, I said nothing.

On July the 7th, Mark and I spent a day at Master Rock Studios listening back to all the masters on 48-track analogue to find out exactly what was on tape. We listened to all the tracks and made a few reference mixes with alternate balances. We decided the bass, for the most part, could be okay, and most of the woodwind were fine, but that we should re-record the guitars, piano and harmonium and review the drums. These sounded far too strong. When I mentioned I had seen Warne, Mark said. "Oh, that's history. Just a mistake. I don't know what happened, but we should be fine now." At this point, Warne was still to be involved in finishing the album.

Recording was to begin on the 20th of August for six weeks. A week before, I rang Mark to check on the basic plan for week one and to see what time he was planning to start. "Warne's no longer involved," said Mark. "He told me the approach would not work and added, 'Phill's just clouding the issue.' I think it's best we just do it ourselves."

On Tuesday the 20th of August 1996, Mark and I arrived at Master Rock and set up the studio again to the January recalls. We then played through each instrument on the master and slave, making fresh, detailed notes as we went. For two days, we erased the instruments that we planned to re-record, and by the end of the second day had surprisingly erased 40 percent of the album, including some sections of drums by Steve Gadd and Vinnie Colaiuta. On Thursday, Martin Ditcham arrived, and over the next few days replaced most of the shaker, cymbal and drum parts. It's always a joy to work with Martin, and this was no exception – his charm, accuracy, innovation and humour made it not like work at all.

With their new feel, many of the tracks instantly settled into their space, but this also drew attention to those that didn't. Within two weeks, we felt that many of the surviving instruments (especially the bass) should also be redone – either to improve the feel or because they now sounded too up front in relation to the drums. The track called *Gonque* (the working title) felt completely wrong, and after many variations and approaches we eventually succeeded in obtaining our desired results by piecing it together from two bars of new drums – manually offset and dropped in every six seconds.

Seeing as how (for the first time with Mark) there were demos of almost all the songs, it was easy to know where we were heading and what was required. The days and weeks were clear-cut, centred, civilized and enjoyable, with medium lighting levels, a wide assortment of food for lunch and dinner, the possibility of a quiet space to work in and a helpful staff. This all added to the pleasure. The only down-side was an erratic air conditioning unit.

During breaks, Mark would remind us both of life at Wessex Studios recording *Spirit of Eden* and *Laughing Stock* – the pizzas or Indian takeaways every night, the endless overdubs in the dark and the smell of cat's piss. He also recalled events from 11 months on the road with Talk Talk, touring the *Colour of Spring* album in '85 and '86. We booked more time, and within two months we had re-recorded 90 percent of the album. On the 13th of October, we took a three-week break.

When we returned to Master Rock on the 5th of November, we continued with the last few overdubs – woodwind (one section that just wouldn't sit right), harmonica and guitars and started recording the vocals. Robbie McIntosh, Henry Lowther and Dominic Miller all came and spent a day playing, telling stories, and in Robbie's case very long, sad jokes. What a gem he is. On the 4th of December, we started two weeks of provisional mixing, back at AIR Studios' Lyndhurst Hall, taking copies away to listen to over Christmas.

Some further adjustments were needed, so with Christmas and a short Japanese tour with Fusa out of the way, I returned to AIR on the 29th of January 1997 to re-mix the album with Mark. We were predominately concerned about the bass end. Our original idea had been to mix the record so that it always sounded quiet, no matter what level it was played at. This proved impossible (for various reasons), but after some experimentation we finally achieved a result we were both happy with.

On the 6th of February, Mark and I mastered the album with Denis Blackham at Country Masters and took our CDs away to listen to. Still unhappy with the bass positioning, we returned to AIR, recalled the songs and gave our mixes a last final tweak. The only song we were not remixing was *Ramah* (the working title), which was just as well, as the Mitsubishi machine decided to eat the end of this master when we weren't looking. We re-mastered with Denis on the 25th and delivered the CD masters and a listening copy DAT to the A&R department at Polydor – there were eight songs, no singles and a possible title of *Mountains of the Moon*.

For me, personally, the album had been wonderful to work on, with easy sessions, lots of good humour and a mutual respect. Mark rang to say he was extremely pleased with the results and wanted to give me a 1 percent royalty. Perfect. This album gave me back my faith in music, business dealings and – most importantly – myself. "I can still do this!" Feeling confident again, I accepted plans to work on various projects with producers Rollo (Armstrong) and Sister Bliss starting in March – these were to include Skinny, Faithless, Dido and Pauline Taylor.

For the next few weeks, the Talk Talk camp was very quiet. Neither Keith, Mark nor I heard from Polydor. Then, one Friday afternoon, I received a telephone call from Denis at Country Masters, "Look, you may be interested in this. I have just had a phone call from a mate of mine at a cutting room, and he is about to CD master Talk Talk. Do you want his number?"

I spoke to Denis' friend at the cutting room, and he told me that he was making up a new master for the factory, working from a safety DAT tape. Exasperated, I realized that this was the DAT I had sent to the A&R department so that they could listen to the album in the office. I rang the A&R office, and after being transferred a couple of times, finally got through to the head of production.

"I don't know what this is all about," he said, "because I have both the DAT and the Exabyte sitting here in front of me on the desk. I have to say though, we can't use Exabytes – I need a 1630," referring to the videocassette mastering system that pre-dated the Exabyte. (By this time, the industry standard for mastering a CD was the Exabyte cartridge – a system devised in Japan and originally intended for computer data storage.)

"But there's only two factories in the world that can't use Exabyte," I answered. "One is in South America and the other, ironically, is in Japan."

"Let me check this out and I'll ring you back," said the head of production.

I decided not to wait. I rang the cutting room again and got all the details – the engineer's name, the studio being used and more importantly, Polydor's booking number. I rang A&R straight back and gave the head of production all the information.

"Yeah, Phill. I'm sorry, it's the girl downstairs. I'll get the DAT back, use the Exabyte you made and send you test copies when I have them."

"Thanks, great," I said, putting down the phone.

June was a difficult month for Mark and me, with one piece of bad news following another. First, we were informed that the album could not come out under the name "Mark Hollis", but had to be a Talk Talk album instead. Mark felt that with Tim Friese-Green and Lee Harris no longer involved, it wouldn't be right to release the album under the name Talk Talk. Then we were told that Lucian Grainge at Polydor Records was not interested in releasing the album at all.

The whole thing was so crazy that Mark and I ended up having a good laugh about the situation.

"Well, if Polydor doesn't release it," said Mark, "then it hardly matters what it's called or who the artist is."

By July, the news briefly changed again. Although Polydor were not interested in releasing the album, both A&M and Mo' Wax Records were. We felt that there would be little trouble in changing labels, since Polydor, A&M and Mo' Wax were all owned by PolyGram. Mark went for a meeting and rang me soon after.

"What do you make of this?" he said. "I have just had a meeting with Polydor and they told me that *Laughing Stock* was deleted soon after release. They don't want this second album, but they have asked me to sign for a third album."

Silence. I was stunned with the news about *Laughing Stock*. "I don't understand," I said. "Maybe it's some corporate plan to sign up artists and then silence them. I hope you told them to fuck off."

"Yeah. Like I'm likely to sign to someone who's saying, 'The first album's crap, the second album's crap, but please sign to us for a third.' Still, the A&M guys are keen," said Mark, "and they'll also re-issue *Laughing Stock*. It'll be great to be with someone who actually wants the albums."

"Well, it would be great if one could buy *Laughing Stock*. I can't believe it's been deleted within three months of release. What a bunch of cunts."

Unfortunately, our excitement was short-lived. Two weeks later, Polydor allegedly told Keith that they would neither release the new album nor give it back to Mark so that he could release it with another label. Mark and I discussed what had happened, but we found it hard to fathom the motives of the record company. Was the deleting of *Laughing Stock* some kind of signal to Mark that he should have toed the line and made his new album commercial? If so, the ploy had failed, as Mark did not discover that *Laughing Stock* had been deleted until he had finished the new album.

While working with Rollo and the singer Dido in August, I gleaned even more information about Polydor's (or their managing director's) attitude. During one of the sessions, Rollo related the following, "A guy in our office had a meeting at Polydor last week, with the managing director Lucian Grainge. Our guy was played a track off the new 'Talk Talk' album and asked what he thought of it."

"Yeah, I like it," he said. "It's really good."

"What, really good?" Said Lucian.

"Yeah, really good. I think it sounds great." Then Lucian asked him, "Is it worth a million?"

My doubts about the critical faculties of Polydor and of record companies in general were reinforced when Mark told me what had happened when the Talk Talk album *Colour of Spring* was finished in 1985. EMI did not like the album and were reluctant to release it. It was not "commercial" according to the record company, and there were no singles. No less than five hit singles were taken from the album, which went on to sell over two million copies. After this massive success, nothing that Talk Talk produced seemed able to please their record companies, who were incapable of seeing any potential in anything other than a *Colour of Spring* – Part 2. The fact that the original *Colour of Spring* album had itself been ground-breaking and innovative was forgotten or ignored – the bottom line was that it had sold two million units. All you had to do to sell another two million units was to make another record just like it.

At the beginning of November, we were finally informed that the new Talk Talk/Mark Hollis album would be released in January 1998. It was released under the name Mark Hollis. In early 1999, Mark decided to retire as a recording artist and suggested that we team up and co-produce other artists. Although we had a few possibilities, including Massive Attack (recommended by Keith Aspden), we finally settled for recording tracks with Anja Garbarek. Unfortunately, on the 9th of April – just a week before we were due to start work – I had a fire that completely gutted the upstairs of my house, requiring Sally, James and myself to move out for four months whilst it was rebuilt. I probably should have pulled out of the sessions at this point, but not wanting to let anyone down I foolishly went ahead.

We set up at Pete Townshend's Eel Pie Recording Studio in Twickenham and initially all went well. Over a five-day period, we recorded two songs using many of the musicians we had worked with during either *Laughing Stock* or Mark's solo project. However, during a string and woodwind overdub session, it all started to get rather difficult. Mark was not communicating well with the session musicians, and I found it all incredibly stressful. I suddenly felt that my priorities were with Sally and my house rebuild and not with an uncommunicative Mark Hollis. After the musicians had left, I told Mark, unfortunately in a rather aggressive and rude tone, that I too was heading home.

We have had little contact since, although I still have great respect for the guy. The 1 percent royalty did not materialize. Along with Tim, Lee, Paul and Mark – all contacts with manager Keith Aspden were also severed.

Robert Plant, Riga, 2001

Phill and Sally, Stevenson Ground, 2007

Chapter 33. Dido
30 May 2007

This is one of the more difficult chapters to write. Had it been written in 1997 at the end of Dido's first album, *No Angel*, it would have been positive and upbeat. Written in 2003 at the end of the second album, *Life for Rent*, it would have been incredibly negative. Now, with 10 years hindsight, I guess it's a bit of both.

My involvement with producer Rollo Armstrong began on Tuesday the 30th of April 1996. I was working in Studio Two at Swanyard Recording Studios near Highbury Corner, mixing my second album for Fusanosuke Kondo with arranger, producer and keyboardist Alastair Gavin. We had started recording the album on my daughter Becca's 21st birthday – on the 18th of March – (another family gathering missed) but I was having a fun time with an excellent band – Pete Lewinson on drums, Steve Lewinson on bass, Kenji Omura on guitar, Yoshinobu Kojima and Alastair on keyboards and Ray Gaskins on sax.

While a piece of equipment was being plugged in and set up by Jason, the assistant, I went out to the kitchen to make a cup of tea. There were about seven people sitting around in reception watching a video on television – *If Loving You is Wrong*. I put the kettle on and wandered over to stand behind the settees to watch. It was a great track – humorous, dirty and great vocals with an excellent black and white video.

When it finished, I said, "Cool track. Who is it?"

"That's us," they chorused, "Faithless."

"Oh, great track," I said embarrassed, and headed back to finish making my tea.

A small, friendly-looking guy around 30 years old came over. "Hi, I'm Rollo. Are you Phill Brown?"

We had a 10-minute conversation – he explained about Faithless, Sister Bliss, Maxi Jazz and Jamie Catto – he was a fan of Talk Talk and *Spirit of Eden*. I had only heard the Faithless dance track *Insomnia* through my son James – the bass end booming through the floor at home.

"We should work together," he said as he headed back to the rest of the gathering. I agreed and went back to my mix.

That weekend, I borrowed James' copy of Faithless' *Reverence*. What a great album.

For the rest of 1996 and into 1997, I worked with Fusa, traveling around Japan again, and got back in the studio with Mark Hollis. (see chapter 32)

Through 1997 and 1998, I joined the Rollo Armstrong and Cheeky Records crowd, with Rollo producing, Sister Bliss (Ayalah Deborah Bentovim) arranging and Goetz and I engineering. The first session with Rollo was at Protocol Studios in Highbury on the 17th of March 1997 – the start of the Skinny album *The Weekend*.

I worked every other week throughout April and May. The sessions were fun and easy, with a great working atmosphere. Rollo's day began early with a swim at the Highbury Baths, followed by an hour or so of office work, finally arriving at the studio around 10:30 or 11:00 a.m. We would work until 11 p.m.

We used an Otari 24-track analogue tape machine combined with an Atari 1040ST computer controlling various Akai S-3000 samplers and free running keyboards. With all the Skinny tracks recorded and overdubbed, Rollo handed the project over to Matty (Matt Benbrook) to finish and mix, while he and I moved on to project number two.

On the 5th of July, we were back at Swanyard Studios to start work on the second Faithless album, *Sunday 8PM*. A great collection of people – Rollo was easy-going, gentle and despite a dodgy, limp handshake, one of the nicest guys I have ever worked with. Feisty Jewish princess Ayalah (Sister Bliss) was full on as a person, excellent when it came to bass lines, keyboards and three-note anthems – an extremely talented musician. Jamie Catto was a rich kid – funny, eccentric and a brilliant ideas man. Finally, Maxi Jazz was a sweetheart – chilled, spiritual and an excellent poet. There was plenty of spliff, humour and hard work. We were rolling again.

These sessions were ideal for me. We worked very fast, often starting with a machined/sampled drum pattern at the beginning of the day, and after adding real drums, bass, guitars, samples, keyboards and a guide vocal, we would put down a good rough mix by 11 p.m. I worked on about five songs, including *Bring My Family Back*, *Postcards* and *Killer's Lullaby*, recording, overdubbing and mixing over a three-week period. Engineer Goetz worked on the dance tracks and anthems like *God is a DJ* and *Sunday 8PM*.

During some evenings on the Faithless sessions, Rollo's sister, Dido, would drop by after work, either hanging out or recording backing vocals along with Pauline Taylor. She seemed very easy, natural and innocent – a true "girl next door" – and it was hard not to like her. Rollo asked me if I would be interested in finishing off and mixing some of the tracks he had recorded with his "kid sister", then added, "There's no deal at this time, so a lower fee would be helpful. I'm paying for it myself."

On the 12th of August, it began. We worked with what was now the usual setup – Otari 24-track analogue with the Atari 1040ST computer and samplers. Musician's performances were recorded straight to tape, with some keyboards (usually Roland Juno) running live.

The tracks were layered up – sampled and triggered drums, real kit, bass lines, keyboards and guitars, weird little sounds and accents – similar to the Faithless sessions. Dido had written the songs over a few years and knew the feel and approach she was after – plus Rollo's production was perfect. We left four tracks free on the 24-track Otari to record lead vocals. These were recorded much of the time with just Rollo, Dido and myself in the control room. This was nothing precious – everyone else would wander off to play pool or get a tea – it was relaxed. We would record three complete vocal performances from top to bottom and then compile. Dido would choose the parts she wanted, and I would bounce the vocal to our fourth free track, dropping in as we went. It was business-like, but unpressured, and I slowly got to know Dido. She was quiet, gentle, funny and sharp. Some evenings her boyfriend, lawyer Bob Page, would call by, and the whole event was like a large family gathering. Many songs were written about Bob over the years, including *Thank You* and *White Flag*.

For recording vocals, and specifically for Dido's lead vocals, I used a Neumann U67 through a UREI 1176 compressor. This information will be relevant later.

We mixed most of the album over a 10-day period at Dave Stewart's studio, The Church (unable to get into Swanyard). I would be left to set up a basic mix while Rollo, Dido, Ayalah and whoever else was there would hang out – chatting and making tea – then Rollo would get involved and work on arrangements and levels. When we had a mix about 70 percent finished, Dido would (with fresh ears) suggest final tweaks, levels and reverbs. It was easy, fast and great fun. The finished tracks had a humour, a chilled vibe and a slight English eccentricity. After Dido was signed, there were a few more months of re-recording and re-mixing of some tracks on the album with different producers and re-mixers, but six of the tracks Rollo and I mixed survived, including *Thank You* and *Honestly OK*.

I continued with Rollo on an assortment of projects during the next 18 months, including Rob Deacon, Pauline Taylor, Tricky and adverts for Vodafone and Kellog's. I passed on The Pet Shop Boys though – one has to draw a line somewhere. Dido's album came out but did not immediately do or sell particularly well. Through 1997 to 1999, I worked on mixing the Talk Talk live album, *London 1986*, and found myself recording the Norwegian group Midnight Choir (*Amsterdam Stranded*) and the Seattle group The Walkabouts – both of these signalling the beginning of a long term working partnership with the professional, talented and delightful Chris Eckman.

Dido and I kept in touch over the following years and she would email me about her early touring adventures down the East Coast of America and her new career as a singer – she had given up her office day job. The album slowly started to sell, especially in America where the track *Thank You* was used in the film *Sliding Doors*, starring Gwyneth Paltrow. I believe she had sold about a million copies when Eminem sampled this same song on his track *Stan* from *The Marshall Mathers LP* and sales went global – nobody expected the eventual 16 million plus in record sales. The follow up to this was always going to be precious.

By 2000, I had drifted away from Rollo and the crew. Grippa had taken over engineering for Faithless (after The Pet Shop Boys' session) and most of Rollo's other projects. I was brought in occasionally to record acoustic instruments such as drums and guitars and for the odd re-mix. I moved on too – helping Marti Pellow from Wet Wet Wet (fresh out of rehab) to record and mix his first solo album *Smile*, and recording and mixing an album for the legendary Arthur Brown. There was a trip to Memphis in 2001 (engineering for Willie Mitchell), a live recording at the Festival Hall with David Gilmour, and the start of work with Beth Gibbons (Portishead) on the album *Out of Season* (with Paul Webb of Talk Talk). While I was traveling around Europe and America, it was exciting to see Dido's phenomenal success – in Seattle I emailed to congratulate her on a sold-out concert at a local arena. She was huge.

A couple of times, I received phone calls from her, "Hi Phill. We're in the studio doing some demos and the vocals don't really sound right. I know it's a bit cheeky, but could you give Grippa a few pointers?" Another time, she rang from America with a similar request. I don't mind people asking me what I do or how to do something specific, and I'm willing to give information on chosen microphones, mic'ing techniques, outboard gear and such, but I also thought, "Fuck that. Why not employ me to record your voice?"

I got back with Robert Plant and co-produced his album *Dreamland* – recording live at RAK's Studio One in Primrose Hill. A stunning band – Clive Deamer on drums (Portishead), Charlie Jones on bass (Goldfrapp), Porl Thompson (The Cure) and Justin Adams on guitars, and John Baggott on keyboards (Portishead). Robert sang vocals on a Shure SM57 in the control room with the Tannoy speakers blasting – a great experience. I continued to work with Beth Gibbons on her album *Out of Season*, tracking for a week at Ray Davies' Konk Studios (on September 11th 2001) or overdubbing for a few days at Westside Studios in Shepherds Bush. Beth would eventually take three years to finish her album.

It was while mixing Robert Plant's album at The Church that I received a telephone call to meet up with Rollo and Dido to discuss the next album. By now, I was pretty pissed off with the reality of the "deal" for Dido's *No Angel* album, but was feeling confident that I would be "looked after" on this album. She had sold about 12 million units at this point, and the success had made her a multi-millionaire. I was still hoping for a lump sum to cover working on *No Angel*.

The meeting was initially a bit confusing. They seemed to be offering a similar deal to last time. They talked about the new approach of musicians and engineers working for free and a credit – something fashionable in the hip-hop scene in America, it seemed. They talked of engineer Grippa's demo fee of £150 a day. I was not sure of what I was being offered and eventually said, "Okay. I will give you a year of my time at £150 a day if I can get some kind of percentage."

"No, we can't give away any points at this time."

I was a bit crushed by this.

"Then perhaps you should pay the same as everyone else," I said. "£500 a day."

This was accepted. I went back to The Church and continued mixing *Dreamland*. No pension plan then?

In September 2002, just after finishing the album *Blue Trash* with the excellent Spikedrivers band, I started Dido's second album, *Life For Rent*. There's an interesting comparison on these two albums. The Spikedrivers (a three-piece) had recorded live – drums, bass, guitar, lead vocals, backing vocals, solos – the lot – and we had recorded to an old Ampex 16-track, 2-inch machine through a rebuilt 1970 Helios desk. I had mixed it manually and it sounded great. With Dido, we were at the front end of the recent technology changes. Rollo had moved away from samplers and the Atari 1040ST and taken to the digital format in a big way. His preferred software was Logic Audio and we had virtually unlimited tracks. Unfortunately, none of them were analogue.

I joined the team at Rollo's studio – The Ark, in Highbury – which originally had been Protocol Studios. This was at the end of their demo and writing period. It was good to see the usual guys there – Faithless' drummer, Andy Treacey; Ayalah; programmer and keyboardist Mark Bates; guitarist Dave Randall and engineer Grippa; plus the new boy, writer/programmer P-Nut. There were a collection of extras – Rollo now had a personal assistant. Dido also had a PA, and she had a manager who had a PA. Everyone had a mobile phone, turned on. In addition, there were three A&R guys – two in London and one in L.A. – who turned up occasionally with opinions and mobile phones, both unwanted. Over the weeks, this way of working created a certain amount of distraction, and I don't think we were as focused as on our recording sessions in 1997. After a week or two of basic recording and programming, we decamped back to Dave Stewart's studio, The Church, in Crouch End.

I'm not going to go into much detail here. Dido had stopped smoking and Rollo had cut down. We were in a little "Californian" environment – with bottled water, salads and bowls of fruit. I worked some weeks and engineer Ash Howes worked others – the approach was purely computerized and digital, with musicians being cut and pasted. We were in the world of stems, and versions multiplied quite easily. There was now no tape and I was never happy with the drum and bass sounds. It was very hard for me to get into any kind of flow or momentum because of the overriding approach of doing so much work "inside the box (computer)" and all the distractions from the assorted personnel.

The SSL was really just a monitor desk, and much of the mixing and fine-tuning was done in the box. I know this is very common now, but I was not used to this in 2002. Another thing that became disturbing was returning to a song a few weeks after first recording it and noticing that some instruments – especially the drums – did not sound as good as I had remembered them. This took a while to investigate, and was later explained by the number of plug-ins being used.

Plug-ins are something I still do not understand today. I work in great studios with wonderful outboard gear and yet many producers, engineers and musicians use the plug-ins in the computer. If Pro Tools/Logic Audio and such recording programs are approached as just a 48-track recording/editing machine, then the sounds are pretty good (obviously depending on the analogue to digital converters). But please do not be tempted to use these "on board" effects and plug-ins. Each tweak of compression, EQ, de-esser, in fact, any treatment at all, will slowly eat away at the original signal. The original could be great... and probably took a while to sort out anyway. As comedian Bill Hicks would say, "I don't want to preach... but guys get a grip."

After nine months, with all the technology you can buy, three sound engineers, four programmers, a few producers and many musicians – *Life for Rent* sounded safe, bland, dense, lacking in air, and to me, a disappointment. Plus my work on *White Flag* was not even credited. I finished my work on the album in May 2003.

As I settled back into life at North Lodge and a brilliant English summer, I was finally certain I did not want to make albums this way. I would love to work with Dido again, but only with the attitude and freedom of the first album.

Strangely, the calls from Dido regarding vocal sounds continued. Her manager emailed one day in 2006 and asked again for my help. I replied by writing down all the information I could remember:

No Angel – Neumann U67 through a UREI 1176, ratio 4:1, medium attack, fast-ish release (3 o'clock).

Life for Rent – Neumann U87 and a remake Neumann M149 through a UREI 1176, ratio 4:1, medium attack, fast-ish release.

Usual reverbs used – delayed EMT 140 plate or Lexicon 480 set to "Fat Plate", three-second reverb, top end rolled off to 1.7, pre-delay of 80 milliseconds.

I ended by writing rather crassly, "Aren't I being generous to you? One day maybe Dido will be generous to me."

Two days later at 5 p.m. on a Saturday, with me unfortunately a bit drunk, Dido's manager Peter Leak telephoned. "I think you need to fill me in," he said. "You seem to have issues and I was not managing her back then. What's the story?" I explained my feelings over *No Angel*, the deal, the lack of fees, no bonus, etc. It all came out. "I was hoping that Dido would have given me some kind of payment for my work on the *No Angel* album," I said. "A 1/4 percent would have been excellent, a lump sum of £20,000 would also have been a lovely gift. I made less than £6,000 for that album – Dido is worth 12 million. And all these requests for information – you should all fuck off."

Peter was gracious considering my rudeness.

"I knew nothing of this," he said. "When Dido comes out to L.A., I will have a word with her about the way you feel."

A few months later, on May 30th, I received an email from Dido, kindly stating that she had no idea what I had (or hadn't) been paid while recording *No Angel*. She promised to send a personal cheque to make up for the oversight. A week later, almost 10 years since first working with Dido, I received a cheque dated 31 May 2007 for £20,000.

Wow, she came through. Thank you, Dido.

Epilogue

December 2023

So that's about it! Over 30 chapters covering 50 years. Many others could have been included – China Crisis (with Walter Becker), Shy Reptiles, Eat, Nan Vernon (with Dave Stewart), 10,000 Things, Beth Gibbons, and Rokia Traoré – and those that unfortunately could not – Robert Plant's production contract had a "secrecy" clause. I can't even begin to explain my experiences with Ray Davies of The Kinks!

There could certainly have been more technical information about recording, but that is not the reason for the book. It's about the emotional reality of sessions, and remembering a period of time that had discipline, performance, and anarchy.

Discipline – having only 4, 8, 16 or 24 tracks to work with and limited outboard equipment. Performance – getting a group of four to 60 musicians to deliver a live recording. Anarchy – general alcohol and drug abuse, coincidence, serendipity, madmen, and the wonderful freedom of the 1970s. In today's 60-track, digitally clean, over-produced records – all this appears strangely appealing.

I am still working, recording with tape where possible, and still using real musicians. There's something that happens when you get five people in a room playing live – the end result is more than the sum of its parts. As Steve Smith told me in Los Angeles in 1975, "…you know [with] this calibre of musicians playing live in a room – it makes their playing better." Nothing has really changed. The song breathes, and I will take a great performance with errors any day over a track that is quantised in time and perfectly in tune. I am very reluctant to use ubiquitous digital processing such as Auto-Tune or other plug-ins on anything.

So yes, I think I'm "still rolling", or at least trying to – and fortunately (most of the time) on good projects. Since finishing Dido, I have made albums with a wide assortment of artists – Chris Eckman (The Walkabouts), The Bambi Molesters (from

Croatia), Colin Vearncombe (of Black), 10,000 Things (a rock band from Leeds that sadly – with the help of their record company Polydor – imploded), Zero 7, The Coral, Christie Hennessy, The Spikedrivers (always a great experience), The Checks, Marti Pellow (a great singer), Kathryn Williams, Rokia Traoré (a tricky Malian Princess), Babasónicos (Argentine rock), Bombay Bicycle Club, David Gray, and Hafdis Huld.

Dealing with record companies and their constant flow of changing opinions is now probably the hardest part of making a record. They waste so much time and money – usually other people's.

Are the major record companies still rolling? No, I don't think they have been for a while. Look at "Radio-Friendly" mixes and the lack of adventure. The problem goes back to the late 1980s and the buying up of smaller record companies like Island, A&M and Mercury. I don't feel you can run a record label the same way as ICI. In the UK, at the moment, it's extremely difficult to get a project or finished album signed or to receive any money for development. Various labels, such as Virgin and Island, have done away with their A&R departments. In truth, it is chaos.

My immediate suggestion would be for them to cut down on the large quantity of assorted staff – especially assistants, co-coordinators, receptionists, and security (do they really think they are going to be invaded?) and to pay a more realistic wage – £160,000 a year for junior A&R is obscene. The savings can then be passed on to recording studios and musicians – where they can be paid enough to survive.

In the UK, at the moment, studios are winning if they financially break even – not a great way to run a business. I also wonder if record companies are more interested in managing data than realising that this is someone's album. I have had three situations these past ten years when masters have been "lost" or "misplaced". They also seem eager to send masters to cutting rooms such as Metropolis at £2,500 a cut, rather than to an independent engineer such as Denis Blackham at Skye mastering, who will do a better job for far less.

The independent record companies are certainly still rolling. Rough Trade, Domino, and Heavenly are companies to admire –

where the boss makes the final decision along with the artist – similar to early Island Records and owner Chris Blackwell.

Not surprisingly, little of my work these days comes from major record labels – most is direct from the artist or producer. Past artists that inspire people to get in touch are usually Bob Marley, Robert Palmer, John Martyn, Roxy Music, and Steve Winwood (from the 1970s); China Crisis, Talk Talk and Eat (from the 1980s); Brian Kennedy, Talk Talk, Mark Hollis and Faithless (from the 1990s); and in the past ten years, Beth Gibbons, Robert Plant and Midnight Choir. Although Dido has sold over 28 million records worldwide, I have never received a single telephone call from any record company or artist because of my involvement on those albums. In contrast, Talk Talk's *Spirit of Eden*, which was seen as a failure at the time of its release, has steadily brought me work for the past 30 years.

In December 2015, I posted that I was finally stopping work and retiring.

The decision was not brought about by any one event but by a series – my dislike for working with the Universal Music Group of Record Labels, bad management, lost record royalties, not wanting to repeat myself, bored and uninspired with 'modern' recording techniques – and I had lost the passion I'd had for nearly 50 years.

Three days later, Maxi Jazz of Faithless telephoned to ask me to work on his new project: The E-Type Boys. "I've got an eight-piece band, I want to record 'live' at RAK Studio One, and I want to record to tape. I think you're the man. We have had a couple of rehearsals and it sounds great." I thought he had seen my post and was messing about; we had not worked together for 12 years. When I realised he was serious, and not involved with Universal, I said yes – so just a three-day retirement!

In January 2016, we recorded the album over two weeks, and the band then went on the road. Some months later, we were back in the studio to re-record the album – the band was now very tight from being on the road. As before, we recorded everyone live to tape. We worked fast and had 90% of the album finished in a week. They went back on the road with Tour Manager Nina Frances.

I now became involved with my brother's new Canadian Trio, the brilliant 'Blurred Vision'.

Many months later, Maxi got back in touch and said he wanted to go into the studio again to re-record the album – "The band is massive." This time, we recorded all the tracks in two and a half days – mostly live in RAK One and a 24-track tape machine. There were a few overdubs and mixing to follow, but what an excellent experience; it was everything I loved about recording.

2016 was a brilliant year. The album *Simple Not Easy* came out in 2017.

So, feeling renewed, I continued to work with artists who were unsigned and wanted to record 'live'. These included singer/songwriter Mark Nevin, The Spikedrivers, Chris Eckman, Chantal Acda, Evi Vine, and The Bambi Molesters. In 2019, I made a wonderful album with my old friend Marti Pellow. Again, it was an eight-piece band playing 'live' in the studio, but this time not recorded to tape – we were back in the world of Pro-Tools. I decided once again to retire, then Covid hit, and the studios were closed anyway – it seemed like good timing.

In the autumn of 2021, I was asked to mix an album by 'Held by Trees' – an instrumental album with many of the Talk Talk musicians. It was beautiful, and I was smitten again. I continued to work, and in 2022 and 2023 recorded or mixed tracks or albums for Chantal Acda, Paul Roberts, Philip Pembleton, and two EP's with Held by Trees.

Maxi Jazz got me out of retirement in 2015, but sadly passed away in December 2022. Is it time for me to retire again?'

Sono, Studio One, Prague, 2023
(Image courtesy of ZuZana Bonisch.
© ZuZana Bonisch 2023)

Glossary

ADT - Automatic Double Tracking; an artificial way to "double" sounds.

Bouncing - sending one or more audio tracks to another open track - see "submixing".

Channel - an audio path, usually found on a console or desk.

Close Mic - to place a microphone very near to a sound source.

Comp - Compile; to take several tracks of the same basic take and pick the best parts.

Compressor - a device that automatically reigns in the dynamic range of a sound.

Compression - the result of using a compressor to reign in the dynamic range.

Console - see "desk" (below).

Control Room - a room in a studio where most of the recording equipment and engineers reside.

Desk - aka mixer, mixing console, soundboard; a device to sum audio channels and provide routing.

DI - Direct Injection; device that connects a line level audio output to the input of a mic preamp.

Digital Delay - an effects unit using digital sampling to create delay/echo.

Doubling - recording two versions of the same part to gain thickness or an effect.

Drop-In - same as a punch-in, engaging record on a channel during playback.

Effects - a catch-all for sounds generated from and added to existing sounds/instruments.

EMT Echo Plates - a specific brand of "plate reverb" (see below).

EQ - equaliser; an adjustable filter to modify the level of selected frequencies - tone control.

Fader - the potentiometer on a console that controls the volume level of a channel of audio.

Filter - component of, or another name for, an equaliser.

Fly In - to record from tape deck to tape deck without synchronisation.

Foldback - monitor amps and speakers for live performance.

Gates - a device that can be set to pass or not pass audio, depending on the input level or key.

Guide Track - an audio track in a session that is used for reference and will be erased later.

Hammond Organ - an electric organ based around a mechanical tone wheel.

Harmoniser - an effects unit that can add harmonised notes via pitch shifting.

Leslie Speaker - a rotating speaker in a cabinet, frequently used with Hammond organ.

Lock Out - a 24-hour recording studio rental where other sessions are "locked out".

Live Room - a room in a studio where most of the musicians perform with their instruments.

Mic - microphone; a transducer that converts variances in air pressure into voltage.

Multitrack - a tape deck capable of recording multiple tracks of synchronous audio.

Overdub - an audio track added to previously recorded tracks.

Panning - placement of the audio signal in the stereo field.

Patchbay - a jack and plug device for audio signal routing.

Plate Reverb - a steel sheet, transducer and pick-up combo used to create artificial reverb ambience.

Pot - Potentiometer; a variable resistor used to control various audio functions, such as volume.

PPM Meter - Peak Program Meter; displays the peak audio volume level.

Preamp - typically refers to a microphone preamplifier, which boosts the mic signal to line level.

Pultec - a well-known, classic equaliser brand.

Scratch Track - see "Guide Track" (above).

Screens - portable barriers used in the live room to isolate musicians and instruments.

Session Musician - a musician hired to perform on a recording session.

Spring Reverb - an effect that uses a spring, transducer and pick-up combo to create artificial reverb.

Submixing - sending parts of a song's mix to a bus where they can be treated or controlled as a group.

Tape Delay - an effect using the gap between tape heads to create delay/echo.

Tape Op - Tape Operator; the assistant engineer or person who is learning recording skills.

Tape Phasing - using two tape decks playing the same material slightly out of time to get comb filtering.

Track - an audio signal that has been recorded and can be played back.

Vari-Speed - a control that changes the pitch, speed and playback of a tape deck.

Voice-over - adding (generally) a speaking voice on top of existing music, like an announcer.

VU Meter - Volume Unit Meter; displays the average audio volume level.

Wah-Wah - a variable EQ filter, usually foot-controlled and used on electric guitar.

Wild - without synchronisation.

Other Books from the Publisher

THINKING ABOUT TOMORROW
EXCERPTS FROM THE LIFE OF KEITH WEST

IAN L. CLAY

DANA GILLESPIE

Weren't Born A Man

FRIENDS AND OTHER STRANGERS: BOB DYLAN EXAMINED

By Harold Lepidus

hank williams & frank sinatra & buddy holly & carl perkins & bobby vee & frankie valli & johnny otis & tiny tim & rick nelson & elvis presley & billy faier & betsy siggins & charlie louvin & earl scruggs & pete seeger & carolyn hester & john byrne cooke & donovan & maria muldaur & john b. sebastian & gordon lightfoot & dom flemons & t-bone burnett & barry manilow & burt bacharach & leonard cohen & chuck berry & nana mouskouri & mavis staples & loudon wainwright iii & paul simon & van morrison & marianne faithfull & tina turner & stephen stills & neil young & jewel & neil innes & otis redding & steve goodman & bryan ferry & robyn hitchcock & chrissie hynde & sheryl crow & whitney houston & al kooper & jeff gold & harvey brooks & george martin & john lennon & george harrison & paul mccartney & the byrds & eric burdon and the animals & the turtles & davy jones & roger waters & the who & stevie wonder & eric clapton & jeff beck & jimmy page & frank zappa & captain beefheart & marc bolan & elton john & billy joel & alice cooper & bruce springsteen & clarence clemons & r.e.m. & john mellencamp & slash & bill graham & dolly parton & joe south & kinky friedman & marshall grant &

www.ingramcontent.com/pod-product-compliance
Lightning Source LLC
Chambersburg PA
CBHW020220170426
43201CB00007B/274